30 WOMEN IN POWER

Praise for the Book

'*30 Women in Power* exclusively and determinedly celebrates woman power. In doing so, it achieves something rare—it presents a complex, nuanced portrait of women in command, showing their frailties and strengths, their failures and achievements. Just like successful men—but [displaying] more grace, hard work and emotional intelligence.'—ADITYA PURI, Managing Director, HDFC Bank

'As the solitary male in an all-woman household, I have always admired women for their ability to handle complexity seamlessly, and to fulfil themselves and nurture others at the same time. This conviction is bolstered by the inspiring stories of thirty high-achieving women. There is nothing so powerful as empowered women speaking in their own voices—and when the editor of their stories is herself an icon, the message becomes that much more memorable.' —ANAND MAHINDRA, Chairman and Managing Director, Mahindra Group

'Naina Lal Kidwai's *30 Women in Power* is a compelling read, and shows us how Indian women are participating in nation-building.'—ARUN JAITLEY, Minister of Finance, Corporate Affairs and Information & Broadcasting, Government of India

'Honest, brave and insightful, *30 Women in Power* is a timely reminder that Indian women can achieve tremendous success despite the seemingly insurmountable odds against them.'—AZIM PREMJI, Chairman, Wipro

'This book is a testimony to the strength and acumen of Indian women, and will inspire women from around the world.'—CHRISTINE LAGARDE, Managing Director, International Monetary Fund

'*30 Women in Power* is a collection of beautifully crafted personal essays of thirty enterprising women leaders. The stories highlight their highs and lows and the life experiences that steered these women to success. It's a great effort by Naina, a super achiever herself, to have put this together. I would recommend the book to anyone who wishes to draw inspiration and motivation for effectively managing the nuances of a successful life.'—DEEPAK PAREKH, Chairman, HDFC

'Naina Lal Kidwai masterfully brings together the stories and experiences of India's most successful women. Whether breaking glass ceilings or busting the myth of a perfect work-life balance, these fearless women take the bull by the horns and discuss these difficult issues in an honest and unflinching voice. *30 Women in Power* presents a complex, nuanced portrait of women in command by showcasing the leadership styles, qualities and achievements that have propelled their careers and inspired us all.'—INDRA NOOYI, Chairman and Chief Executive Officer, PepsiCo

'Mahatma Gandhi likened women's power to "an ancestral treasure lying buried in a corner of the house unknown to members of the family". Our society is belatedly discovering this treasure, and this book sparkles with that discovery in the field of business. Kudos to Naina Lal Kidwai for presenting to us the inspiring voices of thirty extraordinary achievers.'—MUKESH AMBANI, Chairman and Managing Director, Reliance Industries Limited

'*30 Women in Power* shines a light on the outstanding women who are contributing to breaking down gender stereotypes. It is a touching and insightful glimpse into the lives of some of India's most successful businesswomen who, with determination and passion, have succeeded against the odds and become inspiring and respected leaders. Naina collates these narratives and poignant success stories with great warmth and sincerity.'—PAUL BULCKE, Chief Executive Officer, Nestlé SA

'India's top women achievers are a source of inspiration to all of us. The authentic stories of their guiding beliefs, struggles and great achievements were waiting to be told and I can't think of anyone better than Naina, herself an inspiring leader, to have taken on this worthy project.'—PAUL POLMAN, Chief Executive Officer, Unilever

'The time is long overdue to encourage more women to dream the possible dream and encourage more men to support women in the workforce and in the home. Naina's book—a collection of powerful stories spotlighting successful women from diverse backgrounds, careers and aspirations—will help ignite the shift to a more equal world. Women and men will benefit from Naina's efforts as well as her inspiring words.'—SHERYL SANDBERG, Chief Operating Officer, Facebook

'*30 Women in Power* is an absolute treasure of thought-provoking, inspirational stories of successful women in their inimitable voices. A must read for all men and women seeking genuine insights into leadership and motivation.'—SUNIL BHARTI MITTAL, Founder and Chairman, Bharti Enterprises

'[This] book is an inspiring account of the journey of thirty powerful, self-made women to the pinnacles of their lives, backed by another powerful voice. I recommend [it] for both men and women!'—UDAY KOTAK, Executive Vice Chairman and Managing Director, Kotak Mahindra Bank

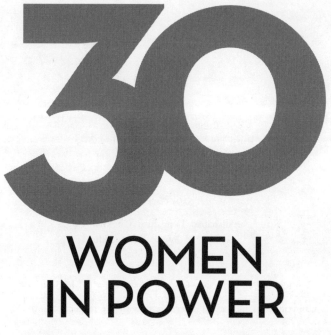

30

WOMEN IN POWER

Their Voices, Their Stories

edited by

NAINA LAL KIDWAI

MAVEN
RUPA

Published in Maven by
Rupa Publications India Pvt. Ltd 2015
7/16, Ansari Road, Daryaganj
New Delhi 110002

Sales Centres:

Allahabad Bengaluru Chennai
Hyderabad Jaipur Kathmandu
Kolkata Mumbai

Edition and Introduction Copyright © Naina Lal Kidwai 2015

Copyright for individual pieces vests with the respective authors.

The views and opinions expressed in this book are
the authors's own and the facts are as reported by them which
have been verified to the extent possible, and the
publishers are not in any way liable for the same.

ISBN: 978-81-291-3580-3

Second impression 2015

10 9 8 7 6 5 4 3 2

The moral right of the authors has been asserted.

Printed by Thomson Press India Ltd, Faridabad

Contents

The Sum and the Substance   ix
Naina Lal Kidwai

Anjali Bansal   1
The Business Builder

Aruna Jayanthi   10
The Kingmaker

Arundhati Bhattacharya   18
The Banker for Every Indian

Avani Davda   24
The Rising Star

Bharti Gupta Ramola   31
The Trusted Advisor

Chanda Kochhar   41
The Bankable Leader

Chitra Ramkrishna   52
The Jewel of the NSE

Debjani Ghosh   60
Digital DNA

Jyotsna Suri   68
The Hospitality Honcho

Kaku Nakhate   73
The Pioneering Banker

Kiran Mazumdar-Shaw 84
The Miracle Worker

Kirthiga Reddy 95
The Face of Young India

Lynn de Souza 108
The Catalyst for Social Change

Mallika Srinivasan 117
The Tractor Empress

Meher Pudumjee 128
The Powerhouse of India

Mirai Chatterjee 137
The Working Woman's Champion

Naina Lal Kidwai 146
The 'First' Lady

Nirupama Rao 158
The Exemplary Ambassador

Pallavi Shroff 167
The Queen of Courts

Preetha Reddy 178
The Patron of Health

Roopa Kudva 184
The High Priestess of Ratings

Sangeeta Pendurkar 192
The 'Cereal' Winner

Shaheen Mistri 202
The Dreamcatcher

Shanti Ekambaram 215
Destiny's Child

Shereen Bhan 222
The Newsmaker

Shobhana Bhartia   230
The Paper Baroness

Sudha Pillai   238
The Development Activist

Sunita Narain   246
The Crusader

Vijayalakshmi Iyer   257
The Inclusive Banker

Vineeta Rai   268
The Admirable Administrator

Zia Mody   280
Big Mamma

Acknowledgements   291
Index   292

The Sum and the Substance
NAINA LAL KIDWAI

In December 2012, a young physiotherapy student was brutally raped; she died two weeks later. The brave heart, appropriately called Nirbhaya (without fear) by the media, roused the consciousness of a nation and its youth. On my part, I was deeply distressed at feeling so helpless and had a strong desire to do something for young women, for us, for my twenty-two-year-old daughter.

Three weeks later, I was elected president of the Federation of Indian Chambers of Commerce and Industry (FICCI). During meetings with foreign dignitaries and chief executive officers (CEOs) from around the world—prompted by the press coverage of Nirbhaya's rape and subsequent articles on the plight of girls in India—I'd often be asked about the state of women in my country. This at a time when India had the highest number of women CEOs of banks (amongst other female CEOs) compared to anywhere in the world!

I believe we need to tell the India narrative better, so that *good* stories about women in this country also get recognition. Moreover, we need to emphasize the fact that such accomplishment is not limited to banking, but is evident across many fields. This is exactly what *30 Women in Power* attempts to do—highlight the success stories in the business economy of India, picking from a mix of industries, presenting a range of professional CEOs, entrepreneurs and heads of family businesses. I have chosen to focus on women who have led large organizations, and there are many more I would have liked to include. Despite my best endeavours, this was not to be. Needless to say, I have consciously left out the entire area of politics, sports and entertainment, where women excel. If we were to document all the successes of women in sectors across India, many volumes could be written, and indeed, should be written!

The essays in *30 Women in Power* are unique, for they convey the dreams, inspirations, challenges and accomplishments of a range of powerful women in their inimitable voices. Each composition is unlike the next, presenting a personal struggle, a well-defined moment of realization or a distinctive style of working. Yet, there are common themes that bind the essays and unite them. There are values emphasized, integral to all success stories.

SIX KEYS TO SUCCESS

Passion Is Essential

When you read *30 Women in Power*, what is likely to first strike you is the passion displayed by each of the women featured, their willingness to push themselves. While Aruna Jayanthi says that the daily challenges at her workplace keep her adrenaline pumping, Anjali Bansal feels that work, even today, is an integral part of her existence and a life without it would seem entirely incomplete. Kirthiga Reddy, on her part, encourages every one of us to remain committed to and enthusiastic about our varied roles:

> I believe it is imperative to take your whole self with you—whether you are at work or at home. I am a full-time professional, a full-time mother, a full-time wife, a full-time daughter, a full-time friend and more.

Ambition Is Not Necessarily Bad

Passion is undoubtedly steered by the ambition to succeed. Kiran Mazumdar-Shaw and Debjani Ghosh are, perhaps, two of the most ardent advocates of such aspiration. While Kiran admits that she was fuelled by drive and vision rather than by expertise when she started Biocon, Debjani asserts that women should not be ashamed to initiate career choices:

> It's time we, as women, accepted that ambition isn't a bad word. To me, being ambitious is what keeps me on my toes and continues to drive me to be the best version of myself. It's what got me my first job and it's what gets every young aspirant a career break—after all, how is one to secure that prized position without displaying drive and interest?

Such ambition certainly helps when you believe you deserve a promotion or an assignment and need to drum up the courage to ask for it. Indeed, in today's competitive world, I'd say that it's vital for women to draw attention to their achievements and ask for a break if they believe it is their due. Chitra Ramkrishna raised her hand each time she wished to work on a project at the Industrial Development Bank of India (IDBI), with the Securities and Exchange Board of India (SEBI) and, later, with the National Stock Exchange (NSE). Sangeeta Pendurkar, while working at Hindustan Ciba-Geigy Ltd (HCG), asked to be part of a strategic project with McKinsey to draft the blueprint for HCG's next ten years. And Roopa Kudva voluntarily made a PowerPoint presentation detailing why she'd be ideal for a post:

> As I completed my presentation, the CEO smiled and said, 'Sounds great, leave the presentation with me.' I did. For a few months, I didn't hear a thing. Then suddenly, one day, the CEO came to me and said, 'Do you remember, a few months ago you had sought the position of CRO? We are happy to offer it to you.'

Experiences of this sort make Kaku Nakhate say that we, as women, must overcome the 'inhibitions that prevent us from asking for a job we covet'. Verbalize your desire for a designation, she says, even if it happens to be that of a CEO.

Humility Is a Hallmark of Success
In *30 Women in Power*, we see that humility is the hallmark of most of these successful women. Meher Pudumjee's entire narrative underlines her unassuming disposition—a virtue she came to fully appreciate during a trainee workshop:

> I realized there was a direct correlation between the size of a house and the trust factor: the larger the house, the less its occupants trusted strangers!...[The workshop made me realize] the power and value of humility; it helped us shed our arrogance, intellectual or otherwise, and understand that respect is not linked to one's economic or social strata. This was a strong lesson, for work as well as for life.

Every woman in this book has admitted to being humbled by accomplishment—from Lynn de Souza, who makes it a point to detach her designation from who she intrinsically is, to Avani Davda, who asserts that her upbringing keeps her grounded and reminds her every day that she is just another normal person:

...my mother made it clear that irrespective of my role outside, once I returned [home], I was just my parents' daughter. Even now, I may be a CEO at work but I slip into a different role once I get home.

Nirupama Rao goes on to say:

Very often in our society, people who have achieved success tend to place a premium on being vainglorious and bumptious. It pays, in my view, to be generous and large of heart and mind; bumptiousness never pays.

Simultaneous with such humility is the fact that our women achievers don't shy away from learning from co-workers, juniors and associates—Mirai Chatterjee says there's never a moment when she isn't overwhelmed by the homegrown wisdom of simple, often illiterate women, while Sudha Pillai maintains that some of the best ideas come from her young staff. Kaku Nakhate agrees when she says that business solutions emerge from all levels in the office hierarchy. Anjali Bansal sums it up by asserting that leadership amounts to having the humility to learn from colleagues. These women never stop learning, acknowledging and giving credit to others.

Integrity Is Paramount

Most of the women in this book highlight integrity in the list of values they cherish; for them, there are no shortcuts or quick fixes, no stopgap arrangements on the road to success. Chanda Kochhar begins her essay by recounting her father's refusal to make concessions for her brother, despite being the principal of the college her brother wished to apply to. She says that while at first dismayed, she came to appreciate the strength of her father's stand; how 'no matter the temptation, he never compromised on his integrity and sense of justice'. Honesty and fair play, consequently, have become her cornerstones.

Preetha Reddy refers to integrity as her moral compass; Nirupama Rao says it's the one quality that helps you remain 'an honest judge of yourself'; and Chitra Ramkrishna views moral rectitude as the foundation stone of the NSE. Chitra says:

...my biggest source of sustenance has been the experience of building an institution which is trusted by market participants because of its high integrity. When we began the NSE, we tried to create a set of guiding principles, so that work ethics were built into the team's fabric right from the outset. Today, all decisions that are made are based on this system of belief.

There Are No Shortcuts to Hard Work

In *30 Women in Power*, our essayists refuse to bank on past plaudits or rely on a surname. Shobhana Bhartia says that her desire to prove herself began when her parents enrolled her in a non-Birla school, where her surname was no advantage and she had to build an identity for herself. Zia Mody, despite being the daughter of Soli Sorabjee, asserts that she has always worked very hard to secure deals. And Mallika Srinivasan says that far from getting a red-carpet welcome when she joined her father's company, she was given a slim corridor for a workspace and a stern directive to make a mark:

> My father...said, 'Sit down young lady, you might be a Wharton graduate, but I do not need one to run my business.' With that cutting remark, he put me in my place. I could have airs and graces as a B-school graduate, but I was talking to a man who had nurtured the company and the group; had held his family, group and all the professionals together post the early demise of his father; and had earned the respect of the business community.

'Only Those Who Dare to Fail Greatly Can Ever Achieve Greatly'

So said Robert Kennedy, and our women in power agree. Each woman (and man) in power has faced immense challenges. Jyotsna Suri saw her hospitality venture being written off by the media and members of her fraternity when her husband passed away. Sangeeta Pendurkar, on starting work as the brand manager for a feminine care range, found herself under immense pressure when, for no fault of hers, a new product was recalled just two weeks after its launch. And Pallavi Shroff describes a 'baptism by fire' in 1980 when her husband and she—still young, still 'novices'— had to start from scratch and set up the Delhi branch of Amarchand & Mangaldas & Suresh A Shroff & Co.

While each of them managed to turn a massive challenge into a stepping stone, the fact is that every woman (and man) in power has also tripped a few times or made a few errors in judgement. Roopa Kudva did not get to join her dream school, Indian Institute of Management (IIM), Ahmedabad, the first time around due to political tensions in Assam. And Shobhana Bhartia mentions a television venture that nosedived:

> We were to launch Home TV… In hindsight, I can spot all the errors—there were far too many partners in the venture; decision-making wasn't streamlined; and the channel had been positioned as a niche undertaking with highbrow entertainment but little content for the masses. One must learn from such errors in judgement. Home TV may be an opportunity lost, but I've come out of it so much the wiser.

Arundhati Bhattacharya, quoting John Keats's unforgettable statement—'I was never afraid of failure; for I would sooner fail than not be among the greatest'—reminds us that 'there is no shame in defeat'. Indeed, what sets the women in this book apart—and *all* successful women apart—is their willingness to dust off the failures, move on to bigger, newer dreams, take fresh risks and keep learning. To believe in oneself is key. As Shanti Ekambaram says:

> I keep telling colleagues—you can do extraordinary things if you believe you can—and that is what drives me. It is not possible to always succeed, so it is important to learn from your mistakes.

REVISITING THOSE CHILDHOOD YEARS

It is no secret that our home environment and our parents shape who we are. The essayists in *30 Women in Power* acknowledge that their childhood years have honed their adult decisions. Interestingly, it is not only mothers who have influenced their inclinations and values but also fathers and teachers who have worked to promote an enabling environment and provide encouragement. The essayists remind us how, as parents or educators, we influence tomorrow's leaders.

In my own life, I am guided by my father's words, 'You must do your best without worrying about the results,' and have been influenced by my mother and teachers; together, they have shaped me as a person. Sunita Narain's interactions with her grandfather and her mother—both gardening enthusiasts—stirred in her a desire to protect the environment; Meher Pudumjee's father's passion for excellence motivated her to place her best foot forward at all times; Nirupama Rao's father's stories of his experiences in the Indian Foreign Service (IFS) drove her to follow him into diplomacy; Sangeeta Pendurkar's parents' insistence that she give her all into every task made her a hard worker; and Bharti Ramola's father's liberality helped her break tradition:

> Papa was determined that I would be economically independent, regardless of the fact that no woman in his extended family had ever worked outside of home. From then on the story is quite simple, really. Between Papa and me, we broke many taboos.

Similarly, Krishna Kumar Birla's ritual of reading a news digest to his children over breakfast chiselled Shobhana Bhartia's passion for current affairs; Kiran Mazumdar-Shaw's exposure to her father's workplace at United Breweries inspired her to become India's first female brewmaster; Soli Sorabjee's work-conversations on the telephone, that Zia Mody eavesdropped on as a little girl, shaped her choice of profession; Chanda Kochhar's high regard for her resilient mother—who rebuilt her life from scratch after her husband's demise—motivated Chanda to embrace huge responsibilities at ICICI; Vineeta Rai's exposure to her father's work as a civil servant compelled her to appear for the Indian Administrative Service (IAS) exams; Roopa Kudva's mother's resolution to embrace a career late in life—and the respect that that earned her—inspired Roopa to commit to a demanding profession; and Mirai Chatterjee's parents' tolerance of new people and ideas and their allegiance to an 'open house' policy shaped Mirai's receptivity to people across class and caste barriers.

These essayists, in their own unique ways, echo Shaheen Mistri's poetic assertion, '…it was the flux of colours that saturated my childhood…that made me a dreamer and a believer.' They also highlight what Thurgood Marshall, the civil rights hero, had said:

> None of us got where we are solely by pulling ourselves up by our bootstraps. We got here because somebody—a parent, a teacher, an Ivy League crony or a few nuns—bent down and helped us pick up our boots.

'WOMEN CANNOT HAVE IT ALL'…OR CAN THEY?

Success is known to come with its trade-offs. And undoubtedly, compromises are made at difference points of time. Women professionals across the world admit that there are numerous demands to juggle, conciliations to be made and sacrifices to consider and weigh on a daily basis. This led Indra Nooyi to assert, 'Women cannot have it all'—a quote that our contributors have referenced, mulled over or rearticulated.

Almost all the women in this book have had to make choices at various stages of their careers between their professional ambitions and personal responsibilities. At times, they've had to forfeit the pleasures of a regular domestic life. Zia Mody, known for her sixteen-hour workdays and her adherence to the statement, 'No sacrifice, no good lawyer', admits:

> There's no doubt that law consumes me completely. It forecloses every other possibility, including an idyllic work-life balance... I remember abandoning my chickenpox-stricken daughter's bedside for courtroom obligations; not being attentive enough to my children and poring over briefs after a quick dinner...

It has been no different for me, as I met the demands of an unremitting work schedule. As for Shereen Bhan, she says that her eighteen-hour workdays have made social events or vacations a virtual impossibility: 'Over time, friends and relatives have stopped inviting me to functions altogether, simply because they know I won't make it!'

Yet, there are times when each of us has had to choose the personal over the professional, decline career opportunities to tend to parents or children—from Shobhana Bhartia, who avoided working full-time until her toddlers grew older; to Vineeta Rai, who chose to reject a prestigious post in the prime minister's office (PMO) to spend time with her daughter and son.

Even while trying to become perfect jugglers, Debjani Ghosh says, 'Women are notorious for falling into a guilt trap by worrying about... compromises and adjustments.' Mirai Chatterjee confesses that she still blames herself and her work schedule for her daughter's ill health, while Kaku Nakhate says:

> I went through [a] phase when my son was young and appearing for his exams. I would get up at 5 a.m. to prepare question papers so that he could...solve them. In hindsight, I don't think my efforts helped very much as he could have done it all himself. But I guess I did it to satisfy my guilt... There are times when you are so overwhelmed by the guilt of ignoring family that the first thought that occurs to you is calling it a day.

And yet, ultimately, not one of them has called it a day. They've built successful careers, enjoyed bringing up wonderful families and pursued the things they love. Perhaps this capacity to stick on and remain content is linked to coming to terms with a single, profound truth, one that both Chitra Ramkrishna and Shanti Ekambaram enunciate—being 'superwoman' is not a prerequisite to success.

THE TRICKS OF THE TRADE

Time Management Is an Art Well Learnt

What has helped our women achievers succeed? Time management immediately comes to mind. And our contributors reveal a few secrets behind this art. Sudha Pillai says:

> As a rule, I have never kept a file for more than twenty-four hours and have tried to clear them in the office itself... bulky bundles of dak and seventy to one hundred files a day was the norm in my last posting, but mostly these were dealt with during the working day.

If Sudha restricted 'office work' to the office, Arundhati Bhattacharya says that time management boils down to making a list of priorities and learning how to say no:

> ...treating everything as top priority is draining and depleting. Even in the daily routine of work, you have to plan for the tasks of the day and rearrange to-do lists to focus on the projects that need special attention... you need to recognize that you don't have to accept every assignment and agree with everyone.

Undoubtedly, what also helps with time management is keeping long hours. While Jyotsna Suri says she'd barely sleep for four hours a day when her hotel chain was being set up, Aruna Jayanthi admits that she sends late-night emails:

> ...once [my daughter] was off to bed at around 10 p.m., I would sit down to work again, often until well past midnight. My team got used to me working during those hours and to getting my emails at midnight. In fact, one evening I didn't work late and one of my colleagues told me the next morning that she was waiting for my response to an email until 1 a.m. and was wondering if I was ill!

As for Chanda Kochhar, she says that she tries tricking time itself by achieving forty-eight hours of work in a twenty-four-hour day, quite literally. While making 'day trips' on official work from Mumbai to New York, she catches a late-night flight from India's financial capital, reaches New York before the sun rises, has back-to-back meetings, takes a flight back home the same night, and heads straight to the ICICI office. While it appears as though she has been away for three days, it's actually just two days because of the time difference!

Choose Your Husband Well!
After keeping long hours, coming back and managing home or putting up with complaints and long faces would be impossible to cope with. Perhaps, in recognition of this, a lot of our women in power maintain that the choice of a marriage partner is vital—indeed, according to Debjani Ghosh, this, too, is a career choice! Various contributors speak of the silent or vocal support of their husbands—be it Kirthiga Reddy, whose husband moved with her to Hyderabad and supports her career unconditionally; or Meher Pudumjee, who says she is happy to have married a man who doesn't feel threatened by her work; or Nirupama Rao, whose husband adjusted to long periods of separation while he served in Karnataka and she abroad; or Sangeeta Pendurkar, whose husband encouraged her to take up an international post, much to her father's dismay and surprise. Sangeeta says:

> I still recall the day when both my husband [Sandeep] and my father were trying to convince each other about their respective views on my accepting this assignment. After a couple of hours of intense debate, my father took me aside and asked me if everything was okay between Sandeep and me! He just couldn't fathom why my husband was so keen that I take up an assignment that would have us living in two different countries, miles away from each other!

Pallavi Shroff, on her part, praises her husband for dividing all responsibilities at home. Mallika Srinivasan is appreciative of her husband not only for encouraging her to take risks and remain intrepid, but also for taking care of her children's upbringing when she had to deal with a crisis. Sudha Pillai reminisces about the early days—when there were no sophisticated childcare facilities—and how her husband would pitch in. And Zia Mody credits her childhood sweetheart and husband, Jaydev, with tweaking his business schedule to accommodate their daughters when they were younger. While very few of us grew up in households where joint parenting was the norm, I can only hope that the practice has become more commonplace over the years.

Make Your Support Networks Your Pillars of Strength

In India, we do have the advantage of extended family support and affordable domestic help, and this definitely makes the dual responsibilities of work and home a little more manageable. Mallika Srinivasan speaks at length about how her family as a whole has rushed to her rescue—be it when she was at Wharton and her mother came along to help her look after her infant daughter; or later, when her husband and extended family voluntarily assisted with various business and domestic commitments as she attended to her ailing parents. While Aruna Jayanthi depended on her parents to nurture her three-week-old daughter, Vijayalakshmi Iyer, during a time of deep personal crisis, sought help from her mother-in-law:

> ...my mother-in-law stepped in and bravely guided me through my duties in life, especially those towards my children. I am proud to acknowledge her immense contribution to my life; I owe every bit of my success to her.

Arundhati Bhattacharya came to rely on the kindness of her colleagues and their spouses when her daughter needed care; Kirthiga Reddy found her classmates and professors at Stanford pitching in and assisting with child-rearing responsibilities; I found solace in that great Indian institution—the ayah; Avani Davda has come to make technology her anchor, with online platforms helping her monitor her child's progress; and Bharti Ramola says she's indebted to their domestic staff for keeping hearth and home together. As for Shereen Bhan, she says:

> ...if I manage to keep long hours at work, it is only possible because of a good support system of family and friends. The last fifteen years would not have been possible without the unconditional support of my parents. My mother continues to be the chief supplier of good food and good sense in my life. She is also my chief fashion consultant!

Our women in power are undoubtedly powered by various inbuilt Indian 'institutions'.

'Me Time' Is Essential to Rejuvenate

Finally, a little word of advice from almost each of our achievers: keep time for yourself if you wish to succeed and remain happy. Preetha Reddy is married not only to her husband and career, but also to meditation, dance and photography. She says:

> You may well ask why I place such an emphasis on meditation. It is because while I am a working woman, I also need time for myself, for my soul and my mind… No day is complete till I find some time to connect with myself. The truth is that we are more than working entities. We need avenues for expression beyond the corporate arena.

In this book, we see that Debjani Ghosh makes time for the gym; Vineeta Rai turns to music during times of stress; Shanti Ekambaram devotes an hour at least four days a week to her fitness needs; Pallavi Shroff likes cooking, spending time in the garden and grabbing a few stolen moments with her grandson; Lynn de Souza, Sudha Pillai and Bharti Ramola sink into the world of books; Sunita Narain runs and swims; Chanda Kochhar catches Hindi films; and I go to nature reserves or for short treks. As Vijayalakshmi Iyer says, 'Life is the most precious gift, so spend at least ten minutes on yourself.' There is no substitute for 'me time'. In my own essay, I have said that work and family are two crystal balls that we, the perennial jugglers, try keeping in the air without letting them crash to the ground. Time for ourselves is a rubber ball which we can drop now and again, knowing full well that we can pick it up at an appropriate time.

To Shatter the Glass Ceiling, Work Hard

Lynn de Souza says that 'every form of engagement—corporate, social, military, legal or governmental—will benefit from having women at the helm'. Yet we have a long way to go in making this ideal a reality, and a lot of our essayists admit to a few harsh truths. Chief among these is the fact that all women have had to work much harder than men to succeed. Besides, some have faced direct discrimination as they were pioneers in male-dominated fields.

Roopa Kudva describes her visits to the sugar factories in Uttar Pradesh and the prejudices she'd confront against women in finance. Kaku Nakhate speaks of how difficult it was to get clients in the stockbroking sector to listen to her, since they weren't used to receiving investment advice from women. Meher Pudumjee describes instances when on answering the telephone, callers would repeat their request to be connected to a sales person—presuming that an engineering manufacturing company would have a male salesman. And Kiran Mazumdar-Shaw, as a woman entrepreneur in pre-liberalization India, would constantly face the glass ceiling as no one would loan her money or work with her. Kiran says:

> When I began negotiating business terms with my suppliers, I realized that many of them felt very uncomfortable dealing with a woman—some even asked if they could discuss prices with my 'manager'!

Pallavi Shroff, too, had to struggle to be taken seriously as a female lawyer:

> There were occasions, too numerous to count, when clients, on encountering me, would tersely say, 'We will wait for Mr [Shardul] Shroff.' True to their word, they'd actually linger for hours in court corridors and in the office, more inclined to kill precious time than trust a woman with their case. During such moments, Shardul would come and tell them firmly, 'Pallavi has been assigned this case, and only *she* will handle it.' The clients would have to take heed.

Vineeta Rai, on her part, speaks of institutionalized gender discrimination, and how much harder it is for women to prove themselves when the establishment doesn't support them. In her words:

> While governments and organizations are quite willing to acknowledge women's practical gender needs (health, education, etc.), they resist confronting strategic issues involving the sharing of power. It is, therefore, not surprising that even after the passage of so many years, our Parliament has not been able to pass the Women's Reservation Bill.

Almost all our women achievers speak of clocking in long hours and thoroughly preparing themselves for every situation. Vijayalakshmi Iyer states that in banking she, as a woman, has had to walk the extra mile to climb the career ladder; Shereen Bhan reveals that she prepares herself thoroughly for her shows, so that every observation is sharp and viewers don't focus merely on 'appearances'; and Sunita Narain, while questioning the concept of 'gender disadvantage', admits that she had been compelled to push her agenda much more aggressively than her male co-workers. Sunita says:

> The fact remains that I work in an extremely male-dominated industry, particularly since I am required to leave the softer world of activism and, armed with scientific knowledge, enter the hard world of business and government... There is no doubt that I have to work harder to explain myself, to constantly prove my credentials and worth. But it is also clear that this has worked to my advantage—when I know that a task will not be easy, I cannot take it for granted.

There are also some like Shanti Ekambaram, Avani Davda and Jyotsna Suri, who, I hope, represent a newer India. While Shanti Ekambaram says that as a working woman her gender has been an asset rather than a liability, Avani says that she has never faced the glass ceiling and has seen numerous women around her do well—indeed, she asserts that the framework of meritocracy cannot be given up in a quest for diversity. Jyotsna goes on to say that one's gender is never an impediment:

> I am often asked whether being a woman posed any gender-specific challenges to me over the years. My answer is always in the negative. I believe that if one has the leadership capabilities, gender has little or no role to play in success.

It is this world that the women in this book, indeed, most women, want—not special treatment, not undue advantage, just a fair shot at success.

Nurture Talent and Watch Your Company Grow

Dipping into their experiences as working professionals, mentors and trailblazers, the women in this book offer some astute leadership advice. And once more, there are intersections and commonalities—from the tips for 'change management' offered by Shereen Bhan and Arundhati Bhattacharya, to the need for faith advocated by Mallika Srinivasan and Preetha Reddy.

Besides this, being in power is also about nurturing talent. Zia Mody believes in encouraging her juniors to express themselves openly (even if it means critiquing her ideas) and mentoring them—a quality that has earned her the moniker 'Big Mamma'. Aruna Jayanthi recommends building strong teams and guiding those capable of taking over responsibilities—so there's always someone to take charge if a leader moves on. Vijayalakshmi Iyer, on her part, has established two hotline portals directly to her office—one for customers and another for employees, so her colleagues know she is available for advice. And Shaheen Mistri believes that leaders beget new leaders—her organization Teach For India's 700 alumni are taking determined steps to better the lives of children by opening schools for the disadvantaged, starting teacher-training institutes or mobilizing resources from the corporate sector.

While Preetha Reddy endorses treating employees as family members, and Shobhana Bhartia says a leader must trust the people she hires, Anjali Bansal emphasizes that a leader takes her team along with her:

> I believe in leading from the front *with* my colleagues. Leadership, for me, is investing in the people you hope to lead, supporting them through their tough times, connecting with them at a personal level, encouraging them to learn and grow, and having the humility to learn from them.

Mirai Chatterjee, on her part, vouches for the power of 'collective leadership':

> One of the important contributions of SEWA [Self Employed Women's Association] has been to help develop grass-roots-level women, so they become powerful and effective leaders. Thousands of local women leaders now run their own organizations and the SEWA movement across the country. Elected from among SEWA members, these leaders are often unschooled, but have home-grown wisdom and intelligence. They have taught women like me about…shared leadership.

On Philanthropy and Giving Back

Our women leaders combine leadership and philanthropy. Some, like Kirthiga Reddy and Anjali Bansal, have volunteered with NGOs (the former with HandsOn in the Bay Area, the latter with SEWA and the Grameen Foundation). Others have gone on to nurture humanitarian or public-spirited institutions, from Shaheen Mistri, who founded Akanksha on the simple belief that within India there exists all that is necessary to give children 'the opportunities to meet their potential'; to Kiran Mazumdar-Shaw, who established a cancer centre to deliver affordable and high-quality care to patients from the lower socio-economic strata; to Sunita Narain, who has promoted sustainable development as the director general of the Centre for Science and Environment (CSE); to Lynn de Souza who, after a fulfilling career as the CEO of Lintas Media Group, started Social Access Communications to use the power of the media to foster genuine connections between profit and non-profit sectors. Lynn says:

> There comes a time when all that one learns in a memorable career, all the experiences—good and bad—all the relationships, all the achievements, cry out to be put to a more selfless purpose... adding value to another being's existence [is] far greater than the value of one more well-delivered presentation, one more award, one more promotion.

Still others reinterpret the idea of charity and say that their work is a form of social commitment—Chitra Ramkrishna views the NSE is a vehicle for financial inclusion; Avani Davda says that she is fuelled by Starbucks's larger vision of giving back to the community; and Jyotsna Suri believes that The Lalit is not just a chain of hotels but a successful catalyst for cultural rejuvenation and energy in low-income areas. While Bharti Ramola speaks of how she has continually been drawn to development issues, both as a consultant and as a promoter/board member, in my own life I know how fulfilling my work in the spaces of the environment, water management and also women's empowerment has been; I've always made time for these activities and for guiding the organizations I lead.

◆

As the number of women multiply at the workplace and their experiences over the years shine through, I am confident that the women who deserve it will get a fair chance. However, they cannot take success for granted and need to prove themselves. I can only hope that an enabling environment will allow men and women to succeed on merit in an equal world.

Ultimately, the outstanding women covered in this book are just a few examples of contemporary Indian women who inspire the world. Their stories—thirty, among millions of others—are meant to enlighten, inform and, hopefully, spur a change in perception. The goal is that we'll bequeath a world to our children where men and women can *both* aspire, where, to quote Shaheen Mistri:

Every girl and boy across our vast nation, all of them, will have the chance to be who they want to be. As all of them discover their own light, like magic, their true colours will come to life. That will be a morning worth waking up for, in a kind, strong and peaceful, a more beautiful India.

This is the India that you and I and every woman featured in this book dreams of. I hope each of our achievements will empower young girls, inform men and transform the destiny of this great nation, our India.

ANJALI BANSAL is the managing director of Spencer Stuart India, which she was instrumental in setting up. She also leads the boards and is the chief operating officer of the company's Asia-Pacific division. Prior to this, she has worked with McKinsey and Company in New York and Mumbai. She serves on the boards of GlaxoSmithKline (GSK) Pharmaceuticals India, Bata India Limited and Voltas, a Tata Enterprise; on the advisory board of the Columbia University Global Centres, South Asia; and as a trustee on the boards of the United Way of Mumbai and Enactus. She has been listed as one of the 'Most Powerful Women in Indian Business' by *Business Today* and as one of the 'Most Powerful Women in Business' by *Fortune India*.

Influenced greatly by her progressive parents, Anjali chose to pursue engineering followed by a degree in international policy and finance from Columbia University. Her foray into professional services began with McKinsey, New York. This was followed by a move to India and, within a few years, an opportunity to start and head Spencer Stuart India. She lives in Mumbai with her husband, Sandeep, and two young sons, Abhay and Anant.

◆

The Business Builder
ANJALI BANSAL

'Karmanye vadhikaraste ma phaleshu kada chana (Young people must work hard with purpose, without worrying about short-term outcomes).' I can still hear my father's words ringing in my ears as he explained the shlok to me. He used the essence of the Bhagavad Gita to get a young girl to realize that she must work to the best of her ability and potential in life, and I imbibed this work ethic from him at that moment.

I have been fortunate to have built a successful and fulfilling career so far, but the journey is still ongoing. Having extremely supportive parents and in-laws and an encouraging husband has made the odyssey till date far easier than I could have imagined.

I was brought up in a progressive environment in Gujarat. My parents did not apply a gender lens to my upbringing and fully supported my multiple interests. As a child and subsequently, in my youth, I had a strong desire to excel academically at school and college, explore the arts through training in classical dance and music and take on leadership roles. I was the head girl of my school, was active in the student body in my engineering college, and led the Ahmedabad chapter of SPIC MACAY. Perhaps going to an all-girls' school helped since we were all encouraged to take up roles of responsibility at an early age.

My upbringing laid the foundation of the gender-neutral view that underpins my professional approach. **Today, when I walk into a meeting room, gender is something I neither think about nor notice**. I believe I am interacting with fellow professionals instead of men or women, and expect them to think the same of me. That being said, I do celebrate the diversity of thoughts and ideas that different backgrounds and experiences bring to a discussion.

My journey to Spencer Stuart has taken many twists and turns. My father was in the Gujarat cadre of the Indian Police Service (IPS) and most of my family was engaged in the civil services or law. My mother had a master's in political science and a keen interest in social service and policy. Thus, it was but natural for me to dream of serving my country and making a difference. For me, the goal of pursuing a bachelor's degree in engineering was to build analytical skills and logical reasoning; the long-term goal was pursuing a career in the public service sector in India. However, my first project at Indian Space Research Organization (ISRO) made me realize that, although I enjoyed maths and science and was quite good at those subjects, I was not an engineer at heart!

Finishing college in the early 1990s in India meant that I was in the midst of a fast-changing political and economic landscape. Confronting a newly liberalized India, I thought that the private sector may be a better path for serving the country with integrity. As luck would have it, I ended up meeting my to-be-husband, Sandeep Singhal, who was completing his master's in business administration (MBA) from The Wharton School, around the same time. I, too, decided to move to the United States (US) and pursue my master's degree from Columbia University, with a dual focus on international policy and finance.

The move to the US was one of the big turning points in my life. I had always thought, while growing up, that I would be in public service in India, and had never considered leaving India. Now here I was, studying business in New York City and contemplating married life in a foreign land. But my love affair with India did not taper off.

◆

While at Columbia, I got the opportunity to intern at Women's World Banking (WWB). Here, I think I should mention that during my teenage years in Ahmedabad, I had always been inspired by Ela Bhatt's Self Employed Women's Association (SEWA). Hence, I did not think twice when I got the opportunity to work with WWB, also founded by Elaben, and a key partner of SEWA. **I was fascinated by how empowering women from the grass roots through microfinance unleashed tremendous social and economic development.** Working as an intern in the mid-1990s, little did I know at that time that one day, upon returning to India, I would chair the board of Friends of Women's World Banking (FWWB), the Indian affiliate of WWB.

Upon graduating from Columbia, I was recruited by McKinsey to join their New York office. I focused on strategy consulting in the financial services space, and did some very interesting and impactful assignments in banking, insurance, equity markets and private equity. I worked with some very smart and driven colleagues and learnt a lot from clients, seniors and various mentors across the firm. The professional exposure was terrific and the learning at McKinsey has stood me in good stead throughout my career.

I got married, settled down in New York and we bought our first home. However, my husband and I had always wanted to return to India to start a family so that our children could grow up in our culture. Recognizing that it was a good time for both of us, professionally and personally, I moved back to India with McKinsey in 2000. Post my return, I continued to serve clients in the financial sector, but the firm also enabled me to pursue my passion for non-profits and financial inclusion by giving me the opportunity to do strategy work for the Grameen Foundation and the SEWA Bank.

The return to India with McKinsey was the second major turning point in my career. Although I was doing well at McKinsey's New York office and had a group of close friends and colleagues (whom I missed sorely after moving), coming back to India during the dot-com bust of 2000–01 and observing the boom years of 2003–07 was a phenomenal experience for me. I was able to combine all my interests and stir them in the big cauldron that this country offered me—ranging from my work in the non-profit space to serving large Indian multinational corporations (MNCs) in the areas of strategy, leadership and corporate governance, as well as participating in the emerging entrepreneurial and private equity ecosystem.

The third turning point in my career came when I was approached by the global leadership of Spencer Stuart to start up and spearhead their India office. I did have some trepidations at the beginning as it was a huge responsibility. However, as I went through the interview process, the senior partners I met made me feel so comfortable that I knew that it would work out. My husband also urged me to take up the challenge head-on and gave me the confidence to believe that I could make it a success. I am glad that, in the end, I let my heart rule over my head, or I would have missed this wonderful journey. That decision to accept the position allowed me to explore my entrepreneurial potential at the age of thirty-four. I also had a lot of support from various senior leaders in the company, with many of them making frequent trips to India to help recruit the team.

The experience of setting up Spencer Stuart India made me realize that even when things appear difficult, nothing is impossible, and taking up a challenge and believing that you can do it can definitely achieve a seemingly daunting goal. There were several defining moments along the way. For example, one of the things I realized early on was that we would need to establish a unique positioning in the market as we were new entrants in an already competitive space. While Spencer Stuart was a powerful brand internationally, we were unknown in the Indian market. Hence, very early on we consciously invested in building intellectual capital, creating a strong advisory board of exemplary Indian leaders and convening gatherings of key influencers and opinion leaders in various fields, while at the same time developing client relationships and serving our clients well. It was a differentiated approach at that time and it helped us accelerate the development of our brand as a thought leader and trusted advisor in the Indian business ecosystem.

In addition, as part of a start-up team, I realized the importance of establishing a work culture and a shared vision and passion. We started the practice of having lunch together every day and that continues to this day across all of our offices; whoever is in the office shares lunch and conversations with the rest of the team, forgetting about titles and designations! This has helped us establish an open, mutually respectful and collaborative culture which overcomes traditional role hierarchies. **An open and transparent environment is especially important in a start-up and the sense of collective ownership in Spencer Stuart's India team has played a big role in the success of our firm in the country.**

Spencer Stuart has been a tremendous firm and my global partnership has a collegial, collaborative and non-hierarchical foundation. In my opinion, to build a high-performance team, providing an environment of trust and a sense of ownership often works better than many tangible incentives. While a clear plan of action is necessary to align a team with the task at hand, it is better to collectively make this plan through constant give and take, rather than hand it out as a directive. I believe that organizations would do well to invest in building such a work culture.

My biggest learning while at Spencer Stuart has been appreciating the power of a team that is bound together with passion for a purpose. The founding team of Spencer Stuart India was united in the passion to build a differentiated business through the highest quality of client commitment and contribution to our ecosystem through intellectual capital and industry efforts. We were able to do this by playing to everyone's strengths, and appreciating the contribution of every single person. We did not set out to have the largest business, being a relative late entrant into the Indian market, but instead to establish relevance by delivering impact to our clients and their businesses.

I am also a firm believer in bringing people together to make great things happen and leveraging the power of collaboration in the broader ecosystem, across industry bodies and companies. Thus, I have built cross-industry collaborative efforts around many of our important initiatives, such as the mentoring programme for women on corporate boards, which aims to help high-achieving women leaders from the corporate, academic, government and non-profit sectors join corporate boards as independent directors. I helped start this programme and now chair it in conjunction with the Federation of Indian Chambers of Commerce and Industry's (FICCI) Centre for Corporate Governance. Similarly, my team and I launched a programme to identify the top forty business leaders under the age of forty, that is, 'the CEOs of today and tomorrow', as also a study to identify the upcoming women leaders in business. **Collaborations allow one to leverage complementary strengths and compensate for skill and resource gaps; they help people work to their strengths to achieve extraordinary results.**

◆

Mentors have played an important role at critical junctures in my life and career. My story would be quite incomplete without acknowledging the significant sounding boards in my life and the thought partnerships that many of my internal and industry peers and seniors have so generously provided.

I continue to give back to our society and ecosystem. Today, I serve on the boards of Glaxo SmithKline India, Bata India and Voltas, and on the boards of trustees of United Way of Mumbai and Enactus. I am proud to serve my alma mater, Columbia University, as a part of the Columbia Global Centers' South Asia Advisory Board. Additionally, I am also associated with the Bombay Chamber of Commerce and Industry as part of the managing committee, and am on the Confederation of Indian Industry's (CII) National Committee for Women. I am a charter member of The Indus Entrepreneurs (TiE) Mumbai and mentor early-stage entrepreneurs.

I am a firm believer in the African proverb, 'If you want to run fast, run alone; if you want to run far, run together', and it forms

the core of my views on leadership—I believe in leading from the front *with* my colleagues. Leadership, for me, is investing in the people you hope to lead, supporting them through their tough times, connecting with them at a personal level, encouraging them to learn and grow, and having the humility to learn from them.

◆

However clichéd it may sound, work is indeed an integral part of life, and life is incomplete without work. This is true for both men and women, and achieving a balance between professional and personal commitments is equally important for both. It is up to each person, man or woman, to determine how to achieve an ideal work-life balance. I have often been asked about this issue, particularly by young working women who are thinking of starting a family. Personally, I feel that my husband's and my decision to return to India to start a family has been instrumental in my having the best of both worlds. **My parents and my in-laws have always made themselves available whenever we need them. I have also been fortunate to have found caring domestic help. With this support framework, I have been able to devote myself to building an institution while raising two young boys**, Abhay and Anant, and never feeling like I have to choose between the two. Establishing such harmony does require very efficient time management, but I feel that India is the best location for a woman to have a balanced career and family life. We are fortunate to have the support of our families as well as domestic staff in this country. Of course, none of this is possible without an enabling spouse, and my husband has truly been my biggest supporter and mentor.

From a personal point of view, **women should be proactive about building the right support structures around themselves. Finding the perfect work-life balance is not a lone ranger's game.** Most working women find that the company of friends and like-minded people offers them much comfort. I was also lucky to have found great mentors who guided me and lent their counsel through the process of finding a balance between home and the office. I would encourage all women to build their own mentor and peer network to reach out to.

From an organization's point of view, flexibility of work hours, convenient office locations, etc., have a huge impact; they enable mothers to continue working and, at the same time, not miss out on moments of their growing child's life. Implementing these policies at Spencer Stuart

India has allowed us to not only retain great female talent but also create a greater sense of mutual commitment. Another important initiative is to have women in leadership roles serve as role models who can guide and mentor other women, especially those in the early and mid-career years.

We have made significant progress in getting and keeping more women in the workplace, even though there's a long way to go yet. Almost 48 per cent of women in corporate India drop out of the workforce mid-career, possibly around the time that they become mothers. Some never come back and some take up 'part-time' careers and abandon the ambitions they had pre-maternity. I faced a similar choice after the birth of my first child. Around that time, I did a dipstick study with fifteen women who were either at a similar stage of life or had passed through it. The idea was to seek out the 'happiness quotient' of these women based on the choices they made vis-à-vis their careers and family. **My research indicated that those who chose to continue with their careers after childbirth had tough lives for the first few years, but tended to be more satisfied with their decision in the long run.** Battling pressure at both ends seemed to not only boost their motivation but also enhance their sense of achievement and joy. The sample research, along with an ever-supportive husband, gave me the encouragement I needed to rejoin work, and I haven't looked back since.

A planner by habit but a realist by nature, I know that few things in life go exactly as planned. Hence, **I try to take each day as it comes, and embrace each opportunity to learn, help and contribute.** In the formative years of my career, I always knew that I wanted to reach 'somewhere' but was not quite sure where. Over the years, I have learnt to have clarity of purpose, while being flexible and agile all the same. I try to make the most of each day and every prospect offered.

◆

- Defining a clear destination, along with maintaining a sense of larger purpose and passion for the journey, takes you far.
- Play to your strengths and surround yourself with people who can help you overcome your weaknesses.
- Work hard, care about people and don't worry about the outcome.
- Don't give up. Failure is a great opportunity for learning. Pick yourself up and move on.

- Have a positive attitude and surround yourself with optimistic people.
- Live life to your best potential each day.
- Seek out mentors and heed their counsel whenever you are faced with tough decisions.
- Acknowledge that personal success is rooted in team success. Make your team members successful in order to achieve personal success.
- Define your own work-life balance based on what drives you, and don't let others guilt you into making decisions.
- Create a support infrastructure and don't sweat the small stuff.

Consistently named one of the most powerful businesswomen in India, **ARUNA JAYANTHI** is a member of Capgemini's group executive committee, chief executive officer (CEO) of Capgemini India and chairperson of the Sweden Country Board, Capgemini Sweden. She is an elected member of the NASSCOM executive council and serves on the board of governors of the National Institute of Technology, Calicut. She was named the 'India Today Woman in the Corporate World' at the India Today Woman Summit in 2013.

While Aruna Jayanthi's South Indian middle-class parents laid great emphasis on conservative values, they also advocated gender equality and encouraged their daughters to make their own choices in life. Aruna chose to pursue maths and statistics, followed by a master's in management (finance) from Narsee Monjee Institute of Management Studies, Mumbai. Her career began at Tata Consultancy Services (TCS), a job she got right out of college, giving her the opportunity to work in Mumbai, the UK and Switzerland. After a few years, she moved to Aptech and then to Capgemini in 2000. She is married and lives in Mumbai with her husband and daughter.

◆

The Kingmaker
ARUNA JAYANTHI

I was born into a South Indian middle-class family from Mumbai with stereotypical values and a focus on education, culture (including a strong belief that girls must learn classical music or dance) and modesty. My father was a marine engineer-turned-entrepreneur and my mother a homemaker, and honesty and hard work formed the cornerstones of our household. Not so typical, however, was their extremely modern and liberal view on the equality of women and of all people, irrespective of their economic or social backgrounds. There was an openness towards Western culture and influence, and a disregard for superstition and rituals, thanks to two earlier generations having travelled widely and lived in Europe. There were no sacred cows or ideas that could not be challenged with logical reasoning. In fact, my sister was encouraged to choose an unconventional path and went to the US when she was nineteen years old to pursue a degree in 'special education'. **The pursuit of wealth or social standing was never important, but the pursuit of happiness, an honest life and a sense of achievement was definitely so. I live by this principle even today.**

My sister and I were left to make our own choices, and I chose the easy option of studying maths and statistics (subjects that required no lab work or long hours, only analytical brainpower), and followed them up with a master's degree in management (finance). This choice ensured that **I had enough time to pursue extracurricular activities in college like drama, dance and music. Looking back, I realize that this is what gave me the confidence to stand in front of a crowd, the ability to laugh at myself and to quickly adapt when things don't go as planned!**

On finishing my degree, straight out of campus, I joined TCS, one of the very few information technology (IT) companies in India in those days. This was the first interview I had given and I was left excited and frustrated at the end of the forty-five-minute-long session conducted by three smart and dynamic people—excited at the opportunity to work in an international environment with people of that calibre, and frustrated because we didn't get to finish our discussion! I took the job (incidentally the lowest-paying job offer on campus) and never looked back. At the age of twenty-one, excitement ruled over money. **That was management lesson number one: interviewing is a two-way process. To reel in good talent, you have to have your best people 'sell' the job and make it sound exciting. Money is important but not necessarily the decision maker.** This rule applies at all levels, starting with college graduates up to senior management.

◆

I wish I could say that I had a grand career plan and knew exactly where I wanted to go in life and what I wanted to achieve. But that is far from true. All I can say is that I wanted a good challenge and to enjoy whatever I did. In retrospect, I can confidently say that I have had that throughout my career.

I spent the formative years of my professional life working in Mumbai, the UK and Switzerland. Fresh out of management school, I was like most other students in their first jobs: thinking that I was special and deserved the best opportunities. But I was brought down to earth right away as, after three months of training, I was handed a terrible assignment. When I protested and contemplated quitting, one of the managers, Manotosh Bakshi, told me to shut up and get on with the job. He said this would give me a great opportunity to learn and see the big picture and that I would thank him some day. I don't know where Manotosh is today, but I do thank him and repeat his advice to all those who are starting out in their careers. In fact, I have heard similar stories from now-successful people who started with less-than-desirable assignments. For instance, Lila Poonawala, the iconic managing director of Alfa Laval India, has said that early in her career, she was pushed out of the shop floor and asked to maintain the gardens!

This leads me to a firm belief that **it is important to look at the big picture at all times. A few months, or even a year or two of doing something unconventional, is not such a bad thing.** When starting off a career that will probably span thirty or forty years, a few months or years do not matter at all—provided, of course, that we give every task our best and use the opportunity to learn and move forward.

After TCS, I moved on to Aptech-Hexaware (which was a joint group at the time). Again, it was an unconventional choice by any standard—I was moving from an established IT services company and the Tata brand to a much smaller organization which was not even in the core IT business. But I was quite charmed by the company's dynamic CEO, Ganesh Natarajan, and saw an opportunity to do something different in a smaller environment... so much so that I quit my job at TCS and landed up in Natarajan's office without even an offer letter! All I had was a job he had described and a salary figure he had written down on a napkin when I had met him for lunch three months ago and had committed to joining his organization. I don't think he really expected me to join, and I guess protocol dictated that he first give me an offer letter, but I wasn't one to wait for such protocol. Naïve, perhaps, but it spoke of the trust I had in the leader. The possibility that a CEO might go back on his word was inconceivable to me.

Working at Aptech was a phenomenal learning experience and I discovered that I could conceptualize new businesses or services, spearhead them, and make them successful. Aptech also gave me my first experience of moving into leadership positions, dealing with the media and analysts, and learning the importance of building strong teams and communicating well. Those were tough times but it was time well spent. Most importantly, **I learnt that people work for people, and being an inspirational manager, connecting with people and earning their trust is crucial.** To most leaders, this trait comes naturally.

The third phase of my career began when I joined Capgemini in 2000. Here, I worked with some very successful and result-oriented people, namely Salil Parekh (who had recruited me), Paul Spence (who was my boss for about five years) and, for the last few years, the group CEO Paul Hermelin. **I found the experience of working in a multinational company very different from anything I had been exposed to before. Their management style varied from that of my old employers, and they placed heavy emphasis on change management,** that is, getting the consensus of the teams and key stakeholders on crucial issues and carrying them and the organization along. We were less than a hundred people in India when I joined the group; today, we are over 50,000 strong and it has been a fantastic journey.

◆

I have to admit, I was quite insensitive to the issue of gender inequality in the workplace until a few years ago. Perhaps this was due to the environment in which I had grown up, studied and worked. My management class in the 1980s had close to 40 per cent women, and most of them today are doing extremely well professionally. It was the same during the early years of my career. **In my extended family, too, some women worked while some didn't, but all of them were very strong in their own right—so much so that there was a running family joke about not messing with the Jayanthi women!**

But over the last five or six years, I have come to acknowledge the fact that there is an issue of gender imbalance in the workplace. There are many women who stop working mid-career due to various reasons, because of which we are losing a big part of our talented workforce. And when there is a war for talent, every good professional counts, man or woman. At Capgemini, we try to do all we can to encourage employees to continue working after taking a break. In fact, **I tell people that it's okay to take a break, as a six-month or one-year hiatus in a career of thirty years or more is nothing!**

I made the choice to come back to work when my daughter was three weeks old, and I was travelling soon afterwards. In fact, I was working within a couple of days of her birth itself, but from home. Of course, I have my parents to thank for this, as they were more than delighted to look after their granddaughter. I recognize that many do not have that luxury and I respect the choices they have to make in similar circumstances. All I can do is encourage them to rejoin work if they truly wish to. One of my colleagues took a break for seven years when her children were very young and spent her time baking cakes and organizing birthday parties. Now back at work, she is one of our most valuable people. Another colleague from our finance team said that she needed to quit as her son was in the tenth standard in school and needed attention, but we convinced her to stay on and work only half-day for the next one year, till the exams were done with.

On the other hand, **I believe that success is not defined at the workplace alone. It is about doing well in whatever one chooses to do.** However, the caveat here is that such decisions should be of one's own volition, not dictated by one's family, society or peers. I see too many people being forced to make a choice for the wrong reasons and I do wish they would stand up and fight for what they really want.

There is also a lot of debate these days about a work-life balance for women. I didn't really think much about it, but was able to negotiate the demands of work and home quite well. I could afford the luxury of taking time off from work for important school events, and being around for my daughter when needed. I think that a part of this luxury was linked to the fact that I wasn't stuck in a nine-to-six job and my schedule was flexible. It was more important that work got done rather than *when* it was done—which meant that I had to put in a few late nights in order to juggle my personal life with my professional. Hence, I would often leave office relatively early, say by 6.30 or 7 p.m., and after a short commute home, spend time with my daughter, get homework done and once she was off to bed at around 10 p.m., I would sit down to work again, often until well past midnight. My team got used to me working during those hours and to getting my emails at midnight. In fact, one evening I didn't work late and one of my colleagues told me the next morning that she was waiting for my response to an email until 1 a.m. and was wondering if I was ill! **We encourage flexible working hours to every possible extent, both for men and women, recognizing that there are times when one needs to balance various priorities in one's personal and professional life.**

Of course, such balance with flexible working hours is possible only when one is not travelling—which I do a lot of. I am away from home for half the month, travelling either within India or internationally. Once, when I didn't travel for three weeks, my family thought there was something wrong and started asking me if all was okay at work or if I wasn't feeling well! They wholeheartedly accept my work and travel schedule. I sometimes think that such support is linked to setting expectations and not feeling guilty about it. In fact, **I often tell women that there is no room for guilt in the choices they make, if they are doing what they really aspire to do. If anyone should feel guilty, it should be those who stop women from achieving what they want!**

◆

About fifteen years ago, a close friend once asked me, 'Do you want to be a king or a kingmaker?' Without hesitation I replied, 'King!' 'Even kings have to be kingmakers and identify the next king if the kingdom has to survive!' he retorted. I have struggled with this concept over the years and **it took me a while to understand that it is not enough to be good in isolation; one has to build a strong team to survive.** This applies across all levels, right from the manager of a small team to the CEO of an organization. 'You are only as good as your team' sounds like an oft-repeated cliché, but following it is not easy, and I learnt this truth the hard way.

Several years ago, I was assigned a role where I performed quite well. I thought I had been reasonably successful and wanted to move to the next level as I felt I had outgrown what I was doing. I went to have a discussion with my boss, clearly expecting a positive response. To my surprise, he told me that it wasn't going to happen, as I had not made the effort to build a platform to the next level; there was no one to take over from me if I moved on. We all like to be the hero (or heroine, in this case) and be seen as the person who can make things happen. We want to grab some limelight and be recognized for driving the success of the company, while getting the occasional pat on the back. And why not? It's a very natural trait, often driven by the fear of someone else taking all the credit.

I guess I had my share of such insecurities, too, but with experience and a burgeoning sense of confidence, they have disappeared. Now I am constantly looking to develop talent, raise the bar, build strong teams, hire people who will challenge me and the other leaders in the organization, bring in new ideas, etc. This is not an easy path to take, and **being challenged day in and day out can be hard, but it has to be done for the growth of the organization. To build an organization, one must first build strong teams.**

◆

I am often asked about the challenges I have faced to get to where I am. It's a question that I find difficult to answer. In the beginning, I used to say, 'None!' This usually provoked a look of disbelief, or perhaps the thought that I don't want to talk about the early difficulties. Now, however, I say that I haven't faced any challenges that have mattered in the long run. **The simple truth is that there is nothing like a good challenge to get the adrenalin going.** When faced with a testing situation, I am inclined to think of multiple solutions and the results they could yield. Where is the time to get stressed about it? Each one of these challenges is an opportunity. Perhaps this is a just a reflection of my extremely positive outlook on life; I am indeed the eternal optimist!

Such optimism also comes from learning and reinventing myself, both professionally and in my personal life. My thirteen-year-old daughter makes me enjoy the simple pleasures of life. We learn how to play the piano together and, I have to admit, I am a slower learner than her but I work harder to make up! I enjoy some of the crazy pop and rap music she listens to and, someday soon, we will go to see a teen band perform. In turn, I try to teach her to enjoy the music, movies and books that I like. I also like keeping pace with new advances in technology, as knowing where it is going and what it can do for us and our customers is important in my line of work.

◆

I have no regard for the many restrictive so-called 'norms' of society. These are often excuses to rationalize actions which might attract some level of disapproval. It requires courage to stand up and fight for what one truly wants. As long as one's actions are ethical, just and do not hurt others, I would strongly encourage everyone to pursue whatever it is that they might want.

◆

- It doesn't matter if your dreams are big, small or crazy. Dare to dream and dare to live those dreams.
- The pursuit of wealth and success is not important. The pursuit of excellence, on the other hand, is critical!
- Learn, learn and learn. There is something to learn from every interaction; we just need to keep our minds open.
- There is only one path from the top, and that is downhill. Never believe you have reached the top or are too powerful to fall.

ARUNDHATI BHATTACHARYA is the first woman and the youngest leader to take over as the chairperson of the State Bank of India (SBI), managing approximately 220,000 staff members and 15,000 branches—this makes her the thirty-sixth most powerful woman in the world (*Forbes*, 2014).

In her nearly four-decade-long career, Arundhati has held multiple roles—in treasury, foreign exchange, human resources, retail operations and investment banking—and been involved with setting up several new initiatives, including SBI General Insurance and SBI SG Global Securities Services.

At work, Arundhati speaks of the need to abandon the culture of QSQT—*quarter se quarter tak*—and is acknowledged for introducing a number of employee-friendly policies. The mother of a daughter, Arundhati admits that while a healthy work-life balance is challenging 'given the pervasiveness of technology', it isn't an impossible dream.

◆

The Banker for Every Indian
ARUNDHATI BHATTACHARYA

I must begin with an admission: **my present vocation wasn't a calculated move; rather, I came to it, or it came to me, through chance and circumstance.** My father had wanted me to pursue 'management studies'. My mother simply said that she wanted what was best for me. But destiny had other plans and ticked the financial services box on my card.

Here's how it happened. While pursuing a postgraduate degree in English literature from Jadavpur University, I joined my peers who were applying for SBI's probationary officer exam. I did it for a lark, and also because I did not want to be left out. As fate would have it, I was selected. Since SBI represented the best in the banking industry and came with good prospects and emoluments, I decided to accept the post of a probationary officer in 1977. Since then, there has been no looking back. SBI has remained a nurturing home for over thirty-seven years.

In retrospect, I realize that banking as a career has been the perfect fit for me—not only because of the extraordinary range of experiences this profession has afforded me, but also because I've found a second family, so to speak, in my wonderful colleagues. Perhaps this is why I have never been tempted to move to more lucrative avenues, though offers and opportunities have been forthcoming. The current generation may look askance at such an approach, but I think something must be said for job contentment and the learning offered by one's work environment.

Besides, **I have been fortunate to have a combination of many roles within one workspace; each assignment along my career path has been unique.** Be it my first assignment at the foreign exchange division at the Kolkata main branch, or the international posting in New York, or the long list of opportunities in a gamut of spheres—retail, corporate, foreign exchange, treasury, rural, new business, human resources and investment banking—or finally, my ascent to the position of chairperson, each career turn has been akin to accepting a new job! There have been challenges— never insurmountable—with every transition. But subsequently, there has also been the joy of knowing that I have done my work with conviction and left my mark.

◆

Even in my early days at SBI, gender was never an issue. In fact, the organization often went out of its way to meet women's career ambitions, attend to their concerns and protect and nurture their spirit; the environment was never threatening. This could be on account of there being relatively few women at the workplace. But this was also a function of the organization's intrinsic belief in inclusiveness.

Today, times may have changed and there may be more female employees, but the encouraging response I received when I first joined needs to be sustained. **I have tried preserving the spirit of inclusiveness in my own way by attending to the problems of our women employees when they come up for my consideration.** This is no easy task. As one reaches the higher rungs of an organization, one loses touch with ground realities; one also misses the smaller complaints, the everyday concerns of colleagues. I've tried forestalling this by keeping communication channels open, offering and receiving constant feedback and being in touch with associates and customers, both internally and externally. In fact, I've started a direct communication channel—SBI Aspirations—a blog that encourages communication between employees, allows for the exchange of ideas and voices the bank's concerns. The response has been overwhelming and gives credence to my belief that fostering a conducive and positive atmosphere will make women and, indeed, all employees significant contributors to any organization; it will allow them to soar without being curtailed by misgivings.

While organizations need to provide the right environment, the onus rests on us as individuals, too, and the values we choose to stick by. These hold us in good stead through personal and professional challenges. In my own case, two values have been instilled in me by my parents and mentors. The first is an unshakeable belief in myself. How vital this is on the road to success! Unless I have conviction in my strengths and my capacity to prepare and think things through, how can I expect others to have faith in me?

The second firm value is acknowledging, confronting and overcoming fears. I believe each of us, in an adult body, has a child within, overwhelmed by insecurities, inhibitions and fears of inadequacy. These fears only get compounded when we are reprimanded by a boss, overlooked for a promotion or rejected during an interview. The first step to overcoming these anxieties is acknowledging that they are real. The second step is facing them head-on. Do not blame yourself and know that there is no shame in defeat. As John Keats said, 'I was never afraid of failure; for I would sooner fail than not be among the greatest.' Most of all, learn, as much as possible. There's no surer path to confidence. And with confidence comes better performance; you automatically minimize the risk of failure.

Equally, **in our fast-paced world, we cannot afford to resist change. If we do, we miss opportunities and worse, deny ourselves the chance to grow.** For instance, in today's wired world, choosing to stay technologically illiterate or remaining aloof from technological advances makes one less worthy of employment. One must adapt to one's time; change is the shield that protects us from the threat of extinction. In this context, change management becomes an especially relevant term; we must make periodic and concerted efforts to ensure that the volume and rate of change at work and at home does not overwhelm or defeat us.

◆

We live in challenging times. Working couples have never had it this tough. Our families are nuclear, our workspaces are globalized bubbles and our lives are hectic and complex. Organizations are more competitive than they used to be, and there is constant need for achievement and social recognition. **Finding a suitable work-life balance was always difficult, but now—given the pervasiveness of technology, its larger-than-life presence in our workspaces and personal lives, and its capacity to blur the line of distinction between office and home—striking an equilibrium has become next to impossible.**

Or has it? I'd say the task cut out for us is more difficult, but we can still find space for our careers and ourselves; we can, even now, segregate our professional and personal lives. All we need to do is align our priorities of work, family, health and well-being, establish a realistic schedule for our workday and stick to it. Besides, **we need to learn to set and strictly enforce boundaries; this is the only way to balance the personal and the professional.** For instance, allot thirty minutes of your workday to follow-ups, and do this conscientiously, so you do not waste time at regular intervals staring at your phone or hovering by your inbox. Do not fritter away time responding to unwarranted emails and missed mobile calls. Strict boundaries sting when enforced, but with time one grows to accept and appreciate them.

Also, remember that **treating everything as top priority is draining and depleting.** Even in the daily routine of work, you have to plan for the tasks of the day and rearrange to-do lists to focus on projects that need special attention. Make this a habit to become an efficient employee and get replenished emotionally and physically.

Finally, to manage time effectively, you need to recognize that **you don't have to accept every assignment and agree with everyone.** Use your priority list to identify requests that simply aren't worth your time. For example, when you have an urgent family matter to attend to, you might be requested by your boss to participate in a conference call. Resolve which commitment is more important, make a case for its relevance and learn to say 'no', even if it is painful at first. Also, there are always ways to make up—for instance, carrying the earlier example forward, if you choose to attend to the family commitment, you can ask a colleague to share the meeting's notes with you.

Equally, it helps having people you can lean on. While sacrifices and compromises at home are sometimes inevitable, professionals can cope when their relatives and colleagues lend them a hand. **A lot of my strength comes from the knowledge that I have the unstinting support of those close to me.**

There was a time when I was posted in Lucknow as the general manager looking after the eastern part of Uttar Pradesh. This belt is fairly backward. Back then, not only was the region incapable of getting traction for business, but it was also unable to absorb credit. To make matters worse, given how vast the geographical terrain is, I used to be on the road constantly, visiting various branches. Once, while I was on a tour, I received the message that my daughter had fallen ill. I longed to be with her, but I knew that, given where I was, going back was not feasible. It would take far too long. What consoled me at that point was my support system—all it took was a few phone calls to guarantee that my daughter would be taken care of even in my absence. The truth is, my colleagues and their spouses always step in when such instances arise. And I try to repay their debt by being there for them when they face personal crises.

I've come to realize that maintaining a healthy work-life balance becomes less of an impossible dream by following five rules:

1. Respect your colleagues and your environment
2. Be appreciative of help
3. Remember the value of humility and remain approachable
4. Listen
5. Be adaptable and open to new ideas and thoughts

The first two rules help create an enduring support system, so you never feel alone. The remaining three ensure that you widen your circle of friends and well-wishers. This makes every challenge more manageable, and you don't have to suffer the guilt pangs of having let your family down.

These pointers are not exhaustive, but they have helped me both with my job and at home. I can only hope that they will provide direction to all the brave hearts—all the women of the world—who wish to claim enriching and meaningful lives.

◆

- Set your priorities in life.
- Learn the art of saying 'no'.
- Develop self-discipline and pick up time-management skills.
- Adapt to change.
- Build interpersonal trust since this helps resolve potential conflicts; besides, when teams work in harmony, they can meet targets.
- Every career ascent is a lesson in humility. Rewards and recognition are meant to act as motivators, not create a false sense of superiority.
- Offer positive feedback. Leaders should assess the core competencies of their employees, strive to build their strengths and assign the right assignments to them. An employee, in turn, excels at her job when she develops a passion for it and receives a pat on the back for her splendid performance.

As the youngest chief executive officer (CEO) in the Tata Group, **AVANI DAVDA** has already carved a niche for herself. Under her leadership, the joint venture between Tata Global Beverages Limited and Starbucks Coffee Company, Tata Starbucks Private Limited, has opened seventy stores in India in over two years. Avani is the only Indian featured in *Fortune* and *Food & Wine's* 2014 list of the '25 most innovative women in food and drink' and was one of *Businessworld*'s C-Suite Women in March 2014.

After completing her management degree from Narsee Monjee Institute of Management Studies (NMIMS), Mumbai, Avani joined the Tata Group as a Tata Administrative Services (TAS) probationer. After completing her training, she joined the Taj Group as a business development manager and grew to become the general manager for marketing at the Taj Hotels. Following her maternity break, she joined R.K. Krishna Kumar's office as his executive assistant. He was instrumental in her meteoric rise within the organization. Avani attributes her work ethic and values to her mother, and lives in Mumbai with her husband, Vishal, and eight-year-old son, Param.

◆

The Rising Star
AVANI DAVDA

The mediocre teacher tells. The good teacher explains. The superior teacher demonstrates. The great teacher inspires.—William Arthur Ward

During a meeting one day, John Culver and R.K. Krishna Kumar—who were closely involved with the creation of the joint venture between Starbucks Coffee Company and Tata Global Beverages Limited—turned to me and said, 'Why don't you start and lead it?' Still focusing on the details of the project, I replied distractedly, 'Yes, of course, but we have to attend to this project update.' I looked up to see both of them laughing. 'No, no, we're telling you to lead it. Not as a project leader, but to actually move into the company,' they explained.

At that moment, I realized the amount of faith both partners had in me. As a young woman, this was an unbelievable opportunity. I was being given the chance to nurture a dream and see it succeed. This project had been my baby and I had worked on it for more than a year before being asked to head it. I still recall that moment every day, and I feel blessed and fortunate to have been guided by such great leaders; my approach towards the business is a result of working with the likes of John Culver and R.K. Krishna Kumar.

What I am today is the result of a series of decisions and life choices. The people I have been associated with over the years have played a large role in shaping my life. I come from a humble middle-class background. Having grown up in Mumbai, I earned my bachelor's degree in commerce from HR College and a master's degree in management studies from Narsee Monjee Institute of Management Studies (NMIMS). In 2002,

I joined the Tata Group as a TAS probationer. As a young graduate, I was looking for an opportunity that would help me develop as a business leader, and not just for a role that would focus on a particular functional area. As a company, the Tata Group offered me this through its TAS programme—a highly recommended leadership programme. It is designed to provide a well-grounded look at different Tata companies and work in cross-functional areas of business. I started in the business development space and then moved to the luxury brand and marketing team of the Taj group of hotels for more than two years, after which I was appointed the general manager for marketing of the luxury hotels. I was responsible for driving and facilitating key strategies and initiatives for the company, as well as leading marketing and business development assignments. Finally, in 2008, I had the good fortune of working with R.K. Krishna Kumar, the director of Tata Sons and vice chairman of Tata Global Beverages and Indian Hotels Company Ltd.

He would become my mentor.

◆

I remember 19 October 2012 vividly. Right outside what is now the Fort store in Mumbai, the business stalwarts Ratan Tata and Howard Schultz announced the birth of Tata Starbucks Private Limited and threw open the first outlet to customers. Led by the sheer passion of the two leaders, the store came alive. We were restless with anxiety and excitement, and **what is amazing is that, even to this day, we feel the same level of anticipation and enthusiasm each time we open a new store.**

All my assignments, from charting the transformation of Tata Global Beverages Limited to working on a joint venture with PepsiCo, have provided me with a range of opportunities to learn and grow as a manager and as a leader. Yet, the real turning point in my career came when I started working for the Starbucks and Tata joint venture. It was so exciting to have the Starbucks leadership from Seattle in India and to glean the synergies of this joint venture—one that went far beyond just a business partnership as the value systems and core philosophies of the two companies mirrored each other. The one thing I have always lived by is that **whatever industry you are in, it is critical to find people who share your values. You cannot work in an organization or team that you are disconnected from.** Common values and intent are what keep you motivated.

Often, this connection between a company and the people who drive it is the difference between success and failure. The Tata Group's corporate values force us to look at business through the lens of compassion and humanity. Combined with Starbucks's strong belief in giving back to the community—be it the community that it serves or sources from or its community of employees—this 'larger purpose' continues to ignite my own passion for and commitment towards the business every day.

I experienced the Tata Group's values and philosophies and its commitment to humanity first-hand by coming in close contact with the Tata trusts and by witnessing the development of the Tata Medical Centre in Kolkata. I also got to see the group's resilience and compassion following the terrorist attack on The Taj Mahal Palace. The 26/11 attacks were emotionally draining and traumatic for me. I attended several funerals in one day. It was painful but it taught me a lot. I was deeply moved by the heroic and selfless behaviour shown by the hotel employees during the attack. We had a young colleague in the food and beverage department who was relatively new to her role, and was staffing the Unilever board meeting in the hotel at the time of the attack. She courageously stayed on with some of the guests and ensured that they got to safety. I was also inspired by the hotel's general manager who, in the midst of personal loss, worked to ensure the safety of the guests and his team. **True leaders are able to remain steadfast even during the deepest crises, and lead their team as a whole.**

It was not just the Tata Group's immediate reaction to 26/11, but also the long-term commitment shown to the victims and their families that touched me. Despite the hotel being shut for renovations following the attack, the management ensured that not a single employee left the group during that time. The Tatas worked relentlessly to set up a trust to help not only those people affected by the attack on the Taj, but also victims and their families from other locations around the city. The way the top management dealt with the crisis left a deep impact on me and helped shape my values as a Tata employee.

I believe that values must never be compromised because these form the soul of a business and are the filters that we use for everything that we do. As the leader of a business, I undertake the responsibility of ensuring that all those who work for us use the lens of compassion and humanity.

Constant innovation is required in the face of changing times to ensure that you are as relevant today as you were yesterday. I consider it a central part of my work to seek out feedback across all departments of the business and from our customers to make sure that we're seizing every moment of opportunity. **The innovations we initiate do not have to be on a large scale—sometimes, something as small as changing the way we're communicating a specific detail to customers can benefit our store partners.**

It is important that goals remain achievable. One of toughest things about my work is the need to exceed the expectations of the partners. I am a disciplined person, however, and I am realistic about setting my expectations. Sometimes I am told that I am brutally blunt, but that works for me—both at work and at home. I am as demanding of my peers and my colleagues as I am of myself. At Tata Starbucks Limited, we are a young dynamic team and everybody has different ambitions. But it is a common vision that motivates us. Besides, there is also a lot of commitment and responsibility shared by my team.

◆

Leadership is not defined by gender: empathy is the real key to successful leadership. When a leader, or a company, embraces an approach that focuses on the care of employees, one sees real success. People often think that there is a glass ceiling in the Indian business environment but, to be frank, I have never faced it. In my years as a working professional, I have seen many women succeeding purely on merit, and leading different functions and roles across companies. They have worked tirelessly for their organizations and have shouldered more complex responsibilities than I have. These women are independent and honest, and they have all approached their roles with the same level of compassion and humanity. These values have shaped the way that they have grown and helped others grow. I believe that if you are focused, passionate and resilient, you will get what you deserve. The journey will be difficult and the trade-offs will have to be decided by you—but success will be within reach.

I don't judge myself through the eyes of others; I have made my own rules. My mother has been my role model all my life; she instilled certain values in me that have helped me find a balance between career aspirations and contentment in life. She also taught me how to stay grounded, and to take into account all those involved while making my decision. I have always led an active life; in my schooldays, I was involved with student council activities, which gave me a certain level of responsibility. Yet, from that point, **my mother made it clear that irrespective of my role** outside home, once I returned, I was just my parents' daughter. Even now, I may be a CEO at work but I slip into a different role once I get home.

But is it possible to achieve that perfect work-life balance? It is the issue most commonly brought up while discussing the lives of working women. I believe that family support is critical to successfully delivering at work, and it is equally important to be disciplined at work to achieve some balance in life. In my opinion, when we enjoy our work, discipline comes naturally. We need to be honest with our families and the workplace to set the right expectations. This is the key to a healthy work-life balance.

Technology also has a huge role to play these days because it has changed the way we function. For instance, schools are shifting towards online platforms; this is a big boon for working parents who are now able to monitor their child's progress from anywhere. Thanks to such technological advances, I can make sure I am involved in my son Param's life, from helping out with his homework to staying updated on what's happening at his school. I always find the time to attend school meetings and other cultural activities too. As far as my social life is concerned, my husband and I bond over theatre and music, and as a family our holidays are sacrosanct. I ensure that I take a week-long vacation each year and love planning my holidays in advance.

I have to say I enjoy the challenges and opportunities that come with my role at Starbucks and the balance that it requires. I genuinely care for and love working in this business. **Interestingly, I didn't enjoy my cup of coffee before Starbucks came into the picture, perhaps because it wasn't the right kind of coffee for me! It wasn't until I was training in Seattle and a Starbucks store manager there made me try the Kenya blend with a lemon loaf that I realized how versatile coffee was.** I then started discovering its various flavours and enjoying the experience along the way.

There are organizations that foster and celebrate women's personal and professional potential. They understand the merits of having women at the helm and believe it is important for people to lead a satisfied and peaceful personal life. I was fortunate to work under a female boss, Deepa Harris, in my early years, and have been given flexibility with my office timings. Deepa is a dynamic and passionate leader who believes in nurturing and investing in her team. When I returned to work after my son was born, she was a pillar of strength and guided me as only a true leader can. Deepa ensured I got a meaningful role and was allowed to balance my career aspirations with my commitments at home. She continues to inspire me in this regard; learning from her example I ensure that, as a leader, I look out for my team and support them through personal milestones. Trying to find a balance between home and the office continued when I began to work under R.K. Krishna Kumar, who encouraged me to spend quality time with my family.

I feel that women shouldn't treat their work as their identity. Having said that, **we form an integral part of the workforce and, increasingly, several business houses have made a conscious effort to include more women in their leadership teams. But as women, we also need to appreciate the fact that a basic framework of meritocracy cannot be given up for diversity.** I really think that it is completely up to us as individuals, whether we are men or women, to drive our career paths in the manner that suits us. There is no one right answer.

You can always maintain some work-life balance in your life if you truly want to. It is this fact that keeps me motivated. All you need to do is to find out what drives you. If you have determination and passion, you will find a way to accomplish your goals.

◆

- Try to find people who share your values so that you don't work in an environment you are disengaged from.
- We as leaders need to remember that the decisions we take affect the people we work with, from our customers to the communities we function in. Our decisions cannot be purely for profit. We must look at a business through the lens of compassion and humanity; long-term vision must never be compromised for short-term success.
- Your work does not define your identity. It is imperative to live a well-rounded life.
- Stretching yourself beyond limits will only lead to problems. The key is to be articulate and realistic about your goals. This has helped me tremendously while fulfilling my personal and professional aspirations.

BHARTI GUPTA RAMOLA is the India Markets Leader for PricewaterhouseCoopers (PwC) and a member of the India Leadership Team. She serves on the boards of BASIX and Srijan, two of India's foremost organizations promoting livelihood development, and was a financial advisor to the National Highways Authority of India (NHAI) during the Golden Quadrilateral programme. She has been a member of PwC Global Diversity and Inclusion Council and chair of the board of Professional Assistance for Development Action (PRADAN).

Hailing from a middle-income family based in Delhi, Bharti was greatly influenced by her father, who encouraged her to read from a young age, taking her to the Delhi Public Library whenever he could. She excelled at school and later at college, where she earned a Physics (Hons) degree from St Stephen's and a management degree from IIM Ahmedabad. Having joined PwC in 1984 after working for ICICI and the Nehru Foundation for Development, she rose through the ranks quickly, becoming a partner in the global PwC network in eight years. She admits to having struggled to balance home and work in the early years and to learning to adapt in her quest for larger roles. She has also learnt to 'ask' for what she wants.

The Trusted Advisor
BHARTI GUPTA RAMOLA

I was born on the Navami before Dussehra, the day devout Hindus in North India pray to the 'kanya kumari'—the young girl—as Goddess. And yet, the announcement of my birth by Baba, my grandfather, to his mother and his wife elicited sighs from the former and tears from the latter. Badi Dadi asked Baba to start saving some more to be able to dower me. Dadi, on the other hand, had lost her first child, a daughter, and had heard of Badi Dadi's first child, also a female, meeting a similar fate. So, I am told she cried because she thought that, in keeping with our Marwari family's tradition, being the firstborn to my parents, I too might not survive.

Perhaps because of this scene at my birth, and certainly because he had watched a close friend's sister die of burn wounds after being returned to her marital home by her maternal relations, **Papa was determined that I would be economically independent, regardless of the fact that no woman in his extended family had ever worked outside of home.**

◆

From then on the story is quite simple, really. Between Papa and me, we broke many taboos. I learnt to read rather early and read a lot, so Papa enrolled me at the Delhi Public Library when I was not yet four. Even today, I remember that first visit and my excitement at finding rooms full of books. I did well at school—a school run by the New Delhi Municipal Corporation (NDMC)—so Papa entered my name in the competition for the National Merit Scholarship. Selected, I went on to study at MGD Girls' Public School, a boarding school started for Rajput princesses by

Maharani Gayatri Devi. I was an eleven-year-old from a middle-income family who could not speak English. Young girls can be cruel and I guess my classmates were no different. I was the eldest of four children and since I did not want to do anything to disappoint my parents or share anything that might cause them grief, my letters home were bland. The funny thing, though, is that other than searing memories of a few nasty incidents, I don't remember my early MGD years with any deep sense of trauma. I was good at studies and got a lot of help from teachers, particularly the maths and English teachers—the former because I knew the subject well and the latter because Miss Mathew, being a very kind Christian soul, took pity on me. She taught me after school and set a separate paper for the midterms for me. I stood second in class for those exams—the last time I stood second for the rest of my MGD life.

In those early years, I did not have a best friend as girls do in boarding school or even a 'gang', so my reading habit came to my rescue. I read everything I could lay my hands on, including the romances that my dorm mates owned and classics that the teachers recommended to me. **Because studies came easily to me and I had no great friends to hang out with, I read for several hours at once, sometimes finishing a book a day. I was the heroine in these books but often the hero, too, when I did not identify with a meek, helpless heroine.** Sometimes, I was both (for instance, in *Pride and Prejudice*, it was hard for me to decide if I was Elizabeth or Darcy!). With time, I also began to be in demand among my peers, at least during exams. I met one of my classmates recently and she recalled how I had taught her how the pulley worked using strands of hair and two pencils!

MGD was a quaint mix of a finishing school and a Jesuit seminary providing a liberal education. We celebrated all religious festivals, read mostly British textbooks and wore traditional Indian clothes on formal occasions. We had a beautiful meditation centre a short distance away from the dorms where we met every week to listen to writers, philosophers and religious leaders or to sing '*Vaishnav jan to tene kahiye*' in the same breath as 'God who touchest earth with beauty, make my heart anew'. Moral science was a compulsory subject and, for at least a couple of years, I remember being asked to keep a diary to write about the kind and unkind things I did during the day. It was hard work to fill it out without some imagination!

◆

In those days if you studied for the Indian School Certificate (ISC), you had a glorious seven months of leave before going to college. I decided to spend these working with Dateline Delhi while doing a six-month course in journalism. Sometimes I think that **my mother gave me this body and this earth; my father gave me the written word; MGD, my intellectual and moral compass; but Dateline was where I learnt of the human condition.** Dateline was full of dropouts, social misfits and rebels, lovingly presided over by Sam Castelino, a.k.a. Abba. Each disrupter was trying to become a journalist. Perhaps these radicals really were all good people, or perhaps I seemed like a baby back then, but they took great care of me and brought me out of my shell. Six months flew by, at the end of which I was offered a job as a cub reporter by *The Times of India*. I was over the moon until Papa got to hear of it; he bluntly told me he would have none of it till I had been to college. When Abba heard this, he sardonically commented, 'So you've decided to stop learning and go to college!'

◆

I joined the physics honours course at St Stephen's. We were the second batch of women at Stephen's, which had been an all-male college for decades. In my physics class of over sixty students, only five were girls (including myself), four of whom were from Delhi schools. When we were to make pairs for lab sessions, the four Delhi girls paired up without any conversation with me. I finally got paired up with someone who had not shown up for lab sessions in the first couple of weeks. While this was annoying then, it was actually the best thing that could have happened as I had to do the experiments pretty much alone and knew them all rather well, unlike some of my classmates who had to take turns to work on them. I did not stay with physics but owe my approach to problem-solving to those three years.

◆

I went on to study at IIM Ahmedabad (regressing in gender terms to ten girls in a class of 180) and after three years at ICICI and the Nehru Foundation for Development, I joined PwC in December 1984 in the management consulting division. **The professional services world was an exclusive men's club then, but so was much of the business**

world, and I did not give this much thought at the time. I had no training in compliance and scant respect for it. I still recollect my first assignment at the firm (to carry out a compensation survey) and how I almost ran away after my final draft report was reviewed by a senior colleague. Instead of an intellectually stimulating session on my findings and the praise I was expecting for my insightful presentation, I received critical feedback for my filing sloppiness and my penchant for incorporating abbreviations and mathematical symbols in working papers. Over time, I learnt the value of compliance while working for a large organization. I also learnt all I know of rigour from my then manager, Ashwani Puri. Through a delayed promotion, I learnt that in a bid to pursue excellence, I was impatient with others and gave the impression of being arrogant. I also realized that I enjoyed the intellectual independence that came with working for a firm like PwC.

I was made partner in the PwC network in 1992—the first woman in India to achieve this in the firm's network and across other large professional services firms in India. I did not then think much about what the organization must have gone through to do this, but over the years I have heard accounts of various discussions from a range of people who were partners then. I am now sure that this milestone in my life would not have been possible without the strong sponsorship of Amal Ganguli, the senior partner in Delhi then, and Ashwani Puri, with whom I worked, as also the active support of many others whose names graced our letterhead.

◆

I am often asked what it was like to be the first and only woman leader at PwC for a number of years. My answer has always been this: they should ask the firm's male partners how they felt, because I did not give this fact any thought. I had grown up in a man's world; I was used to the idea of being the only woman in a room full of men. For me, the challenge was my impatience to bring about rapid change within the system. I had a very Western approach to management—I wanted merit to trump seniority and a strong performance management system to be set up for all. I was also very blunt, a particular affliction in India.

I used to joke that not sharing locker rooms with the partners was a real disadvantage because a lot of decisions happened outside formal meetings. But over time I learnt that, while I could not share

locker rooms and did not wish to, I could join the 'addas' held in the evenings at off-sites; I was accepted by my male counterparts without reservation.

◆

While growth at work was a cakewalk in those early days, finding my balance at home was really hard. **Having grown up in a traditional Marwari family, I knew that I was expected someday to fulfil the roles of wife, mother, daughter and daughter-in-law perfectly. This was fine until I had Divi, my daughter. After she was born, I went through a rather rough and confused time, often feeling inadequate and unsure of myself.** I was ready to walk out of my marriage since my husband, Sushil, who was singularly driven, was too busy setting up a chemical plant in Bhiwadi to be of much help, either with day-to-day routines or with the emotional rollercoaster I was on.

Then a book came to my rescue—as books have often done in my life. Called *Women Like Us* by Liz Roman Gallese, it was about the women of the Harvard Business School (HBS) class of 1975. This was the first class of HBS to be 10 per cent female. Liz conducted numerous interviews with these women ten years after graduating from HBS and shared, in particular, the stories of six women whom she considered representative of the class. When I chanced upon this book at the American Library, it had been eight years since I had passed out of IIM Ahmedabad; I had been married for seven years to the most liberal man I know, had a beautiful three-year-old baby, was on track to be made partner and, in spite of it all or *because* of it all, was completely overwhelmed by everything I thought I had to do well.

I still remember a few of the stories from the book. One highlighted the case of a woman who was doing really well in her career, was more 'male' than the men around her, and appeared to be hitting a glass ceiling because she was perceived as being too aggressive. Another story was about a woman who was doing better than her husband, who had taken over the 'mom' tasks. She felt that her personal life was not going anywhere and hence did not feel successful. Out of all the women, the one who seemed the happiest was doing well at work, had two (or maybe three) children, two dogs, two nannies and a husband with whom she had a good relationship but who was focused on his career. She seemed to have the best work-life balance and was the most positive about success in her career. This was because she felt in charge of everything she wanted to do rather than getting overwhelmed by her goals (or so it seemed to me). In particular, she did not seem to expect her husband to do all the things she could not; instead, she organized herself so that she could get them done by someone else.

This book somehow shook me out of my self-pity. **I figured that while women (like those in the book and me) aspired to have great careers and perfect homes in a single generation, perhaps it would take more generations for the men in our lives to share our tasks to make that perfect home.** So, as I still wanted to have it all, I decided to set my goals around my daughter and my work. I also made a firm resolution that I would view both these crucial aspects of my life as things I had to manage by myself, and not feel overwhelmed. I stopped expecting my husband to see that I was carrying most of the burden at home and raising our child while he built his career single-mindedly. I started communicating with him about some of my expectations from him regarding chores. (Of course, he did them cheerfully when he could!) I also gave up my quest to be perfect in all spheres. **I stopped trying to be the perfect homemaker (a little dust under the sofa was fine!), the perfect wife (I did not find it necessary to turn up at all of my husband's work-related socials), the perfect daughter or the perfect friend.** I got professional help around the house, more sanity in my schedule and began to enjoy my work, the time spent with my daughter and, after a while, even my relationship with my husband. Last, but not least, I sought the help of our family and others while bringing up Divi. Our two sets of parents; Sushil's widowed aunt; my siblings, Anil, Arti and Salil; our driver, Makan Singh; and several nannies all contributed to raising my daughter. It was as Hillary Clinton once said, 'It takes a village.' I am very grateful to my large village for helping Divi become the centred and lovely person she is.

◆

From the time I was ten, the taxpayers of India paid for my education and at least a part of my keep at the best educational institutions in this country. Hence, my idea of leadership has been to engage with the development process in the country. I spent a couple of years at the Nehru Foundation for Development after IIM, but I was too young and perhaps not entrepreneurial enough to feel like I was making much of a difference. Back in the corporate world, I have been continually drawn to development issues, both as a consultant and as a promoter/board member. My life story would not be complete without acknowledging my debt to PRADAN, Srijan, BASIX, B-ABLE and DueNorth—the first two non-governmental organization (NGOs) and the rest social enterprises—for letting me be a part of their journeys to address some of the most intractable problems of our times. I have learnt much from the men and women who work in these organizations and from their clients, including lessons on commitment, leadership and inspiring others.

My work as a consultant and in the space of promoting and supporting development organizations has led to a substantial evolution in my idea of leadership. **In the beginning of my career, leadership was all about individual drive and excellence. Inspired by poets, writers and artists, I thought that to be a good leader, I needed to lead by example. So I had to work more, know the subject better, learn faster, write well, speak better. Over the years I have learnt that this is not enough to inspire others or to achieve personal, business or societal goals.**

One of the finest examples of leadership in action I have seen is in the case of Deepak Dasgupta, chairman of the NHAI when Atal Bihari Vajpayee decided that India would build world-class highways to connect the length and breadth of the country and launched the Golden Quadrilateral (GQ) programme. PwC was an advisor to the NHAI on its first public-private partnership (PPP) toll road procurement and the broader programme, and I was leading the project. We had the processes and documentation ready to invite the private sector to bid but interdepartmental conflicts and egos of the individuals involved made it very difficult to move forward. We spent an enormous amount of time in interdepartmental meetings at the Government of India level where officers would keep asking for more analysis, changes to the documentation, etc., with the approval to move forward getting inordinately delayed. As the financial advisor, it was my job to focus on getting value for money from the PPP project and to protect the NHAI and its chairman from criticism about the processes. So we were very careful in our dealings, which was also the cause of some delays. During every project review meeting, I would explain to the chairman why more diligence was required on a project or why a particular project needed to go back a couple of steps. Whether in interdepartmental meetings or meetings with his advisors, Deepak Dasgupta was always courteous and kept his cool. He would listen patiently and hardly ever pushed back, even when the demand seemed unreasonable. At the end of each meeting, however, he would hold me back and ask me to figure out how we could get the project done faster. In the first few meetings, I wondered if he had heard a word of what I had said or why he was not reacting to the comments made by junior officers in other ministries. But over time, as we overcame most obstacles and the NHAI moved forward with most of the projects, I realized that Deepak Dasgupta was what Jim Collins calls a 'Level 5 leader': someone who combines genuine personal humility with compelling professional will. He didn't care about the small battles because he was focused on winning the war—that is, rolling out the GQ programme.

I am not quite there yet, particularly with the humility quotient, but I know where I want to be and I intend to keep working at it.

◆

So, does a glass ceiling exist? **My experiences while trying to climb the management ladder at PwC, to my current role as the India Markets Leader, tell me that the glass ceiling does exist, but not quite as an impenetrable rock placed above women's heads by men.** We women must take some responsibility for not making it beyond the ceiling as well. In my case, for instance, I was programmed to let my work speak for me and did not articulate my ambition (research tells us that while some men are like that, too, more women face this challenge). However, over the years it became obvious to me that if I did not speak up, no one else would for me. I also realized that, beyond a certain level, people get promoted not just for capability and potential but also because they are trusted. Most of us tend to trust people like ourselves rather than those who are different—for instance, as a leader, you want to pick a team that will support you and back you up, and for that you need people whom you know and understand rather than those who have a reputation for being very smart and capable but difficult and unpredictable. In my case, I learnt to articulate my ambition, reach out to those who were doing the selecting and demonstrate that not only was I capable, I could be trusted to be a part of a team. Having said this, we have a lot of work to do with men as much as women in our quest to address the issue of diversity, both as a matter of natural justice and a talent-management initiative.

◆

- Believe in yourself, set goals and go after them. You can do it.
- Reflect on and understand how others see you. Do not mould yourself to fit a stereotype, but understand the gap between what you want to achieve and how your image restricts you. Once you do this, you will find the personal and professional resources to move forward.
- Excellence is an attitude that achievers have—recognize that.
- If you are a student of physics like me, you will know that balance is transient. So, by all means, look for it every day but do not make it your most important goal!

CHANDA KOCHHAR is the managing director and chief executive officer (CEO) of ICICI Bank Limited, India's second-largest bank and the largest in the private sector. She is widely recognized for her role in shaping the retail banking sector in India and for her leadership of the ICICI Group, as well as her contributions to various forums in India and globally.

Chanda began her career with erstwhile ICICI Limited in 1984 and was elevated to the board of directors of ICICI Bank in 2001. She was instrumental in establishing ICICI Bank during the 1990s, and subsequently headed the infrastructure finance and corporate banking business in ICICI Limited. In 2000, she took on the challenge of building the nascent retail business, with a strong focus on technology, innovation, process re-engineering and expansion of distribution and scale. The bank achieved a leadership position in this business. During 2006-2007, she successfully led the bank's corporate and international banking businesses during a period of heightened activity and global expansion by Indian companies. From 2007 to 2009, she was the joint managing director and chief financial officer during a critical period of rapid change in the global financial landscape. She was elevated as managing director and CEO of ICICI Bank in 2009 and is responsible for the bank's diverse operations in India and overseas. She also chairs the boards of the bank's principal subsidiaries, which include India's leading private sector life and general insurance companies.

Chanda was conferred with the Padma Bhushan, one of India's highest civilian honours, in 2011.

◆

The Bankable Leader
CHANDA KOCHHAR[*]

When she was a young schoolgoing girl in Jaipur, Chanda Kochhar's brother, older than her by seven years, decided to apply for an engineering degree. Back then, her father, Roop Chand Advani, was the principal of the local Malaviya Regional Engineering College. Expectedly, her brother applied to her father's college, and also, just to be doubly sure, to faraway Baroda. To the family's great dismay, once the results were announced, they learnt that he had passed the Baroda test with flying colours, but had missed admission to the local college by a mere half a per cent. This is when Chanda's father's colleagues approached him with a suggestion: Why not offer the children of faculty members the privilege of a relatively lower cut-off score? Her father agreed that it was an excellent idea, but then he slipped in a caveat—the recommendation would be implemented a year down the line. So it came to be: Chanda's brother went off to the neighbouring state of Gujarat. As a young girl witnessing this turn of events, Chanda remembers feeling let down by her father. Why would he deny his son an opportunity that was well within his reach? Why not let the boy reap the benefits of a new rule? It was only later that she came to appreciate the strength of her father's stand—how, no matter the temptation, he never compromised on his integrity and sense of justice. **While she imbibed honesty and fair play from her father, Chanda credits her mother with teaching her the value of tenacity and adapting to her environment.** When she was just thirteen, her father had a sudden heart attack and passed away. It was the end of life as she knew it—of light-hearted mornings at St Angela Sophia School,

---

*This essay is in the third person at the author's request.

or afternoons devoted to playing with friends or participating in All India Radio programmes. Her mother, on her part, now found herself responsible for three growing children—Chanda was yet to appear for the tenth Board exams; Bharti, her older sister, was halfway through her medical degree; and Mahesh, her brother, was still pursuing his engineering course. As a child of Partition, Chanda's mother had watched her own father rebuild his life from scratch in India, and so she knew something of pulling through tough times. As a bereaved homemaker, it took all the fortitude and ingenuity she possessed to arrive at a viable plan for the future. She discovered her flair for dress designing, found a job in a small textile firm and made herself indispensable to her employers. She then decided to move with her children to Mumbai, a city that housed her extended family. She became Chanda's role model, showing her how to shoulder responsibility and roll with the punches.

For the kids, adjusting to Mumbai was by no means easy. In Jaipur everyone knew everyone else; Mumbai was impersonal, and it took time and effort for strangers to become acquaintances. Yet, Mumbai was also a dazzling metropolis, buzzing with activity—with the call of business and trade. It was inevitable that Chanda's childhood dreams of becoming an Indian Administrative Service (IAS) officer would fall by the wayside. Inspired by the city she now inhabited, she pursued economics at Jai Hind College and a master's in business administration (MBA) in finance from the Jamnalal Bajaj Institute of Management Studies. As she topped her class, she knew that her father—who had urged his children to pursue their dreams, regardless of gender—would be proud.

◆

Chanda Kochhar's first place of employment was destined to become her permanent home. Back in 1984, fresh out of B-school, she sought the post of a management trainee. The Industrial Credit and Investment Corporation of India (the former avatar of ICICI Bank), impressed by her number-crunching skills and her focus, hired her; so began her first assignment as a trainee in project finance.

Over the years, Chanda grew rapidly within the organization. N. Vaghul, then the chairman and managing director of ICICI, keen to empower young employees, offered her her first big undertaking six months into her employment—computerizing the entire client information storage and retrieval system for the organization—a prestigious task even by today's standards. Then, in 1993–94, he chose her to be a part of his core team to learn the brass tacks of commercial banking. Then, in the mid-1990s, she was selected to head the newly formed infrastructure industry group and later, the major clients group—which meant handling the top 200 clients of ICICI.

After having run the corporate business for some time, the turning point in her career came with the new millennium—K.V. Kamath, the CEO who succeeded Vaghul, asked her to head retail operations. It was a risky proposition by most people's estimates, and she is known to have asked: 'Why should I move from handling 50 per cent of the bank's business and profit in the major clients group to handling a mere 1 per cent of the bank's business in retail? It makes no sense!' In reply, Kamath merely smiled and said, 'Because I want you to make retail 50 per cent of the bank's business, too.' And that is exactly what happened. **She worked hard, dreamt big, took informed risks—at a time when India had about 300 Automated Teller Machines (ATMs), ICICI decided to set up *3,000* ATMs across the country.** In the next six years, true to Kamath's vision, with a strong focus on technology, innovation, scale, process re-engineering and the expansion of distribution, they ramped up the retail business to about 67 per cent of the bank's balance sheet, growing it from ₹200 crore in the year 2000 to ₹100,000 crore in 2006. ICICI became the largest retail financier in the country.

In fact, Chanda was lucky to have K.V. Kamath for a mentor. Early on, as the head of ICICI's western regional office, she made a brief presentation to him on the changes she had made in the functioning of the workplace. Kamath was quick to say, 'Who did you ask before making the changes?' Chanda remembers mustering some courage and softly saying, 'No one.' Kamath congratulated her for having the courage to take initiative.

The other defining moment in Chanda's life was the 2008 meltdown. The Lehman Brothers had filed for bankruptcy, the world economy was unravelling, and although ICICI's exposure to the Lehman catastrophe was less than 1 per cent of its balance sheet, there was panic in India. Despite the Reserve Bank of India's (RBI) assurances and the then finance minister, P. Chidambaram's measured advice that there was no cause for worry, thousands queued outside ICICI's ATMs to withdraw money from ICICI Bank. Chanda—now as ICICI's joint managing director and chief financial officer—decided to take some decisive steps to quell people's anxiety. First, after putting herself firmly in her customers' shoes and reflecting over what they needed to know, she reassured them via the media. 'You are free to withdraw your money,' she said, 'but it's a knee-jerk reaction, since there is no crisis.' Next, **she instructed her staff to empathize with the fears of the bank's depositors, offer them a seat and a glass of water, give them a patient hearing and guide them; some of ICICI's branches were open till midnight because she didn't want a single customer being turned away.** Finally, Chanda ensured that all their ATMs were full of cash—not an easy task in a nation as immense as India! Her team had to plan to the last detail with precise mathematical calculations: if one customer were to make a transaction every three minutes at every ATM, and were to withdraw an average amount of cash, how much cash was needed on a daily basis? And how many armoured trucks had to be called to move all that money from their cash chests to the distant ATMs?

Most importantly, as the spokesperson of ICICI, she made it a point to remain calm in her demeanour and approach. She even remembers, in the middle of the upheaval, taking a couple of hours off to attend her son's squash tournament. This wasn't a calculated move, but it went a long way towards restoring customer confidence. According to her, mothers at the tournament, even those she barely knew, decided that if she could attend a tournament in the middle of a 'looming catastrophe', the bank was clearly doing fine! Within twenty-four hours, the crisis was averted and they managed to restore some calm.

◆

Banking is the business of commanding confidence. In December 2008, even as K.V. Kamath moved on, Chanda secured the top job at ICICI—as managing director and CEO—after a stiff selection process. She was later informed that four things worked in her favour—the fact that she was, by temperament, unruffled, no matter the crisis; her ability to simplify strategy, without letting it get weighed down by jargon; her belief in being a hands-on leader; and, most importantly, that she had grown with the organization and knew it inside-out.

The position of managing director and CEO, however, could not have come at a more fraught juncture. Businesses across the globe were in a state of turmoil; in India, the RBI was consistently pushing up interest rates; and ICICI, she believed, needed to reinvent itself.

Until that point, ICICI had been the icon of breakneck growth at a frenzied pace. When times were good—when the country's gross domestic product (GDP) was growing at 9 per cent, and retail banking was unpenetrated territory—ICICI could afford to ride the growth elephant and seek market expansion, size and scale.

But **in the global environment Chanda had inherited, she realized that they had to reorient the strategy, focusing on the four Cs—capital conservation, cost efficiency, CASA (current account & savings account) deposits and credit quality.** Therefore, when she took over ICICI from K.V. Kamath, she chose to spend the first year consolidating and positioning the balance sheet for the next phase of growth.

Earlier, ICICI had assertively pursued credit card and personal loan businesses; now, Chanda instructed her colleagues to cut their losses from those verticals. Earlier, they had recruited an entire army of direct selling agents (DSAs); now, they chose to focus on branches and internal teams for both business acquisition and collections. From working for an organization that always grew at 35–40 per cent each year, team members found themselves using terms like 'profitable, balanced growth'. If they felt demotivated, Chanda would remind them that **growth could mean various things; it wasn't just about growing the balance sheet.**

Two years and many battles later, the numbers proved the wisdom of that decision. Unsecured loans as a percentage of total loans came down from around 11 per cent in mid-2008 to less than 3 per cent in 2010. The net non-performing assets ratio reduced from around 2 per cent to 0.9 per cent. And the return on assets, which had been less than 0.9 per cent, had crossed 1.3 per cent. These were milestones in the bank's remarkable turnaround, and set the foundation for a long-term profitable growth model.

◆

When asked about the role gender plays at the workplace, Chanda believes that being a woman should neither hinder nor grant one the right to demand privileges at work. **If one wishes to enjoy the opportunities men do, if one expects a level playing field, one needs to fulfil the same responsibilities, whether it involves travel or working late. There can be no gender-driven excuses.** Chanda recalls how, in 1996, the day she returned from maternity leave, K.V. Kamath gave her one of her most challenging assignments—ICICI was introducing a new product linked to the prime lending rate and she was to market it to corporates in the western region, with an ambitious target. K.V. Kamath, of course, knew that Chanda had an infant at home. She, too, could have complained about her domestic commitments, but she chose not to because she did not think she had the right to ask for special concessions as a woman. She has always viewed every responsibility as a testimony of the organization's faith in her. Consequently, Chanda squeezed everything she could out of her time in office, multitasked like she never had and pushed her team to the limit. They achieved the annual target in just three months.

Chanda has often said that ICICI is a completely gender-neutral organization—indeed, the company has always had women in senior managerial positions, from Lalita Gupte, Kalpana Morparia and Shikha Sharma to Renuka Ramnath, Vishakha Mulye and Madhabi Puri-Buch. **Chanda herself has strong views about the equality of sexes—she remains firm in the belief that all selections and promotions should be merit-based.**

Of curse, she is aware that society as a whole isn't governed by these values. Chanda still remembers the response she received when, in the early years of her career, she visited factories to inspect the projects that ICICI were funding. Onlookers stared and employees were visibly uncomfortable; she was the only woman around. So unaccustomed were they to female visitors that there wasn't even a women's loo!

It is this, she believes, that disconcerts professional women—apart from the fact that families demand that women be caregivers and nurturers. As a result, these days, while women are enthusiastically accepting entry-level positions, there are several—hemmed in by the gender-specific responsibilities of marriage and home—dropping out at mid- and upper-management levels. Chanda considers this to be unfortunate, since she thinks women are much more flexible than men, adapt better, come with higher emotional quotients and are expert multitaskers.

◆

In today's world, Chanda states, a leader has to balance the big picture and ground reality; she can't get so preoccupied with an enticing dream that she forgets a looming crisis, or focus so entirely on a momentary upheaval that she misses distant opportunities.

Additionally, she says, **a leader must have one eye on the broad trends—what is happening out there, what is the next volatile**

development that can hit the organization?—and one eye on day-to-day operations. In her experience, this isn't easy, since in a wired world, the broad trends themselves are short-lived phenomena—anything one wishes to implement needs to be carried through in less than ninety days if it is to remain relevant!

Moreover, Chanda has observed that as one climbs the career ladder, there is a risk of insulating oneself. Communication alone can keep one abreast of all developments. To remain clued in at all times, she holds regularly scheduled employee discussion meetings. These are not performance reviews; rather, they are frank discussions with about twenty employees randomly picked from various parts of the organization. These employees are assured that everything they tell her will be viewed as confidential, and merely for her to absorb—and she states that she has had some wonderful and enlightening conversations with them on the work environment, customer-responses, transfer policies and gender issues. According to her, her team members know they can talk to her, and that she will listen.

Most of all, **Chanda thinks that a leader has to be hands-on**. In 2008, when the global financial crisis hit, she, as the joint managing director, oversaw every tiny detail—from highlighting the strategy for dealing with small depositors coming to faraway branches; arriving at how best to handle regulators and large investors; listing out the twenty-five most likely questions the media would ask, and answering them; to recommending ways of de-stressing harried bank managers—this was the level of detailing and execution!

Chanda believes that every leader should communicate clearly. When she decided to rebalance the bank's portfolio as the new managing director, it was a big adjustment for the staff. Chanda wanted them on her side; she hoped they'd understand her vision. The only way of achieving this was by constantly and consistently communicating with them. ICICI has more than 60,000 employees, so she followed a formal trickle-down approach. She started with the senior management team, in groups and in one-to-one meetings, not only explaining why this was the right call in the current situation, but also highlighting how each of them could contribute individually. She then travelled to regional offices and branches, and conveyed her strategy to the staff there. Finally, she communicated through the organization's own internal media to reach out to those she hadn't been able to speak to. She is confident that this went a long way towards helping her gain her team's confidence.

Chanda also regularly visits ICICI's branches; she considers it important to talk to those working there, and also to customers. One of her most meaningful encounters, she reminisces, was when ICICI was changing many of the customer processes; she spent an entire day not just visiting a branch but standing in the reception area watching the trainee who greeted and directed those coming through the door. Chanda had assumed that all the trainee had to do was ask customers, 'Hello, may I help you?', and steer them to the right counters. But she learnt that this seemingly simple job was actually quite complicated—for the trainee encountered all kinds of questions, from how to apply for a life insurance policy, to how to file claims on the death of a relative! Far from being a straightforward role for a beginner, this task was meant for someone with enough experience to deal with complicated and unstructured queries. Chanda realized that since this was the bank's very first point of interaction with its customers, this role required a high level of skill and experience. Customers deserved nothing less.

Ultimately, though, Chanda believes that **the decision about where the organization will go has to come from a single leader. She doesn't think that a dozen people can take a big decision—if a leader seeks that kind of involvement, there will be a dozen choices and no solution!** While taking a final call, though, a leader has to ensure that she has a keen understanding of everyone's opinion within the organization and outside; has absorbed and assimilated all the significant points; and has conveyed her vision and the reasons guiding it to her team.

◆

Apart from being the managing director and CEO of ICICI Bank, Chanda Kochhar is a member of the India-Japan Business Leaders' Forum and US-India CEO Forum; the deputy chairperson of the Indian Banks' Association; and on the boards of the Indian Council for Research on International Economic Relations and National Institute of Securities Markets. The inevitable question that follows is how she manages to do it all.

The answer, she says, is simpler than one thinks: **achieve forty-eight hours of work in a twenty-four-hour day.** Chanda often makes 'day trips' on official work from Mumbai to New York. Catching a late-night flight from India's financial capital, she reaches New York early in the morning, attends back-to-back meetings, takes a flight back home the same night and heads to office the morning after she lands. While it appears as though she has been away for three days, it's actually just *two* days because of the time difference! This is what it sometimes takes for her to juggle multiple commitments.

At other times, it's a matter of her being supremely organized—constantly planning and perennially multitasking—and holding on to her belief that she can and will achieve the impossible. She recalls reading the *Satyanarayan Katha* during her forty-minute journey home. She goes through mails when she has a ten-minute window of free time. She also stays in touch with her children from work, and attends to work calls quite often from home. During weekends, she divides her time between watching the latest Hindi film with her family (always a stressbuster, she says) and reviewing presentations and replying to emails.

As a working woman, Chanda acknowledges her mother and in-laws for their support, especially when her children were younger. **Her children are 'pillars of strength' too—she recounts how, when her daughter, Aarti, was growing up, she'd pitch in and look after her younger brother, Arjun; and neither of them ever whined or complained.** Most of all, though, Chanda thanks her husband, Deepak Kochhar, for backing her. She met Deepak when they were both at B-school; he was a classmate, and soon became a close friend. Two years after she joined ICICI, they got married. She calls him her strongest supporter. Even today, she says, not much has changed; he is always encouraging her. Despite having an enormously busy schedule as a wind energy entrepreneur, he played an equal role in raising Aarti and Arjun, and, according to Chanda, has always been there to urge her to pursue her ambitions.

While it may sound as though she has managed to strike a work-life balance, Chanda admits that there are times she has missed her son's sports tournaments to attend a meeting; or left her ailing daughter's bedside to avert a work crisis. On other occasions, in the early days of her career, she would delay taking a work call because her kids needed help with a cut-and-paste project; or would rejig her schedule to attend a parent-teacher meeting. Either way, the primary feeling she has constantly battled is *guilt*—for not always being there for her children.

Yet, Chanda says that one of her most cherished memories is when the newspapers announced that she had become managing director and CEO of ICICI Bank, and her daughter, Aarti, then in the US, sent her an email that moved her to tears. Aarti said, **'You never made us realize you had such a demanding, stressful and successful career. At home, you were just our mother.'**

At such times, Chanda states, it does seem possible—one can claim the best of both worlds.

◆

- It is important to know the organization one works for.
- Show initiative.
- A leader must learn to take quick decisions. As the head of an organization or project, one does not have the luxury of waiting for every scrap of data and analysis before taking a decision.
- Embrace challenges. Confidence is vital if one is leading an organization.
- It is imperative to ensure that stress doesn't weigh us down. If, as a leader, one allows stress to filter down the organization and reach the team, one is only wearing away the organization's core.
- Keep communication channels open.
- Every good leader must talk to her staff about her vision to earn her employees' trust.
- As the head of a business, staying in touch with one's customers is a must.

After her early days at the Industrial Development Bank of India (IDBI), **CHITRA RAMKRISHNA** was selected to be part of a small team that prepared a blueprint for the Securities and Exchange Board of India (SEBI).

Later, she found herself as part of a core five-member team that was to create the National Stock Exchange (NSE). Chitra, as an architect of one of the world's biggest stock exchanges, was elevated to the post of NSE's managing director and chief executive officer (CEO), succeeding Ravi Narain in 2013; she became the third woman to head an exchange in the Asia-Pacific region.

Nominated by *Fortune* as one of the fifty most powerful women in the world, and awarded the Forbes Women Leader of the Year (2014), Chitra's advice to women is especially interesting. She says, 'You do not need to do it all!'

◆

The Jewel of the NSE
CHITRA RAMKRISHNA

In my career of nearly thirty years, I have often been asked how I came to choose the financial services industry. The question always makes me pause since the fact is that I did not choose this space, nor did I have an agenda about where I would be two decades later. All I was clear about was this—I wanted to be a part of something big and meaningful, that would have a large impact and where I would have a share in the decision-making process. I've been fortunate—all three conditions have been fulfilled.

I was born to parents who were highly enlightened. **From an early age, we, the children of the house, were brought up to believe that irrespective of our gender, financial independence was a necessary goal**; a professional qualification to equip us for a career was imperative. So it came to be that by twenty-one, I secured my chartered accountancy degree. And shortly thereafter, I found myself at the IDBI.

◆

In retrospect, my stint at the IDBI was the first major breakthrough in my career since it provided me with exposure to large projects with nationwide reach and the opportunity to be part of something meaningful early on.

The IDBI was unlike what I would have imagined of public sector organizations at that time. I had assumed that they were institutions with rigid and reserved hierarchies. Instead, within the IDBI, I was proven entirely wrong; employees were encouraged to interact with the leadership. In fact, whenever a new assignment or an opportunity was at hand, all of us had a chance to volunteer and ask if we could be part of the project.

We had a rare freedom—the freedom to choose. All we had to do was ask.

I recollect the time between 1988 and 1990 when the IDBI put together a small team to work on the setting up of SEBI. A few volunteers from the IDBI were sought to work on this project. I jumped at the opportunity and voiced my desire to be involved. Because there were not too many takers for the job at that time, I had the chance to be associated with the legislative framework of SEBI at the formative stages. I returned to the IDBI in 1989 and by 1991–92 the SEBI Act saw the light of day.

A similar thing happened during the setting up of the NSE. Twenty-odd years back, when it was no more than a glimmer of an idea, the IDBI was asked to do some spadework for getting the organization started. Once again, I raised my hand and expressed my enthusiasm for the task. Once more, I was assigned the project. **If my career stands testimony to one fact, it is this—if you ask, doors open.**

◆

It has been quite a journey from when I was one of the five hand-picked by the legendary S.S. Nadkarni, then chairman of the IDBI, to set up the NSE from scratch.

Building the NSE was by no means easy. We confronted every conceivable obstacle in our path. For one, when I started the new assignment, I knew little about the business of bourses. Moreover, it was 1992, which will go down in the history of India as the year of the 'Big Bull' scam in the stock markets. On the one hand, we had to battle the trust deficit and perception problems it had created for brokers. On the other, the broking community itself viewed us with some suspicion as a team of naïve bureaucrats creating an unrealistic institution. And then there were the stipulations of the government of the day, keen to set up a stock exchange that would be free of the problems witnessed by the existing exchanges; a professionally run bourse that would conduct trading transparently and would ensure that price discovery was transparent and electronically driven was the need of the hour. This was a tall order! Besides, the Bombay Stock Exchange (BSE) was already an established institution and it was not clear how easy or difficult it would be to bring a new business model in the industry and how long it would take to reach a leadership position.

Clearly, when we started the NSE project we had no idea how large it would become! We had only three things going for us. One, **we were**

perceived as a bunch of outsiders. Since we had nothing to lose, we could experiment. Second, we were guided by the vision and determination of S.S. Nadkarni and R.H. Patil (formerly an IDBI director). They led us, yet gave us the space to execute every task independently. Third, we were quick to market.

In this context, an incident immediately comes to mind. In the early days, when S.S. Nadkarni would visit the NSE's office in Mumbai to check on the progress, he'd walk around mulling over the future state of affairs. How did we plan to trade? Those were the days of poor telephone connectivity. The BSE conducted trading under the open outcry system, where brokers would talk to each other or rather, shout at each other, gesticulate wildly and transact on the pit. All of us at the NSE knew that if we had to take on the might of the BSE, we would have to switch to satellite-based technology. One day, S.S. Nadkarni asked us bluntly when the exchange would be up and running. The team was quick to respond: 'In a few months.' S.S. Nadkarni was likely sceptical, but within that narrow time frame, the NSE was functional and came with the best of technology. This set the benchmark for the NSE's work culture. **To date, we follow a quick-to-market module.**

In the initial days, we didn't really set ourselves a volume target. Our focus was getting the trading platform and back end systems right. We also needed to keep broad market stability in mind to push through regulatory functions. Consequently, we had to play twin roles—on the one hand, develop the market for trading and on the other, develop business for our members.

Even as we worked long and hard, the times favoured us. The demutualization of exchanges visualized by regulators and policymakers brought about a paradigm shift in the operation of capital markets. The separation of management and ownership helped establish a framework in which the conflict of interest in handling the dual responsibilities of commercial and regulatory aspects was reduced. This move was ahead of the curve and enabled the introduction of new products and a more robust market infrastructure.

We grew slowly, but decisively. Around March 1995, the NSE had 135 companies and the daily average turnover for equities was barely ₹17 crore. Today, it has over 1,600 actively traded companies and the average daily turnover in the cash segment has grown 43 per cent annually to around ₹15,000 crore. To put all of this in perspective, the NSE is not only the leader in the Indian markets, but has also carved a space in the global exchanges arena, having made inroads here with fifteen-odd markets trading in exchange-traded funds (ETFs) based on the Nifty.

Working for the NSE had taught me about the absolute need to have innovation as a part of our vision. **We need to look for ideas that have the potential to become trends and remain open at all times to technological advances.** Within the NSE, we've embraced a pan-India VSAT (very small aperture terminal) network; facilitated screen-based trading, so retail investors located across cities and in remote corners of the country have trading access; built the infrastructure and legislative framework for India's first depository; and pushed for a technological backbone that is scalable and unassailable.

◆

Being a part of the team that built the NSE brick by brick was the first major turning point in my life. The next pivotal moment in my career came most unexpectedly in November 2012, when Ravi Narain told me that I was to be his successor. Soon, I realized that being the CEO of an organization is a wholly different ballgame and unlike being the second-in-command!

I took up the post of CEO, albeit with some trepidation in my heart. **As the third woman to head an exchange in the Asia-Pacific region (after Sri Lanka's Colombo Stock Exchange and China's Shenzhen Stock Exchange) I was aware that I was in a position of both privilege and enormous responsibility.** Besides, given the real-time nature of this business, the challenges that we face on a daily basis need no enunciation. Everything that we do is customer-centric and we continue to push ourselves each day to provide a superior and an integrity-led experience to investors.

Indeed, my biggest source of sustenance has been the experience of building an institution which is trusted by market participants because of its high integrity. When we began the NSE, we tried to create a set of guiding principles, so that work ethics were built into the team's fabric right from the outset. Today, all decisions are made based on this system of belief.

I think **building a business is all about focusing on a need, bringing talented people together, and creating something of lasting value for society at large. For me, working at the NSE is not just a job; it is a commitment to public service.** I view the exchange as a vehicle for the financial well-being of the people of India. It provides an ethical platform for people to trade and thus drives financial inclusion and literacy among the under-represented. Financial education, therefore, has always been a top priority for the NSE and we have helmed various education and awareness programmes to improve the financial well-being of the common citizen. The final objective is to empower our youth by inculcating the habit of saving from an early age and developing financial and investment capabilities. It is this larger vision that drives us and makes us a successful institution.

◆

As a leader, it is your responsibility to share your commitment to and wholehearted love for your job with your team at every opportunity. This is what I learnt by observing the leadership team at the IDBI and the NSE. I was surrounded by people who shared a common vision and a collective passion to realize it and this inspired everyone. As a team, therefore, we knew we could achieve just about anything.

I believe that the qualities that make a great leader—integrity, vision, relentless commitment, even tenaciousness, and, of course, passion—are attributes demonstrated by individuals irrespective of their gender. Having said that, I believe **women bring unique strengths to homes and to the workplaces. They collaborate, communicate and reach out. They're responsible.** With their compassion and inclusiveness, they empower those colleagues who are timid or unsure. I have seen scores of women leverage these strengths for entrepreneurial success, not just in metropolitan cities, but also in the rural hinterland, where uneducated or semi-skilled women display enterprise and resourcefulness as breadwinners, saving and investing to keep their families secure.

Not surprisingly, today, a lot of our regional heads at the NSE are women and do extremely well. While I'm happy about this, I also know that the banking and financial services industry isn't representative of India. Within the manufacturing sector or in non-metropolitan areas women still struggle to find a foothold.

Organizations need women at the helm, now more than ever, and have an important role to play in empowering their female workforce—be it by advancing the careers of female staff, nurturing them in the system, handing them positions of responsibility once they prove themselves or offering them level playing fields.

Currently, few sectors display progressiveness; they do little to provide women with equal access to leadership opportunities and fail to tap into the huge potential of gender diversity at the workplace.

In my own instance, when I embarked on my career, two things worked in my favour. First, the financial sector is largely gender-agnostic. Second, if you have been a part of an establishment from the very beginning and have grown with it, you don't confront the challenge of having to be heard. Instead, you can focus your energies on day-to-day professional assignments.

◆

While a lot more women enter the workforce today, they also tend to drop off midstream. Women invest time and effort, first securing an education, then establishing themselves within their respective professions. If there is a way of helping women ride through some of life's crossroads, we will be able to retain a lot more woman power at middle and senior levels.

Women's capacity to stay on at a job has a lot to do with the support systems available to them to help balance their responsibilities at home and at work. **While young employees are enormously confident about decisions at the workplace, many of them return to nuclear families and find themselves without succour. With requisite support systems in place, it is easier for women to make hard career decisions**; it's also just a little easier to achieve some work-life balance. If workplaces can provide environments that are empathetic to these needs, they will be doing much to enhance the participation of women.

Women will also have it a little easier if they stop attempting to be superwomen. We have extremely unrealistic expectations and end up being doubly harsh on ourselves. My advice to women is: You do not need to do it all! Also, **taking a break to enrich yourself personally or professionally is perfectly fine. I have seen men taking career breaks to add value to their lives, so why shouldn't women be at liberty to do that?** Organizations need to offer their staff such flexibility.

◆

In our country, even today, women's empowerment is linked to the basic challenge of gender equality. **It is only when all individuals, irrespective**

of gender, are given the chance to hone their capabilities and are offered equal access to basic opportunities like education that women's empowerment will become more than a fight for survival.

I wish to tell all women: There will always be things that you don't know. There will always be a risk of failure. But there is greater risk in holding back. What you need to do is to take a giant leap of faith and grab every opportunity that comes your way! Be open to new ideas and the world will open itself to you.

◆

- Passion, not profit, is the biggest driver.
- The need for integrity cannot be overemphasized. While things have changed significantly in the financial services industry and indeed, across all sectors, in the last thirty years, the basic principles of hard work, honesty, and a quest for excellence have remained the same.
- If you create value for your stakeholders at large, profits will follow.
- Innovate. While there will always be competition, it is innovation alone that will grant organizations distinct identities.
- Ask, if you seek opportunities for growth.
- If you're an outsider, you have more room to experiment and prove detractors wrong.
- You do not have to do it all!

In 1996, when **DEBJANI GHOSH** was asked during an interview where she saw herself two decades later, she answered, 'As the head of Intel India.' Today, as Intel India's first female managing director in South Asia and vice president in charge of sales and marketing, Debjani is known for her commitment to success.

This commitment has its wellspring in her unconventional childhood, when she travelled across multiple countries—changing schools every few years and learning to imbibe the best of each cultural nuance she was exposed to. She was brought up to believe she could achieve anything she desired, just as any of her brothers could. Such conviction spurred her growth within Intel; today, she is rated as amongst the twenty-five most powerful women in India (*Fortune*, 2013).

A master of business administration (MBA) in marketing from the S.P. Jain Institute of Management and Research, Mumbai, one of Debjani's passions is encouraging equal opportunities at the workplace. She laments that women are 'told how best to become great wives and mothers, but never great CEOs or sportswomen', and hopes for a time when more women occupy leadership positions in corporate India.

◆

Digital DNA
DEBJANI GHOSH

Napoleon said that 'patience, persistence and perspiration make an unbeatable combination for success'. When I look back at my career and observe those moments when I've had to overcome challenges, I see how vital these ingredients have been.

Indeed, climbing the corporate ladder is never easy and the difficulty is exacerbated in the case of women. We have to be ready to deal with daily difficulties—be it stereotypical mindsets about gender, juggling family and work, unequal pay or, worst of all, self-doubt.

Perhaps, my struggle has been eased to some degree on account of the parental support I've received. **Right from the time I was a child growing up in a family with several boys, my parents made it a point to treat me as an equal.** Through words and deeds, they taught me to believe in myself and make a difference. Dad's constant refrain was, 'The right question is not whether you can do it, but whether you *want* to do it.' How valuable these early life lessons are when one has to compete in the male-dominated corporate world, without being apologetic or scared!

◆

In 1996, when I joined Intel in India, it was not the behemoth it is today. The organization had just five people!

My reason for joining Intel was purely guided by the heart winning over the head. It was the only company where I was interviewed by a woman, and an amazing one at that. She was Deborah Conrad, the head of marketing for the Asia-Pacific region at that point in time and one of the first professional women I had met.

Deborah was strong, extremely confident, passionate about her work and successful! I was in awe of her from the moment I walked in. Sitting in front of me was someone who had achieved what I wanted to; Deborah was real proof that it was possible for women to get to the top while remaining passionate about what they did! I knew at that very point that this was the company I wanted to work for. Nothing else mattered. And I am so glad I decided to go with that instinct.

Joining (what was then) a tiny organization was, in its own way, an advantage—a smaller team meant a culture of entrepreneurship, fluid learning and a larger range of opportunities to choose from. The first few years at Intel saw me gaining new experiences and skill sets, and building a strong network of colleagues and mentors.

Further, **when I joined Intel, I was one of the few women in the organization and the information technology (IT) industry as a whole. I decided to use this fact to my advantage rather than complain.** I came to see that as long as I was well-prepared and bringing value to the table, being the only female in the room was not a problem. In fact, it helped me put my distinct perspective as a working woman to better use.

When it comes to women professionals, especially in leadership roles, gender-based behavioural stereotypes remain a challenge. We are expected to be gentler than our male counterparts, emotional, less aggressive, just because we are women. And if we don't comply, we are considered intimidating or not easy to work with. This is one gender-related conception that I have struggled the most with. **I have never understood why it's perfectly okay for a man to raise his voice when making a point, or thump the table, but not for a woman.** What we forget is that each woman is an individual with unique behavioural traits and characteristics; as organizations we should leverage that to our advantage.

◆

A professional woman has to face distinct challenges. But these trials aren't showstoppers—merely speed-breakers that must be overcome.

Some of the biggest challenges are self-created. I've noticed that, more often than not, women hold themselves back, fearing they are not ready for the next role. To me, the elephant in the room is the one in our heads. And that elephant takes birth in our heads from childhood when **we're told how to become great wives and mothers, but never great chief** executive officers (CEOs) or sportswomen. We're expected to be domestic goddesses, whether or not we have career ambitions. And that's where our guilt trip starts—when we find ourselves as excellent professionals struggling to perform as exemplary homemakers.

Women, consequently, suffer crises of confidence across industries. They feel remorseful about the time they spend at work; they undermine themselves and foil their own aspirations. The moment they stray from the 'defined' path of matrimony and maternity, women across the board ask: are we really capable? Are we being fair to our families? Are we doing right by our employers? Is it okay to want more professionally or will that make us ambitious? Is ambition a bad thing? These are questions women have to grapple with on a continual basis. **My advice to all young women is: do not worry about what others think, but about what you think and believe**. That is the starting point of change.

Then there is the other extreme—of committing ourselves to our careers to the extent that we forget about our own needs; we lose 'me time' and 'us time'. I believe that the subject of a work-life balance is extremely personal and something we need to figure out on our own. For me, it's more about work-life *integration*, given that we live in an always-connected world and the lines between our professional and personal lives are blurring fast. **I try scheduling the time I need for myself—be it at the gym or in the company of books—and do not leave such pursuits to chance.** It helps me get into a habit and manage time better. I am also very disciplined about keeping weekends free for family and ensuring I take some time off once or twice a year to just do the things I enjoy outside work, like travelling. There is no right or wrong answer, but we do need to unwind and follow the dreams that exist beyond the office space; it helps to plan for these interests, so that we don't ignore them.

◆

I believe that leadership isn't dependent on position, power or gender. Rather, it is linked to being the best version of you. It is about rising to the occasion when you are called and leading from the front. All of us have the potential to be extraordinary; we just need to believe in our ability to deliver results.

Equally, a leader is willing to take off her blinkers and embrace the best talent—irrespective of the shape, size, age or gender it comes in. **The competitive edge of an organization is defined by its ability to**

find, hire and retain the best people, and leaders have to identify such genius.

Authenticity is the third defining trait of a leader. With today's rapidly changing business environment, employees are likely to be nervous; they need reassurance and clarity. A leader, therefore, has to offer genuine comfort, not merely by communicating effectively but by leading by behaviour. Indeed, **more than grand tokens, it's the small gestures that build trust and confidence within teams.**

◆

While growing within Intel, I have gathered valuable insights as a professional and also as a working woman—call this the tenfold path to success, if you will.

Ambition is vital for climbing the corporate ladder; embrace your ambition and view it as a strength, rather than as a weakness. I've learnt this lesson within my own home—while my mother is a brilliant homemaker, I've had remarkably different aspirations. Rather than thwarting these dreams, my family has nurtured them. Rather than telling me to follow in my mother's footsteps, I've been taught to be proud of who I am. It's time we, as women, accepted that ambition isn't a bad word. To me, being ambitious is what keeps me on my toes and continues to drive me to be the best version of myself. It's what got me my first job and it's what gets every young aspirant a career break—after all, how is one to secure that prized position without displaying drive and interest?

Share your dreams with your family and loved ones. I've always said that marriage is one of the most important career decisions for a woman. Yet, it's amazing how many young girls enter matrimony without knowing the kind of support they'll get from their future spouse and extended family. If you seriously intend having a career, ensure that you speak to your spouse and family members to set the right expectations. This also helps you build that much-needed support system—a must for every working woman.

Pinpoint the trade-offs you're willing to make, and make your peace with them. The fact is that whether you're a man or a woman, you cannot have the best of both worlds. A good work-life balance is possible, but some trade-offs need to be made by everyone. For instance, I've given myself the space to outsource cooking and housekeeping, so I can focus on work. Similarly, with my team, I've set clear expectations—the weekend is family time, and unless there's an emergency, I do not want to be disturbed. Women are notorious for falling into a guilt trap by worrying about these compromises and adjustments. We need to stop doing that!

Find a job that challenges you to be the best version of yourself. The definition of a 'perfect woman' is a moving target. It differs for each individual based on personal dreams and aspirations. At the end of the day, a 'perfect woman' is one who can be the best she wants to be.

I must quote from my own experiences. After completing my MBA and working for a couple of years in Ogilvy and Mather I chose to interview with Intel—not because I was a technical person or wanted to become one, but because I was passionate about how technology could be used to change lives. Given Intel's history of relentless innovation and its commitment to making technology an integral part of our lives, I decided to follow my passion. Eighteen years on, I feel energized, enthused and on my toes, much as I did when I was a newbie. I feel excited about being involved with the space of technology—a space that doesn't allow you to become complacent, expects you to constantly adapt to keep pace with new revolutions and reminds you that what worked yesterday will not work today.

I was lucky that I found my passion and the perfect company early in my career. Not everyone is as fortunate and it takes a while to find the right job. Grant yourself the luxury of time, but don't stop looking out for the perfect opportunity. And when it comes, seize it with both hands and give the future your very best. Nothing can act as a substitute for hard work and conviction.

Leave gender out of the equation once you enter the workplace. Work hard, work smart and don't expect to be treated differently because you are a woman. The first step to equality is viewing yourself as an equal, worthy of the same treatment, compensation and rewards as men.

Having said that, our strengths and weaknesses are unlike those of men. I actually believe that in today's business environment, being a woman is an advantage. As women, we are better programmed to handle ambiguity and chaos—a highly valuable skill set in today's frenzied world. Be aware of this advantage and grow comfortable in your own shoes.

Accept that if you're a professional woman, you have to work a little bit harder than your male colleagues to prove yourself. So be it. Hopefully one day this will change, but till then, don't waste time fighting it or using it as an excuse to get demotivated.

My earnest advice to all professional women is: do not give in to the victim mindset. Being surrounded by men at work doesn't mean you can't shine. If you are the only woman at the table, use it to your advantage. Chances are you will be heard more closely; ensure that your ideas are sound, and you've won half the battle.

Celebrate your accomplishments. I see that a lot of women are not comfortable taking credit for what they have accomplished. We need to stop selling ourselves short. Of course, we don't need to become obnoxious, self-obsessed or consumed by 'me and myself'. But when we have done something well, we ought to put our hands up and acknowledge it. Our work gets noticed; this earns us the respect of our peers and managers, as they know what we are capable of.

You cannot achieve your goals by accident. You need to plan for every success. In order to make your dreams of 'having more' a reality, you must be clear about what you want, where you want to go and by when you'd like to get there. At Intel, we call this a development plan—a plan that structures your thoughts by listing your short-term and long-term objectives, citing your strengths and the gaps that need to be addressed. It's extremely important for every professional to have a real development plan as it shows seriousness and intent.

Once a plan is in place, nothing can act as a substitute for hard work, consistency and passion. And it is important to add a healthy dose of integrity to the mix. To succeed in today's volatile and fast-changing environment, we need people who are flexible, adaptable, creative and have the courage to take risks. Imbibe these traits.

Communicate clearly and consistently. A development plan is as effective as the discussion you have about it with your manager. The best way to show intent is by talking about your goals, your strengths and your weaknesses with your manager, and discussing the steps you need to take to go to the next level. Not communicating with your manager will mean s/he won't know you're interested in growing, and so, when the opportunity opens up, your manager will look at people who are not just capable, but also interested in the job! Don't get left out because you were too shy to tell your manager what you wanted.

Devote time to building your networks. Networks offer tremendous support and help enrich one's professional journey. Take the initiative to find the right mentors and sponsors—achievers who can help you develop the right skills to achieve professional goals and also provide you with the right opportunities to increase your visibility and impact. Someone had once told me, 'Don't look at networks and mentors merely as a means to get ahead. Look at them as sources of tremendous learning opportunities;

thanks to them, you connect with like-minded people who can share their experiences and knowledge with you.' And no, your mentors and sponsors don't have to be women! Find the person you can learn the most from.

Most of all, remember: it's true that we, as women, will need to work harder and smarter. It's true that at times, we will face the infamous glass ceiling. But **the best thing about a glass ceiling is that it's made of glass. And glass can be shattered. Just believe that you can do it!**

◆

- There is no substitute for patience, persistence and perspiration.
- Don't write off small organizations. Tinier teams can foster a culture of entrepreneurship and offer a larger range of opportunities to choose from. Join an organization based not on its size, but on the extent to which it can let you become the best version of yourself.
- Ambition is not a bad word. Embrace it. Celebrate your accomplishments.
- Keep time for yourself and the things you love doing, while accepting the inevitable trade-offs.
- A marriage is one of the most vital career decisions.
- Do not fall into the victim trap. If you're the only woman at the table, use it to your advantage. If you have to work harder than male colleagues, so be it!
- Each of us has the potential to be extraordinary.

DR JYOTSNA SURI is the chairperson and managing director of Bharat Hotels Limited, and has been instrumental in the creation and successful rebranding of The Lalit Suri Hospitality Group's luxury hotels. She is also the president of the Federation of Indian Chambers of Commerce and Industry (FICCI) and has been named one of the 'Top 50 Business Power Women in Asia' by *Forbes Asia* in 2014. A supporter of several social causes, including the successful education programme Project Disha, Jyotsna also works closely with NGOs like The Subros Education Society, Savera and Khushi.

Married to Lalit Suri, Jyotsna was a mother and homemaker for the early part of her marriage, but her husband's decision to break away from the family business and set up a hotel in Delhi changed that rapidly. Thrust into managing a business where the stakes were extremely high, Jyotsna learnt the ropes quickly, becoming joint managing director in just a few years. She took over the reins of the hotel when her husband was incapacitated for almost two years after a bypass surgery and again later, when he became a Rajya Sabha member. After his death in 2006, she took over as managing director and runs the conglomerate with her children.

◆

The Hospitality Honcho
JYOTSNA SURI

I was born into a business family, was educated at the Lawrence School—a co-educational boarding school in Sanawar—and thereafter graduated from Miranda House, Delhi University, with an honours degree in English literature. Between home and school, I led a wholesome life and drew my daily principles from my parents and teachers. I got married early, had four children and got busy taking care of them. I was not a professional career woman and it was only in 1981, when my husband, Lalit Suri, decided to exit his family's automobile business to set up a hotel in New Delhi, that I started working.

Since we were not trained hoteliers and it was our money on the block, this venture was like a labour of love that required a major investment of our time. **I would put in long hours at work to learn as much of the business as I could, while continuing to balance the demands of my young children. It was a tough balancing act, and the days would blend into one another—get up early, send the children to school, get to office, go back home in the afternoon to take care of the children and then return to work at night, often getting just four to five hours of sleep on a daily basis.** This habit of waking up early has now become a way of life; it helps me maximize productive hours to get the most out of each day.

Though I started as a director in the company, my ability to grasp the nuances of the hospitality business quickly elevated me to the role of joint managing director. In 1990, Lalit had a triple bypass surgery and was incapacitated for almost two years. His recovery was very slow as he was an insulin-dependent diabetic. This was perhaps the roughest phase of my life, since I was juggling my workload while taking care of a sick husband and four young children.

Things got better after his recovery, though, and we started expanding. Lalit had the inherent ability to spot a good proposition and then follow it up with guts and perseverance. By now, I focused on developing the new hotels and managing the existing properties, while Lalit focused on finance, relationships and further expansion.

When Lalit became a member of the Rajya Sabha in 2002, I was virtually operating as the CEO of the company. This proved to be a godsend later, as it didn't take me very long to find my feet when I assumed the role of managing director in 2006 after losing Lalit. Despite the overwhelming circumstances, my immediate concern was to stabilize the business as well as secure my family's future. My son, Keshav, only twenty years old at that time, was completely devastated; my daughter, Deeksha, who had got married a month prior to Lalit's death, was unable to come to terms with the loss; and my other two daughters, Shradha and Divya, were pregnant and very fragile. To make matters worse, rumours were rife that the business was being sold off as I was unable to shoulder the burden. Many people, including some media persons and members of my fraternity, wrote us off, but I was determined to prove them wrong. Managing the hotels was the least of my problems as I had handled that responsibility for years; my two new priorities were the group's finances and managing its external relationships, since Lalit had been in charge of those aspects of the business. I spent a year understanding these roles, while working on consolidating the business further.

After getting a handle on these new aspects, I turned my attention to the development of hotels, since there were many in the pipeline, with most of the projects being time bound. The company grew from strength to strength and, from the seven operational hotels when I took over, we are today one of the largest privately owned hotel chains in India, with eleven operational luxury and two mid-segment hotels. In fact, we will soon make our international foray with a hotel in London.

One of the key decisions I took after taking over as managing director was to rebrand the group. Our hotels had gone through several name changes in the past and I felt that we were now experienced enough to establish our own brand. In 2008, we rebranded the group as 'The Lalit', as a tribute to my late husband who was the founder of the business. People in the industry were apprehensive and wondered if we would be able to pull it off, but for me it was a well-thought-out decision and I was confident that it would work. My team and I worked on the rebranding exercise for over a year. We also hired two agencies, which specialized in branding and marketing, for this exercise. Six years later, the brand has been very well received and has established itself firmly on the hospitality map in India.

As we continued to develop hotels, I felt a responsibility to the people in the immediate vicinity of our properties and realized that what mattered was not just building hotels but also the business destinations. I, therefore, planned initiatives that involved the local population—showcasing their handicrafts, culture, sports and food. The people of these regions came forward with great enthusiasm and The Lalit is now a successful catalyst for cultural rejuvenation and energy in low-income areas. Some of the events that we have held annually as part of my Developing Destinations initiative include traditional polo in Dras, which is the second-coldest habitable place on earth; ice hockey in Leh; a shikara-thon in Srinagar; a tipaiya-thon in Khajuraho; and kabaddi for boys and girls in Bekal (Kerala). I also spearheaded a Green Initiative through which we have planted 150,000 saplings in Bangalore, 100,000 in Khajuraho, and 50,000 in Delhi.

◆

I am often asked whether being a woman posed any gender-specific challenges to me over the years. My answer is always in the negative. **I believe that if one has the leadership capabilities, gender has little or no role to play in success. At the end of the day, the responsibilities of a leader remain the same—establish and articulate a vision, and then lead and inspire a team to achieve it. Anyone who possesses these qualities can rise to head an organization.** Whether it is a man or a woman, both face the same challenges and roadblocks while conducting their business.

I follow the same principle in my organization and give equal opportunities to both men and women. Today, my daughters as well as my son are working with me and are in charge of important portfolios in the company. I would love to see more Indian women coming out and holding senior positions in organizations. Women have some inherent qualities that make them successful leaders. **A woman's ability to multitask is a great asset and comes in very handy at the workplace, especially at the senior management level, where one is constantly juggling several initiatives and wearing different hats while still moving with singular focus towards a goal.**

Patience is a virtue that every leader should possess. Building an organization from scratch requires a lot of nurturing. As a leader, I look for strengths and weaknesses in each of my team members and delegate work accordingly. The ability to manage people and deal with egos while remaining unbiased is a must if one wants to run a professional workplace where every individual is respected and given equal opportunities to grow. **Dedication, passion and the ability to inspire others is what tend to distinguish a leader from a follower.**

The two people who have been an inspiration to me are Mahatma Gandhi—a man who singlehandedly inspired a diverse nation to fight for freedom—and Aung San Suu Kyi—a strong woman who fought relentlessly for what she believed in, despite seemingly insurmountable odds. My husband has been, and will continue to be, a great inspiration to me. His vision, foresight, generosity and time management skills were truly admirable, as was his utmost faith in me.

My life's mantra is to never give up. No matter what life throws at me, I take it as a challenge and overcome it. The road to success is never easy, and it is up to each individual to persevere through all obstacles and dig a unique path.

◆

- Take whatever life gives you and make the most of it. It is up to you to determine your destiny.
- It is important to have a long-term vision for your company and a practical step-by-step approach to achieving it. This must be articulated to your team so that work is delegated accordingly.
- Manage your time well to get the most out of each day. Develop and hone the ability to multitask as it helps you find a balance between work and home.

KAKU NAKHATE took over as president and country head of Bank of America Merrill Lynch (BofAML) in March 2010, and the bank hasn't looked back since, despite the slowing economy. She has consistently been a part of *Forbes*'s '50 Most Powerful Women in India' list and, in 2014, *Business Today* named her the 'Distinctive Female Leader in Investment Banking' in India.

Kaku recalls her businessman father taking her to his meetings when she was young because he believed that this would give her great insight into how a business works. Meanwhile, her mother provided her much-needed encouragement all through her school life and pushed her to work harder. After studying business management at the Narsee Monjee Institute of Management Studies (NMIMS), Kaku started her first job at DSP Financial Consultants (which later became DSP Merrill Lynch or DSPML), where she learnt the ropes of investment banking. In 2009, she briefly left BofAML to join JP Morgan Chase as vice chairperson of their India operations, only to return to BofAML a year later.

◆

The Pioneering Banker
KAKU NAKHATE

Since my childhood, my father had harboured the ambition of seeing me become a lawyer. He had great respect for the profession and often took me, his only child, along to meet his lawyers, auditors and tax consultants. A successful businessman, he wanted to expose me to the various aspects of running a business and the complexities that come with it, as he believed that first-hand experience was important if I wished to decide the course of my career. For a docile girl born into a large Kutchi joint family with its own business, and surrounded by half a dozen cousins, this exposure had a significant impact.

We were a well-respected family in the community with a flourishing cotton ginning and pressing business, but **my father always insisted that I become independent.** Perhaps his determination to make me stand on my feet sprang from his own life-changing experience: at sixteen, after his father had passed away, he had taken on the responsibility of running the family business.

◆

My parents were exceptional and I owe a lot to them. **My father always wanted me to 'dream big', but at the same time had built a fortified revenue stream for each of us to sail through life easily.** Simultaneously, he was clear that every cousin should know the nuts and bolts of our business. I wanted to study commerce and, to this end, joined RA Podar College of Commerce and Economics in Mumbai. Alongside my degree course, I took up chartered accountancy (CA) and worked part-time at my father's office. My weekly schedule was simple: have lots of fun in college and head straight to my father's office afterwards to gain work experience. As always, he insisted that I tag along with him to every external meeting—a tradition I hated at the time and realized the importance of only later. It was such diverse exposure that strengthened my decision-making capabilities at a fairly young age.

My mother, who was very strong-willed and determined, helped me grow and supported me through my school years. Her encouragement meant a lot to me, as some of my cousins were far brighter. **At a time when parents usually told their children, 'You should do better', my mother always said, 'You *can* do better.'** That boosted my confidence and spurred me to perform well. My mother was also well-regarded in the community—she held our joint family together and had an aptitude for connecting people, especially for business. For instance, she would take an acquaintance to a trader to buy cloth or order spices for thirty families with the noble intention of saving that individual's money and time. In today's parlance, this could be termed as 'reaping the network for greater good'. My mother didn't pursue higher education, but if she were to run a business, she would have fared much better than me. I realized how fond people were of her when 5,000 mourners, most of whom I had never met, turned up at her funeral. She connected the dots across society and did a lot of charitable work, both in Mumbai and Kutch. She was a role model for the family.

It's little wonder that my parents have been my main source of inspiration. They taught me to have strong values and to never compromise on them. I was told to speak up if I didn't think something was right, and avoid getting coerced into treading the wrong path. Whenever we fought tax appeals, even if the costs were high, my father said that we had to fight for our principles and not give up.

◆

Everything changed when I decided to stop pursuing CA and joined the Narsee Monjee Institute of Management Studies (NMIMS) for my management degree. Competing with friends who came from strong engineering backgrounds or who had rich work experience after graduation did stump me initially. (Incidentally, one of them is now my husband, whose intelligence and out-of-the-box thinking occasionally sweeps me off my feet.) **The quality of the debates, the exposure to large companies and my interaction with passionate professors shaped my outlook to life.** It was at NMIMS that I learnt about the stock market, honed my presentation skills, became bold and confident and learnt to articulate my thoughts with clarity. My biggest source of inspiration was a business professor whom I idolized. His flair for and deep understanding of the stock markets was infectious and, soon, I passionately started analysing investment opportunities and following the Sensex.

Companies still coveted management graduates at the time and I got placement offers from Hindustan Unilever (HUL), DSP Financial Consultants and Citibank. The choice was easy as I followed my heart. I grabbed the offer from DSP Financial Consultants, a boutique investment banking firm, as I knew that every day of my life would be exciting. Different sectors, different companies, new trends, valuation metrics— there was so much to learn every day!

DSP also had a very vibrant and young feel to it, and I liked the people I met. We clicked and I thought I could learn a lot if I stayed with the firm. It was absolutely the right choice for me, as the firm encouraged the spirit of professional entrepreneurship. My boss, Hemendra Kothari, continues to be my idol as I learnt a lot under his mentorship, more than I can quantify. He granted us the freedom to express ideas; fostered and preserved a vibrant work culture; stood up for the firm's values in business dealings; and contributed to the development of employees in the industry and the community. These are lessons I cherish even today. In fact, **I would advise youngsters who are about to embark on their first jobs to avoid viewing money as a priority; rather, they should focus on getting roles that build a strong foundation for their careers.**

When I joined DSP in 1989, I did not think that I would become the CEO one day. I was placed in the research team, where DSP was a pioneer. The activity in investment banking was new back then, but this offered me a good foundation for my career. Two years later, bored with my desk job, I raised my hand and asked to be shifted out. The firm was accommodating and allowed me to spend half a day in the research team and the other half with the equities team.

But it wasn't easy to break into what was then a man's world. Initially, I started covering public sector insurance companies for their investments in shares and securities. **The chief investment officers were not used to receiving investment ideas from women.** To make matters worse, I was young and had no experience in the industry. It was tempting to give up, and perhaps many would have, but I never did. I would always tell myself, 'I can do better; one day I will prove to them I am the best in class.' My colleagues were my sounding board for investment ideas and healthy debates helped us discover new emerging corporates to invest in. Two years later, I was making more in brokerage fees from insurance clients than any other firm on Dalal Street at that time.

At DSP Equities, we had regular sessions to discuss new clients, and all of us, even the junior-most members, actively contributed to these sessions. The meetings taught us to put everything on the table and helped us admit to things that were not working—an extremely important practice within organizations. If one could not land a particular client, someone else from the team would take on the responsibility of having a crack at the account. These sessions reiterated the importance of teamwork and helped build successful business strategies.

◆

A few years into the job, I was offered the opportunity to work for Merrill Lynch in New York, the finest firm on Wall Street, but chose to stay in India for my family. I have not once regretted the decision—being in equity sales, my role was international in any case and constant travel and interaction with clients and colleagues did enough to broaden my horizons. **Today, I encourage employees who show an interest in working abroad to find an overseas assignment in our company. Learning about different cultures and working in other countries only sharpens one's business acumen and empowers one to take on new challenges.**

With liberalization and new players coming in, I got many job offers, but I didn't consider them as I enjoyed and valued the freedom at DSP, which was the market leader. The company had a good partner in Merrill and, with their assistance, we introduced many firsts in investment banking and global markets, which helped shape our industry. A growing organization gave us the opportunity to do many things beyond our assigned jobs and this equipped us with strong skills. Running the business end-to-end was satisfying.

Things began to get difficult only around the time that Merrill decided to increase its stake to that of a majority partner. As professionals, we made many presentations on business valuations, but both shareholders felt that we were favouring the other side. During this period, I learnt about negotiations and the art of stakeholder management, and how we as a team had to win the trust and confidence of both sides. At the same time, as senior leaders, we had to hold the team together and get on with our daily assignments. Managing the situation was a tough balancing act, but it was the best experience of my career.

◆

You cannot paint everything with the same brush, and strategies have to be tweaked periodically for every business. I learnt early that, with India opening up to international business, we would have to work hard to excel—there was no room for slacking. I also accepted that every client was different and had to be serviced differently to get the best results.

In 2002, our head of global equities, Rohit D'Souza, visited India for the first time to evaluate the business and the size of our five-year-old wallet. We had made decks of presentations and lined up many external and internal meetings with the clear objective of making him appreciate the tremendous effort that had gone into building a market-leading franchise over the years. He attributed our success to the team's passion and energy, which made us all proud. He also pointed out that curtailing our technology costs was a mistake and that smart technology was a business enabler—a lesson that has stayed with me to date. He asked me to spend more time understanding our global trading platforms to build a strong and stable onshore platform, which could bring in consistent revenues from a new algorithm-savvy set of clients. He asked me to arrive a couple of days earlier for my next trip to the US to meet clients. I didn't know the agenda, but as he had taken the effort to help me, I complied. In those two days, I met many technology experts who introduced me to state-of-the-art trading platforms—the speed of accessing markets in nanoseconds led to profits and losses. I was mesmerized by these internally developed trading technologies that crossed tonnes of stock through the day for our clients, losing the least possible volume to the street. The fact that we were the leading powerhouse for equities clearly showed. Seeing is believing, they say.

Sometimes, finding success is all about getting the right kind of exposure and finding a good mentor. **It is extremely rare to find bosses who encourage their employees to look beyond their traditional roles in the organization, so Rohit's initiative was a real game-changer for me.**

◆

The trip to the US was an eye-opener. We were left with no doubt that we had to rebuild our trading platform in India to achieve speedy and accurate trade executions and remain ahead of the curve. I came back and spoke to my team and we embarked on this new mission. However, we decided to do it differently—instead of just asking the technology team to work on the new platform, we got business representatives—dealers, sales traders and salespersons—to contribute their thoughts to the project. Our neo-expert team reached out to our counterparts in the US, the UK, Japan and Australia to learn about their best algorithms across asset classes and understand risk mitigation tools. We improvised, innovated and rebuilt our Indian platform, taking advantage of these global discoveries. This helped our firm speed up the deliverables, contain costs and get more time to work on new ideas specific to the Indian markets. Yes, for all of us actively involved with getting it right, the project was time-consuming. But today Merrill Lynch's system is well ahead of the competition—and it all happened because somebody showed us the way things worked in a mature market. **We could have asked the US office to set everything up for us, but we took charge and married the best international practices to the Indian way of doing business. We aimed to be glocal in nature, so we built a glocal solution for our clients.**

◆

In 2009, after the global merger of Bank of America and Merrill Lynch (BofAML) was announced, I was given a bigger role and asked to head the combined global markets business. There were constant discussions in the office regarding how the merger of two large global entities would evolve, and there were two contenders vying for the corner office. Since I was already reporting to the chairman of DSPML, I thought I would at least be considered for the top job. However, the CEO got selected without me being asked. I felt let down. In hindsight, I should have raised my hand for the top job as I was already running a major part of the business, but I didn't, and so I lost out.

That's when I decided to re-evaluate my ambitions. When JP Morgan offered me the post of vice chairperson of their India operations, I decided to consider it seriously. It was time for me to get out of my comfort zone and take on a new challenge. **My bosses were surprised when I put in my papers and asked why I had not asked for the top job if I had been genuinely interested in the position. I realized then that I had assumed that my work would speak for itself.** BofAML wanted to retain me, but I had already committed to JP Morgan and felt ethically bound to join them. In retrospect, I believe that if you have career aspirations, you should share them with your senior management. It is often our own inhibitions that prevent us from asking for a job we covet.

◆

In many ways, walking away from DSP Merrill Lynch after twenty years wasn't easy. It was the business that I had grown up with and nurtured. But three months of gardening leave offered me a new perspective. I spent a few precious moments with my darling son, Riday, who was studying for his class ten exams at the time. It was well-timed in a way. He understands me perfectly, often offers simple solutions to my complex problems and makes my life easier.

At JP Morgan, as part of my role as vice chairperson, I was responsible for running the equities, futures and options businesses, as well as leading the firm's worldwide securities services business in India. I had a seat in the global equity management team, which developed the worldwide equity business for the organization. As vice chairperson, my role made me reach out to new people, connect the dots, mentor leaders and strengthen our onshore franchise. Contrary to my belief that I would take a long time to settle in, given that it was only my second job, I actually settled in very quickly, thanks to the confidence the senior management at the firm had in me. In a short span of time, we brought in big revenue streams. This increased my confidence and I was able to get people across the globe to subscribe to our strategy and execute it. After being in one company for so many years, it was encouraging to see that my leadership skills weren't circumscribed by the place I worked in.

In 2010, I was offered the role of president and country head at BofAML. I was doing well at JP Morgan, so I wondered if I wanted to change streams at this point and risk failure. After all, if I accepted the job, I would be leading a corporate bank, and all my experience till then was in financial markets. What finally convinced me was a conversation with BofAML's head of global banking and markets, Tom Montag, whom I respect very much. Tom told me, **'It's not your job to decide whether you are the right fit. We are taking that risk. We want your leadership and strong execution.'** This radical piece of advice lent a new perspective to the situation and made me realize what a great opportunity this was. My son's strong belief that I could do it and my mother's and husband's support motivated me to finally take the plunge and say yes.

My first year as CEO was tough. The integration of the employees of the erstwhile Bank of America with Merrill Lynch had to be completed. **I needed to build a cohesive team to be able to run a strong India franchise. Seamless strategy and execution was the call of the hour.** To make things more challenging, as I've mentioned, I had not worked in the space of corporate banking before, which meant that I had to win the trust and respect of my colleagues. Staring at me were two options—I could either get actively involved with global markets which I used to run before, rely on my designation and wait for escalations to reach me in businesses I did not know well; or roll up my sleeves and immerse myself in the newer businesses, and learn them end-to-end while broadly overseeing the global markets segment. I chose the latter option and worked closely with our global corporate and investment banking teams on live deals and global transaction solutions for our key clients. Of course, this had to be achieved without compromising on governance, compliance and risk—the most important priorities for any country head. On the personal front, I must acknowledge the emotional support I received from my husband, which helped me sail through those difficult first few months when I settled into the new role. **An important tenet of leadership is keeping things simple; while you can have an ego, you should be open to learning all the time.**

As I recollect, my first step in this unfamiliar territory was reaching out to the clients and getting their direct feedback to assess our strengths and weaknesses. It was important to incorporate the regulators' feedback regarding growing the bank's operations the right way. Teamwork, employee engagement and winning my colleagues' confidence were vital to achieve success. Each time I explored new ideas and executed them, most of them worked well. This is not to say that I did not have doubts along the way, but I didn't shy away from accepting responsibility and taking tough decisions.

It was during this time that the Indian economy took a hit, as did the banking sector across the world. We had to embrace changes in the way we did business while continuing to grow; cross-selling, return on assets and return on equity were the new buzzwords in the firm globally. We decided that clients and employees had to understand these new ways of doing business—a move that benefited us in the long run. The path was clear—all I needed to do was adapt to the situation and lead from the front.

Therefore I would go with bankers and ask for a cross-selling deal, explaining the importance of this to our key clients while trying to win them over. My strong and able team helped meet our targets. Our global partners strengthened my commitment to this new style of functioning. Soon, it became a way of life for all of us.

Learning and trying to pursue excellence keeps me going. When you encounter a challenge, you need to get to the bottom of it and understand what your organization and senior management teams expect from you. Equally, it's important to articulate the same message down the line, even if you have a different opinion. Remember, you can't keep questioning your boss constantly. What you can do is present your point of view to him or her with valid reasons. Do not be afraid of losing your job. If you are a natural leader, you will find the way forward.

Currently, BofAML is doing very well, but we can't rest on our laurels and become complacent. There is always a new idea on the street that can affect your business and nibble at your revenues. You have to empower employees so they continue sharing their ideas and improve a franchise. You also need to hire the right talent at all levels who can bring fresh thoughts and energy to the firm from time to time. **I strongly believe that ideas come from all levels of the organization and need to be encouraged.** It is our duty as senior management to provide an environment where employees, more so at the bottom of the ladder, are not afraid to share their suggestions; this can go a long way towards improving a process or a product, or creating a new business.

◆

Maintaining some work-life balance is never easy. I am employed in an industry that is growing at a rapid pace and my firm is the industry leader. Given the long hours of work, there are times when you are so overwhelmed by the guilt of ignoring your family that the first thought that occurs to you is calling it a day. I went through that phase when my son was young and appearing for his exams. I would get up at 5 a.m. to prepare question papers so that he could come home from school and solve them. In hindsight, I don't think my efforts helped very much as he could have done it all himself. But I guess I did it to satisfy my guilt.

This is when you realize how critical the support systems in your life are for your growth. I was blessed to have a very accommodating mother-in-law as well as a mother who took care of my wonderful child as he grew up. I am sure that the values they have imparted will hold him in good stead in the future. Also, I have an extremely supportive and understanding husband who has guided our child beautifully through these years; this has been an additional boon. It is only because of my wonderful family and the help I have had at home that I have been able to commit to fifteen-hour workdays and sometimes travel for half the month.

I have realized that to succeed, you have to overcome all fears and work through the problems you encounter along the way. **But you also need to have the courage to voice your familial commitments when the time arises; you are certain to find champions around you who will extend support. I remember telling my bosses that I could not travel when my son was appearing for his exams and they readily accommodated my request.** My colleagues would step in for me and projects would go on seamlessly.

I work too hard and have little work-life balance. But my efforts have not been in vain. Over the years, I have stood up for the right values, which have helped me wade through the tough phases. My experiences, both at work and home, have helped me grow as a person and continue to hold me in good stead in my job today.

◆

- Take on different roles at a young age. Rotate your jobs till you earn where your heart lies. If you are passionate about your job, success will follow.
- Push yourself when you become complacent and let your aspirations guide you. This is how you will create a path to success. Be open to different suggestions and criticism and remain open to change.
- Make innovation a part of your philosophy.
- Seek mentors and keep learning as you grow. Good mentors can champion your cause in the organization and help you explore newer and better opportunities.
- Voice your ambitions to the senior management, as they can guide you only if they are aware of your goals.
- Be positive to minimize heartburn. You will go through bad times, but they will not impact you as much if you remain optimistic.
- As a leader, you must create an environment that is conducive to change. A dynamic organization with lots of opportunities cannot hold back talent.
- Respect cannot be forced; it is always earned. The more senior you are in the organization, the more you need to learn.

KIRAN MAZUMDAR-SHAW is the founder, chairman and managing director of Biocon, one of the world's leading biotechnology companies. Named among the most powerful people in the world by *Forbes* in 2014, she also became the first Indian to be awarded the prestigious Othmer Gold Medal by the Chemical Heritage Foundation for her contribution to the field of biotechnology. Moreover, Kiran has also received the Germany-based Kiel Institute for the World Economy's coveted '2014 Global Economy Prize' for business. Her most cherished awards are the two prestigious civilian national awards, the Padma Shri (1989) and the Padma Bhushan (2005).

After a chance meeting with Leslie Auchincloss, the founder of Ireland-based Biocon Biochemicals Limited, Kiran started a subsidiary of the company in the garage of her home in Bangalore with nothing to her name other than a brewmaster's degree, ₹10,000 and the determination to make her venture succeed. She continues to push the boundaries of research and has been instrumental in Biocon creating affordable medicines for diabetes, cancer and autoimmune diseases, as well as in setting up the Mazumdar-Shaw Cancer Centre (MSCC) and the Mazumdar-Shaw Centre for Translational Research (MSCTR). Kiran is married and lives in Bangalore.

◆

The Miracle Worker
KIRAN MAZUMDAR-SHAW

'Two roads diverged in a wood, and I—I took the one less travelled by, and that has made all the difference.'

These immortal lines of American poet Robert Frost sum up my long and eventful tryst with biotechnology—a tryst that started when I went to Australia to train as a brewmaster, a vocation unexplored by Indians and more so by women the world over. **When I returned to my country as its first woman brewmaster, intent on pursuing a career as a brewer, I found that the industry in India was a male bastion where I was unwelcome.** It was an accidental encounter with the Irish biotech entrepreneur Les Auchincloss that saw me start Biocon in 1978 in my garage. Auchincloss wanted a partner in India who was entrepreneurial and understood the business of brewing. I was reluctant at first because the thought of starting and running my own company had never crossed my mind. However, since he infused a tremendous sense of confidence in me, I eventually decided to take up the challenge. Hence, **I prefer to call myself an 'accidental entrepreneur'!**

When I started Biocon, I was twenty-five years old with no business experience and limited financial resources. In the 1970s, entrepreneurship was an unusual career choice for women, and biotechnology was unheard of as an industry sector. I was daring to start a business in a male-dominated society and that too in a sector that no one was familiar with. Fuelled more by drive and vision than by business expertise, I approached the venture with the single-minded aim of succeeding.

My drive and determination were a result of my upbringing. I was greatly inspired by my late father, Rasendra Mazumdar, who was managing director and master brewer for India's largest brewery, United Breweries. I remember visiting him at work while I was growing up in Bangalore and being fascinated by the brewery's unique processes and smells. A man far ahead of his times, he believed in the equal treatment of men and women and always encouraged me to take the road less travelled. Hence, I grew up believing that there was nothing my brothers could do that I could not.

I studied at the Bishop Cotton Girls' School in Bangalore, after which I wanted to become a doctor, but unfortunately did not have the grades to gain admission in a medical college. Like many of my friends, I expected my father to secure a seat for me by paying a capitation fee. To my surprise, my father refused to do so. He told me, 'I have provided you with the best possible school education and if your efforts have not helped you gain admission into a medical college, it means you haven't worked as hard as someone else who has made the grade. **Money is not the currency with which you buy favours but the currency with which you make a difference to society.**' His words of integrity taught me an important lesson in meritocracy and in not having a sense of entitlement. Since then, they have inspired me to strive for excellence and be second to none.

My father also taught me to persevere in the face of adversity with the mantra 'failure is temporary but giving up is permanent'. This is why, when I experienced the initial hiccups that all start-ups in India faced during the pre-liberalization period, I simply became more determined to make my business work. I started building my company, Biocon, with a sense of purpose and spirit of adventure. I knew that we could make Biocon work if we followed a strategy of differentiation and leveraged our early-mover advantage. Instead of being hampered by what we did not have, I tried to use what we did and maximize results through home-grown innovation.

My strong grounding in the biological sciences, followed by a practical academic course in fermentation-science based on brewing technology, enabled me to pursue biotechnology with a deep understanding of the life sciences. I was also able to apply my scientific know-how across domains.

Along my entrepreneurial journey, **my ability to face and learn from failure has helped me a great deal. It is a trait that most entrepreneurs need to have in order to succeed. They also need to understand—as I did over time—that risk and failure are intrinsic to any business.**

◆

When I started Biocon India for manufacturing industrial enzymes for food and textile makers around the world, all I had was ₹10,000, an office in our home's garage in Bangalore and the determination to make things happen. At that time in India, there was little or no appreciation of enterprise and entrepreneurial talent, least of all for a woman peddling an unknown technology. But I was determined to build a world-class biotechnology enterprise—I wanted to show the world that it was possible to produce high-quality, high-technology products in India based on cutting-edge R&D (research and development). I also wanted to build a company where women scientists could pursue their research dreams, where women professionals could work shoulder to shoulder with their male colleagues and where men and women had mutual respect.

However, recruiting for my company was a big challenge, my gender being one of my greatest handicaps. I couldn't get anyone to join me, not only because I was a woman but also because mine was a start-up company. I couldn't even get a secretary to work for me. **I still remember how candidates, who came for the interview in response to the newspaper advertisement I had put out, were shocked to see me operating out of a garage. They then looked around for the person in charge as they assumed that I was a secretary and were somewhat crestfallen to learn that I was, in fact, the managing director of the company.**

Besides hiring new employees, I had many other hurdles to cross, among these being poor infrastructure. Enzyme manufacturing for industrial application involved sophisticated fermentation procedures, which demanded abundant good quality water and uninterrupted power supply for precision and control. However, the power supply in Bangalore at the time was erratic at best. We also had little access to superior quality water and had to struggle to import high-quality research equipment due to procedural hurdles.

My troubles did not end there. Enzyme technology was a new concept back then in India. There was scepticism about the commercial viability of eco-friendly but expensive enzymes that sought to replace cheap chemical processes. My challenge was to get the market to accept biotechnology and change age-old practices. When I began negotiating business terms with my suppliers, I realized that many of them felt very uncomfortable dealing with a woman—some even asked if they could discuss prices with my 'manager'! It took sustained effort on my part to educate these people and develop their confidence in me. Once I negotiated good business terms for them and they saw their own enterprises doing better thanks to Biocon, these suppliers respected me much more.

With no access to venture capital, money was scarce and high-cost; debt-based capital was all I could aim for. I applied for loans at several banks and, in each instance, was turned down. Having faced an impenetrable glass ceiling as a woman brewmaster, I did not let gender discrimination stop me. I persevered and finally found a banker who was willing to bet on my biotech dream.

It was a chance breakfast meeting with Narayanan Vaghul, then chairman and managing director of ICICI, that enabled me to not only raise the necessary finance but also obtain venture capital on attractive terms. Vaghul was keen on initiating the concept of funding first-generation entrepreneurs through equity rather than debt financing, and my enzyme business fit his criteria perfectly. I had failed to convince others to back my dream, but had miraculously succeeded in getting ICICI to share my risk! **Getting people to buy into your vision is difficult, but once they do, it enables you to sprout wings and fly.**

I was single-minded in my determination to see my venture succeed. I believed that we could focus on one step at a time and make things happen if we adopted a sensible and adaptable approach. I have never been one to give up easily, which is why I simply became more determined to make it work.

Over the next decade, I steadily built my biotechnology business and, thus, established my credibility. By 1990, Biocon was already a leading exporter of enzymes from India and I was also substituting imported enzymes in many an industry in India. **Our R&D in enzyme technology was recognized internationally and we were innovating several patented enzyme technologies for various industries the world over. So much so that when I finally sold my enzymes business to Novozymes in 2007, they conceded that some of my enzymes were impossible to compete with!**

Having attained success in industrial enzymes, the next part of my journey was using the innovative power of biotechnology in the space of biopharmaceuticals. In 1998, we strategically decided to leverage fermentation and recombinant DNA technology to ferment biopharmaceuticals like insulin and monoclonal antibodies. **Biocon's mission now became distinctly different from what it had been when the company was founded—from wanting to 'green the world' through eco-friendly enzyme technologies, we wanted to 'heal the**

world' by developing affordable life-saving drugs for patients across the globe.

I decided that Biocon would make a difference by targeting those diseases that were chronic, and where medical needs were yet largely unmet. To this end, Biocon leveraged India's value advantage and scientific excellence to continuously speed up the process of 'lab to market' of new and differentiated biopharmaceuticals. The endeavour was to push for innovation while keeping it affordable and accessible.

◆

What spurred me on this mission of healing the world was the realization that a significant proportion of the world's population does not have access to essential medicines and, where health care does exist, it is unaffordable. This is especially true of India, where a major part of the population does not have access to even basic health care, and almost 3 per cent of the population moves into the medical poverty trap each year. The vicious circle of poverty, malnutrition and illness is aggravated by expensive medical care.

The challenge was formidable, given India's enormous disease burden. Our country is at the epicentre of both communicable and non-communicable diseases—from diabetes and cancer, to heart disease, tuberculosis and HIV.

I decided to pick up the gauntlet to fight diabetes and cancer, which are life-threatening conditions and require expensive lifelong medication. As advanced biotherapeutics (drugs derived from living organisms) such as recombinant human Insulin (rh-Insulin) and monoclonal antibodies were beyond the reach of most patients in India who needed them, I decided to focus on affordability.

Indeed, with India emerging as the nation with the largest population of diabetics, it was important for an Indian company to take on the disease and offer cost-effective and easily accessible treatment. (India currently has over 65 million diabetes patients and the number could cross 85 million by 2030.) In 2004, my academic knowledge of brewing technology truly paid off when Biocon, using fermentation, successfully launched its generic rh-Insulin for diabetes at one-fourth of the cost of imported insulin. This was a huge achievement, as India had been entirely dependent on importing insulin before this discovery; now, insulin is much more affordable in the country. This technology has since then been exported to several markets across the globe and is providing high-quality yet affordable insulin to millions of diabetic patients.

◆

As with diabetes, developing countries like India also have a disproportionate number of cancer patients. The annual incidence of all forms of cancer in India is about a million, with head and neck, lung, and breast cancer leading the way. Added to this is an increase in the number of cancer cases in the country partly due to increasing life expectancy and better diagnosis. Cancer is a debilitating challenge for India, both financially and as a disease.

Moreover, it has been observed that low- and middle-income countries like ours face the 5/80 cancer disequilibrium. While 80 per cent of the cancer burden is faced by low- and middle-income countries, only 5 per cent of the global spending on cancer happens within this bracket because most patients cannot afford the treatment.

My own introduction to the world of cancer was when my best friend was diagnosed with breast cancer in 2002. I saw the struggle that she went through—the fear, the financial burden, the treatment, the suffering and the disease itself. What was even more hard-hitting was the fact that even though my friend was fairly well-to-do, she found the treatment costs financially crippling. **My friend ran through her life's savings in the six years that she battled her cancer, to which she finally succumbed. If this was her predicament, imagine what cancer does to a poor person fighting the disease!**

It was this realization that motivated me to invest in cancer research to deliver affordable health-care access to cancer patients. Biocon launched its cancer research programme in 2002. The emerging importance of targeted therapies based on monoclonal antibodies caught our interest and we started a research programme to develop an anti-EGFR (epidermal growth factor receptor) antibody primarily for cancers of the head and neck—one of the most prevalent cancers among poor people in India. Subsequently, in 2006, we launched India's first monoclonal antibody for cancers of the head and neck at one-fifth of the cost of imported products. We have, as a result, expanded access to millions of patients who can now afford this therapy, which is gratifying.

◆

From the very beginning I wanted to be a change agent in society. When I started Biocon, I was driven by the desire to create a business that would leverage science for the benefit of society through affordable innovation. That has always been Biocon's raison d'être. I have encouraged a corporate culture that is anchored in dedication to excellence and a strong social conscience.

I started out with the ambition of being a doctor, but strangely life took me on another path. I now believe that as a researcher and an entrepreneur, I have been able to touch so many more people. I have got from life much more than I could even have imagined and I now think it's time to give back to the society.

My philanthropic goals and business goals are closely aligned with my crusade against cancer. On the philanthropic front, I focus on diagnosing and researching the disease as well as caring for patients. I established the 1,400-bed Mazumdar-Shaw Cancer Center (MSCC) in Bangalore in 2009 with the vision of delivering affordable and high-quality cancer care to patients, especially to those who belong to the lower socio-economic strata. I also set up the Mazumdar-Shaw Center for Translational Research (MSCTR), a non-profit research institute that is pursuing innovation-led translational research, at the MSCC in 2014. MSCTR is one of the first such research hospitals in India and I truly believe that it will play a transformational role both in early detection and treatment by personalizing therapies, as well as by developing solutions for better health outcomes.

◆

I have always believed that citizens' engagement is critical for the success of any country and, as a conscientious Indian citizen, I have always participated in nation-building exercises for the greater good. More recently, I have been actively involved with restoring the glory of my city, Bangalore. With like-minded citizens from various walks of life, I have set up the Bangalore Political Action Committee (BPAC), which is pushing for better governance in the city by mobilizing the educated middle class and the elite; together, we hope to fully engage and work with political leaders to establish strong policies with the aim of ensuring a superior quality of life for the people of Bangalore.

◆

I have traversed a great distance since my early start-up days and I am fortunate to have had a family that has offered me considerable emotional support, and friends who have always stood by me. For both men and women to succeed in their careers, it is important to have their family and friends backing them. For women, especially, balancing home and work may become difficult without adequate support.

A large number of people in India still believe that, for women, marriage must take precedence over a career. It is also common to see highly qualified women give up their careers and settle for a traditional homemaker's role in order to conform to familial expectations. **I believe that starting a family should not be a deterrent to a woman's career goals. There is no reason for a woman not to get back to her work environment after taking maternity leave.** Women should be encouraged to develop family support systems or explore the option of day-care centres to raise their children. In fact, many companies today cater to the needs of mothers and have crèches on their campuses to allow them to return to work.

It is my firm belief that knowledge makes no gender distinction. Today, you see a large pool of women scientists, engineers and managers in various streams who have succeeded much like their male counterparts. **It is true that if you are a woman employer, people are more likely to doubt the stability of the company than if you are male. But the moment you start succeeding, these credibility perceptions are immediately dismantled.** I am proud to say that today, Biocon employs over 7,500 people, about 15 per cent of whom are women. Of the 3,500 scientists whom work with us, about 30 per cent are women.

To be successful, I believe you need to be genuine and compassionate, besides being intellectually savvy. It is also important to pay special attention to your interests and enjoy your free time as much as possible. For instance, my love for art not only helps me relax but also keeps me intellectually stimulated. I have been known for encouraging new artists and own a fairly large collection of art today. I also listen to classical music or watch sports whenever I feel the need to destress.

I have always felt that women, with self-confidence, determination, hard work and business acumen, can chart their way to the top. I am proud to be a woman and strongly believe that the world belongs to those who want to make a difference.

◆

As an entrepreneur, I have always found challenges exciting. Challenges, I believe, contain the seeds of opportunity, which in turn give birth to innovation and progress. When one is driven by the spirit of leadership, such challenges become milestones on the path to success.

I believe the real leaders are those who spot opportunities where others see challenges. They are committed to creating value from these opportunities, not just for their own organizations but also for society at large. I believe that it is only with a commitment to humanity and a passion for making a difference that true leadership is born.

Leaders who have made a difference and steered their organizations to new horizons have rarely been conformists. Spurred by the courage of conviction, they have the zeal to confront all odds. They are the entrepreneurial risk-takers and innovators. It is this spirit that enables them to stand apart.

True leaders can also come from any walk of life—they are visionaries with a sense of purpose, who persevere and have a passion for change. They know that leadership is not about control but about being able to inspire people with values and vision.

We must channelize the innate leadership instinct that all of us possess and try making a difference in our own lives as well as in the lives of others. This will not only result in self-empowerment but also help society prosper through all-round economic growth.

◆

Today, thirty-six years down the road, Biocon is a global biopharmaceutical powerhouse. But, to me, that is merely symbolic of our leadership. My vision is for our research programmes for oral insulin or antibodies for cancer and autoimmune disorders, to bring transformative change in treatment paradigms. **Affordable blockbuster drugs with a 'Made in India' label that can change the lives of millions of patients around the world will truly stand testimony to our foresight.** As a first-generation entrepreneur, I am intensely conscious of the fact that I must do my bit for society. Making a difference in health care has always been my calling. My efforts are geared towards changing lives for the better by ensuring affordability and access to health care through Biocon's products.

◆

- As a pioneer, I have understood the power of differentiation to build leadership. I have always chosen to lead rather than follow. This has created tremendous brand value for Biocon. To this end, we have focused on affordable innovation to make health care accessible to patients across the globe.
- I believe in challenging the status quo and have benefited exponentially from reinventing the business every five to seven years—for example, we have grown from producing industrial enzymes to biopharmaceuticals; and from the original mission of 'greening the world' we have embraced the ideal of 'healing the world'.
- Regulatory risks and research failures are integral to our business. The ability to manage and mitigate risks and failures provides us with a competitive advantage and prevents both reputational and business impact.
- Innovation has been my hallmark and I have consciously built a culture of creativity across all levels of the organization. We have a large and diverse portfolio of patents that has built a strong value base for the organization; these are being periodically monetized.
- Leadership is about being recognized in the global firmament and I have invested strategically to secure Biocon's reputation internationally. Today, Biocon is recognized worldwide for its global scale in fermentation-based bulk drugs and insulin production.
- Driving sustainable growth by having a competitive advantage is a strategy I have encouraged in the organization. Be it new technologies, intellectual property or scale, we have successfully created value.

KIRTHIGA REDDY is managing director of Facebook India and was the first employee of the company in the country in 2010. She has been featured in Fast Company's list of the 100 Most Creative People in Business, 2013, and is one of *Fortune India's* 'Top 50 Most Powerful Women in India'. Kirthiga is also vice chairperson of the Internet and Mobile Association of India (IAMAI) and serves on the Stanford Business School Management Board and the Indian School of Business's (ISB) Next Generation Leadership Board.

Born into a middle-class family, Kirthiga spent her childhood moving from city to city due to her father's job at Lloyds Steel. On graduating from the Mahatma Gandhi Mission's College of Engineering, Nanded, she went on to study computer engineering at Syracuse University and moved to the San Francisco Bay Area, California, with her husband to work for Silicon Graphics. She quit her job to get a master's in business administration (MBA) from Stanford University and had a child one year into the MBA programme. She now lives in Mumbai with her husband, Dev, and two daughters, Ashna and Ariya.

The Face of Young India
KIRTHIGA REDDY

The first time I was featured in one of the 'Top 50 Women in Business' lists, one of my colleagues asked, 'Did you always know what career path you would chart and was it always a goal to get onto one of these lists?' The answer was, 'Of course not.' I did not know growing up that I would pursue an undergraduate degree in computer engineering, that I would decide to go to the US for my master's in engineering, and that I would stay in the US for fourteen years—initially working on the engineering side and, after my MBA from Stanford Business School, moving to the business side with product management. I had no idea that I would eventually move back to India to take on my current role as managing director of Facebook India.

I was born into a middle-class family, the younger of two daughters. My father was the oldest son, born seven years after my grandparents' wedding and after many pilgrimages. When my older sister was born, my grandparents were somewhat disappointed that it wasn't a boy but the dominant sentiment was that of happiness at the birth of their first grandchild. When my mother was pregnant with me, the whole family was convinced that it would be a boy and had chosen the name 'Karthik' after Lord Karthikeya, a family deity. **When I was born, my grandparents refused to come to the hospital to see me because I wasn't a boy. As my mother wept, my dad consoled her saying, 'If we have a third child, I want it to be a girl, and we will name her Kanchana.'**

For the most part, my parents raised us no differently than they would have raised two sons. One exception was the belief that daughters would stay with their parents until they were married. My father moved cities every few years as part of his decades-long tenure at Lloyds Steel, and we moved with him. We lived in large metros like Chennai and Mumbai, mid-sized cities like Nashik, Nagpur and Tarapur, and small towns like Dandeli and Nanded. From my dad, I picked up his strong work ethic, the value of 'planning my work and working my plan', and the spirit of making the most of opportunities. My mother gave me spirituality, the ability to see cheer no matter what the situation was and a can-do attitude. My sister and I fought like cats and dogs growing up, as most siblings do, and became best friends as we grew older, especially during our college years.

The Indian societal norm of following a career path in engineering or medicine led me to choose the former. **I did not have the domicile needed to apply to state colleges and hence went to a small private college called Mahatma Gandhi Mission's College of Engineering in Nanded, which offered me a full scholarship. When I graduated second in the university with the 'Jewel in the Crown' award from the college for all-round excellence, it was testimony to the impact a small group of committed academicians could have and an affirmation of making the most of the opportunities given to you.** My father's work took us to Nagpur right after my graduation. It was here that I landed my first job with Yashawant Kanetkar, author of the book *Let Us C*—still a bible in many engineering colleges. We developed anti-virus software, delivered training courses, and I also had the opportunity to partner with him on the software featured in subsequent books like *Exploring C++* and publish articles.

I began to think about getting a master's degree and hesitantly spoke to my parents about my desire to do so in the US. My father was thrilled that I would be the first one in the family to go abroad. My mother said, 'Go for it! But just get married before you go.' Thereon, we began the search for the perfect groom. I was engaged to Dev four days after we first met and married a year later. In him, I found my soulmate.

◆

After completing my master's degree in computer engineering from Syracuse University, Upstate New York, I moved to the San Francisco Bay Area, California—the place to be for technology roles. I accepted a job with Silicon Graphics, then a US$2 billion worth, 9,000-employee strong, high-performance computing company known for great technology and exceptional people. **One of the best pieces of advice I received**

early in my career was from my manager, Betsy Zeller, who said, 'Kirthiga, focus on the success of your clients, your organization and your team. Your success is but a by-product.' This was liberating. Job descriptions became largely irrelevant. My work really became doing whatever it took to make our clients, organization and team successful. One often wonders how much to push a certain cause, and this framework gave me the conviction to be persistent about things that mattered because the goal became clear. This philosophy was key to my success, and I soon became the youngest director of engineering in my organization. I was twenty-eight years old.

As director of engineering, I began to get more and more involved in business decisions and it was a world that fascinated me. I decided I wanted to get an MBA as a way of honing these skills. It wasn't an easy decision to make—it would involve leaving a job I had worked hard to get. I spent several sleepless nights wondering if I should pursue a full-time MBA, a part-time MBA or an executive MBA. But Dev was firm in his support and conviction. 'It's better to look back and regret having done something than look back and regret not having done it. What's two years in a decades-long career?' he said. I will always look back at my decision to apply for the programme as one of the best choices I've made in my life. I had the privilege of studying at the Stanford Business School and it gave me the foundation I have today.

After business school, I knew I wanted to work for a start-up in a growing space. **While it is assumed that after graduating from one of the best business schools in the world, a title or a compensation raise is mandatory, I took a 40 per cent pay cut and went from being director of engineering at Silicon Graphics to being a senior product manager at a mobile software start-up called Good Technology, which was a Kleiner Perkins, Benchmark Capital company.** This was another hard decision to make. I sought the counsel of Jana Rich, then a principal at Korn Ferry International, on whether the decision would be detrimental to my career and whether it would be seen as a step-down. She asked me if it was a short- or long-term investment. If it was short term, it was absolutely the wrong move. However, if I was looking to bet long term on the success of the company, I would learn and grow quickly with the organization. Four years later, we were acquired by Motorola for US$500 million. I was the director of product management then and I had absolutely loved the journey of building, learning and growing with the company. The pay-off was also much higher than what I would have received had I chosen a role that was a more natural progression after business school with an associated compensation raise. Of course, this wasn't a given when we started. Hence, **it is important to work with an organization where you can build skills and relationships that will stand you in good stead in the long run—even if the business itself fails.**

The next phase of my career was an opportunity with Motorola to relocate to India and lead the cross-functional Good Technology division in a general management capacity. By this time, Dev and I had our two girls, Ashna and Ariya. With almost all our extended family based in India, it was a perfect opportunity to experience being back in the country. However, while we had mentally considered this to be a temporary move, it rapidly transitioned to being a long-term decision as we found our professional and personal worlds coming together back here. I began to yearn for my early start-up days—the pace, the environment of high growth, teams working cohesively and closely on a common mission—and it was then that I was introduced to Sheryl Sandberg by a business school classmate. Facebook had become an integral part of my life after my move to India as it helped me stay connected to my life of fourteen years in the US and reconnect with friends from India. It was at the top of my list of companies that I would be privileged to work with. At that time, Facebook did not have concrete plans to open an office in India, but Sheryl and I decided to keep in touch.

Instead, I joined a turnaround company, Phoenix Technology, driving P&L (profit and loss) for their SaaS (Software as a Service)-based business unit and leading global teams located in the US, India, Japan, Korea, and Taiwan. Just about the time the SaaS unit was sold, Facebook announced its intention to open an office in India. It almost seemed meant to be. A set of gruelling interview sessions and many months later, I was offered the position of director and head of Facebook India—an offer I was glad to accept. Hence, I became the first employee of Facebook India. I am in my fifth year at Facebook in 2015, and each day continues to be the best yet.

◆

Big visions and aspirational goals inspire me. At Silicon Graphics, our technology was part of many big-ticket endeavours like the landing of NASA's Mars Pathfinder. At Facebook, it is the company's mission of giving people the power to share to make the world more open and connected that drives me to come in to work each day and give my very best.

When we started building Facebook India, a key goal was to build an organization that would 'Be Open', 'Move Fast', 'Focus on Impact', 'Be Bold' and 'Build Social Impact', all of which are part of Facebook's global values. Many cautioned me that, for example, building an 'open' culture was not a realistic goal, given India's cultural hierarchy. However, we knew that building the right culture was paramount to achieving our ambitious goals in India. We invested in the art and science of building culture. Continuing with the example of the 'Be Open' goal, we spent time with each employee, discussing what 'being open' meant to Indians. We decided to build the skills needed for people to have crucial conversations. Leaders at Facebook were at the forefront, talking about their mistakes and areas of opportunities they were working on in team meetings, over email, and in company-wide all-hands. We created intentional safe spaces for people to have hard conversations. They also publicly acknowledged people who gave them critical inputs that helped them become better leaders. **We fostered a 'leadership by all' culture, where it was not about what the managers did or did not do, but about cultivating a collective sense of ownership.** And judging by the amount of constructive input I receive directly, I know we succeeded! This is also reflected in metrics like the amount of peer feedback shared directly during our regular performance summary cycles, the norm of asking the elephant-in-the-room questions and the high bar set for accountability. If we didn't have the overarching vision of 'building an organization that reflects our global values', we would not have had that fire in our belly and the persistence and determination to get there and continue to consistently better ourselves.

Today, one of our key goals is to help our clients leverage consumer transition to digital and mobile. To quote former Intel chief executive officer (CEO), Andy Grove: 'Market share is won and lost in periods of transition.' As an industry, we are currently in the midst of a massive shift in how people consume content. For instance, in 2013, for the first time ever in the US, digital overtook TV as the medium where most content was consumed. The last time such a transition had happened was in the 1950s when TV overtook radio. **When it comes to marketing, companies need to be where consumers *are*, not where they were.** As an organization, Facebook went through a massive transformation to become a mobile-first company. Our ability to be at the centre of this industry shift driven by changing consumer preferences and technological advancements, and play a pivotal role in helping our clients grow their businesses, is enormously exciting and drives me each day.

People inspire me. I was once asked what type of recognition meant the most to me. I thought about the promotions, the awards and the opportunities offered to me over the years but, in the end, it boiled down to one thing—people. When people who have worked with me or reported to me over the years reach out to ask for counsel during critical junctures—both personal and professional—I appreciate the faith they place in that outreach and feel a deep sense of satisfaction that I was able to gain that trust in the time we worked together; that they still reached out after more than a decade of having worked together. As leaders, the impact we are able to make on people and families as we lead the organization through its ups and downs is hugely gratifying.

Last, but certainly not the least, people inspire me by the impact I see them making every day. I leave each calibration session during our regular performance review cycle feeling extremely proud, especially when I hear about the kind of impact that people who are right out of school and working in their first job are making! They, more than anyone else in the organization, set the bar for me in terms of how high I need to aim.

My family and friends inspire me. I am blessed to have a circle of family and friends who routinely believe in me, more than I sometimes believe in myself. When I tell my mother about a presentation I am worried about, her answer is always, 'Oh, you will be awesome.' When we were faced with the decision of moving from Bengaluru to Hyderabad for the Facebook opportunity just as Dev started his real-estate business in Bengaluru, we talked about it for a long time. I told him that this wasn't about my career versus his. It was important to make it work for both of us. We considered several options, including him continuing his work in Bengaluru and me moving to Hyderabad and one of us commuting over holidays. In the end, however, Dev said, 'I can tell how much this role means to you. Let's just make the move and we'll figure the rest out.' When you have that kind of support behind you, it is a huge responsibility to do the best you can and make it all worthwhile.

◆

I believe there are five qualities or approaches that define leaders:

Vision. Big visions and aspirational goals attract energy, make the energy contagious and inspire action. A critical part of leadership is defining a bold vision for the company, organization and team; articulating the vision; fostering an environment where people make the vision their own; and keeping it at the forefront in all that we do. My natural style gravitates to the 'get things done' action orientation. I have to constantly remind myself not to assume that the vision has been internalized by all, and remember that talking about the 'why' we are (or are not) doing something is often more important than the 'what'. In addition to defining what we will do, it is critical that we also identify goals we will not spend time on, to make sure we are focused on the highest priority targets and are not stretching ourselves too thin—I call these 'NOT' goals. Make setting 'NOT' goals a part of the regular visioning and goal-setting process. These 'NOT' goals are not things that you would not do anyway. They are usually areas that offer fantastic things to do when evaluated in isolation but are not the best and highest-impact tasks to carry out, all things considered. For example, when we started our sales support and marketing focus in India, we concentrated on three key verticals: e-commerce, fast-moving consumer goods (FMCG), and Tech and Telco. Other verticals, such as financial services, were also full of opportunity, but we needed to sharply focus on a few key verticals, demonstrate success and then pick up new verticals like financial services (our NOT goal in the initial phase), which we have since done.

It's all about people. Once the vision is in place, it's all about people. When business goals are aligned to getting the right people in the right positions, and understanding what forces drive them, their careers, goals and personal aspirations—that's when magic happens. Even when we cannot do things that are completely aligned to each person on the team, it is critical to be directionally aligned. Research shows that the answer to the question 'Do you have the opportunity to do what you do best every day?' is one of the biggest drivers of employee satisfaction and productivity. As leaders, it is important to prioritize people-related items—hiring the best, developing the best, recognizing the best and having regular one-on-one sessions focused on learning goals and career aspirations. This is an era of servant leadership. As leaders, we are here to serve our teams.

Execution and discipline. 'Say what you are going to do. Do what you say. Close the loop.' I am constantly astounded by how something that sounds so simple can be so hard for people to do in practice. As leaders, it is essential that we help build execution skills in the organization. This can be broken down to helping people understand what 'done' means (for example, shipping the first draft of a presentation may mean 'done' to someone, while it may mean 'presentation is reviewed, feedback incorporated and ready to ship externally' to someone else), agreeing on interim milestones to track and holding a high bar on accountability. Assess the execution quotient of your organization and invest in skills, culture and processes to create a high-performance team with flawless execution capabilities. I urge every leader or aspirant to really invest in building this execution muscle—through prioritization, follow-through and communication. This could make the difference between a good career and a great one.

Give people the power of 'voice'. Stephen Covey talks about 'voice' as the eighth habit of highly effective people. Jack Welch talks about the importance of candour in his book, *Winning*. Such candour is reflected in values like 'Be Open', 'Be Bold', 'Move Fast' and in small bytes of real-time feedback. It embodies the spirit that one has to want to make a difference or cause a change that one thinks possible. If I had to pick one attribute that has particularly led to my growth as a leader, it's having the confidence to use my voice (fuelled by the conviction that I am driven by the success of my clients, organization and team—that is, it is not about *me*), and focusing on creating a culture of empowering others to use their voice. Investments in understanding personality traits (using tools like Colors, Myers Briggs) are important aspects of giving people the power of voice. We also need to build organizations with the capacity for taking risks and encouraging failures. If we aren't making mistakes, we aren't trying hard enough. We just need to learn from mistakes and iterate rapidly.

Communicate. Communicate. Communicate. Gone are the days of one-way, top-down communication. A leader today is increasingly accessible. At Facebook, this is reflected in our office spaces, where everyone sits in an open floor. There are no cubicles, no offices for anyone, including Mark Zuckerberg, our founder and CEO, and Sheryl. Personally, I love a space that's at the centre of the office so I get a sense of the flow of information and ideas, and am physically easily accessible. Other practices include office hours where anyone in the company can sign up for a quick informal chat, skip-level meetings and mentors, replicating the open Q&A session Mark does every Friday for the company at a country level or Facebook tribes like 'Ask Kirthiga' (a forum conceived and created by one of our analysts). In addition to ensuring accessibility of communication, leaders need to invest in building their own communication skills—a skill I believe is one that no one should ever stop working on, no matter how good they are. Conciseness, clarity, and conviction are key aspects of communication. I work with mentors and coaches—both formal and informal, external and internal—for continually raising the bar on my communication skills.

Being a leader is a privilege. A responsibility. Cherish it. Enjoy it. Deliver on the promise of being a leader to 'Change lives. Change organizations. Change the world'—a tagline from the Stanford Business School that is deeply ingrained in me.

◆

A work-life balance gets stressed the most during childbearing years. In my case, for the first few years after marriage, we were not ready for children. When we thought we were ready, we postponed it for the smallest of reasons—a conference to attend, a pre-planned vacation whose timing may conflict with pregnancy, etc. Then, when we were really ready, we found, to our great dismay, that it doesn't just happen when *you* are ready. Ashna was born seven years after we were married. But the joy and richness she and Ariya, born three years later, add to our lives, and the appreciation we feel for having them, put all trade-offs into sharp perspective. My takeaway from this experience is: **there will *never* be a perfect time to have children. The corollary is that if you want to have children, it is *always* a good time to have children!**

Ashna was born a year into my two-year Stanford Business School programme. Frankly, it was the best time to have a baby! We partied more after she was born than before—she had the habit of staying up late into the night so we had to be out with her in any case. She had 365 aunts and uncles—all my amazing classmates! Someone or the other was always ready to take care of her when I needed to study, or if we needed to take a much-needed break once in a while. I finished my MBA on time and graduated as an Arjay Miller Scholar, in the top 10 per cent of the class.

Ashna and I both walked on to the stage together to get my degree, both of us in graduation gowns and hats. Dean Joss jokingly told me, 'Please just don't ask for an exemption to the Core Classes if and when she joins Stanford Business School because she "attended" them with you when you were pregnant with her!'

Ariya was born two years after I joined Good Technology. When I had to return to work after my six-week maternity leave was over I wept, loath to leave my six-week-old infant at home with her nanny. **Since my job required me to travel, I rapidly began researching ways in which I could nurse Ariya during her first year, as I had Ashna. I wondered if this was the moment everyone talked about, when one had to choose between professional goals and personal ones. Then it dawned upon me—I didn't have to make a choice!** I travelled with Ariya for the first year after she was born. Fortunately for me, every place I went, things somehow fell into place. For example, in North Carolina, my colleague's wife who used to run a day-care centre offered to take care of Ariya as I timed meetings and sessions around her nursing schedule. It was amazing to see how, when one makes up one's mind to do something, nature conspires to make things happen.

To me, this was an illustration of the power of AND versus the tyranny of OR. In this example, **I did not have to choose one: professional ambitions OR personal goals. I could pursue professional ambitions AND personal goals. I began to embrace the power of the AND more and more.** For instance, after Ariya was born, I wasn't able to continue volunteering at the Stanford Children's Hospital (something I did weekly), given the unpredictable schedule that raising two young children brings. Since I missed the community involvement pillar in my life, my friend introduced me to HandsOn Bay Area, a wonderful organization geared for busy professionals, where you could sign up to volunteer a few hours at a time to various causes as availability permitted. I chose activities where I could take the children, and from the time Ariya was three months old, Ashna, she and I have gone to soup kitchens together, planted native California saplings with an organization called MAGIC, taught at an English as a Second Language (ESL) training course, helped with Halloween and Christmas parties for the Grandparents Resource Center organization, and so on. While the choices I made may not be the right choices for everyone, the overall message is: **'Embrace the power of AND versus the tyranny of OR'**—a takeaway that holds true in both the personal and professional spheres.

I have also had the privilege of working with organizations that have invested deeply in developing women leaders. I started Motorola's Women's Business Council Bay Area Chapter and I'm now the sponsor for Facebook's Asia Pacific Diversity initiatives. Through business school and sessions at work, I began to appreciate the need for women and men to be aware of research-backed gender differences, and to consciously adapt, based on their self-awareness of where they fell in the spectrum. For example, I fall under the generalization of 'women who don't like to negotiate for themselves'. In fact, **my husband once told me: 'It's amazing how well you negotiate for everyone but yourself!' Margaret Neale, the professor of management at the Stanford Business School, talks about how women don't ask, and how they are damned if they do and damned if they don't. Through tips from experts like her, I remind myself to be conscious of my natural inclination to shy away from negotiating for myself and to push myself to do better.**

I believe it is imperative to take your whole self with you—whether you are at work or at home. I am a full-time professional, a full-time mother, a full-time wife, a full-time daughter, a full-time friend and more. If I am going through a particularly busy phase at work, I talk to my girls about it, and they offer me the most practical advice on how to balance work and life and are wonderfully accommodating during the 'work-heavy' phases. Similarly, if I am, for example, worrying about my father's health, my Facebook family is wonderfully supportive and the pillar of strength that keeps me going.

A final thought—be sure to make the time to enjoy the journey. I remember a family weekend getaway with some of my best friends from business school that I was very much looking forward to. I worked extra hard over the week to make sure I would be able to unplug over the weekend. I must have slept for an average of no more than four hours a day that week. We packed enthusiastically, chattered all the way on our drive to the vacation home in Big Sur, California, met up with the two other families there, made dinner, finally sat down together...and I fell asleep on the dinner table. Hence, make sure to leave enough energy to enjoy and appreciate the very things we work so hard for. Know what you want to invest in, know what to say no to, reserve time for the things that are most important to you and live life fully.

◆

- Focus on the success of your clients, organization and team. Your success is a by-product.
- Make your partner a true partner.
- Remember the power of AND versus the tyranny of OR.
- Dream big.
- Be aware of gender differences and consciously make the necessary adjustments.
- Make the most of the opportunities given to you and create opportunities when possible.
- Don't forget to enjoy the journey along the way!

LYNN DE SOUZA is a multifaceted media personality. A national tennis champ, who followed up her master's in business administration (MBA) in marketing with a twenty-five-year-long career in advertising media, working for Ogilvy, Grey and Lintas, she is one of the most influential women in the country. She features regularly in the power lists of top business publications.

A brief sabbatical to study veterinary nursing in Australia in 1998 was followed by a five-year stint at Lintas, where Lynn was in charge of the integrated marketing, health care and knowledge management functions. At this time she joined the animal welfare movement as a trainer and volunteer, and built a veterinary hospital and shelter on her ancestral land in Goa. Besides animal welfare, Lynn is also actively involved with the upliftment of girls and women in India, and has founded and chaired the Women's Leadership Network for Interpublic Group in India. She concluded her advertising career in 2012 after a four-year term as chairperson and chief executive officer (CEO) of Lintas Media Group and set up Social Access Communications in 2013, India's first communications firm working purely for social causes.

◆

The Catalyst for Social Change
LYNN DE SOUZA

A WALK IN THE HILLS

It was a cloud-soaked September afternoon walk along the hillsides of Ambavane. The year was 1988, and the gentleman by my side was arguably the most revered entrepreneur and strategist in advertising at the time, Ravi Gupta. As he pointed out various aspects of the countryside that were of interest to him, in line with his then budding passion for agriculture, he punctuated his discourse with career advice that I consider the most valuable advice I have ever received. A treasured nugget that saw me through the decades that ensued (and still does), delivered in his famous gruff baritone, was: **'Sweetie, never ever equate the chair you occupy with the person you are. The day you do that, you are finished.'**

I had joined Trikaya a few months earlier and, for the next seven years, Ravi Gupta was to become a boss, a mentor and an unparalleled source of inspiration to me, as he was to so many of us who had the good fortune to work for him. When I left to join Lintas in 1995, to work at a bigger job in a bigger place, it was with his active guidance and encouragement. At my farewell party, he called me a leader, a champion and a friend. He lost his battle against cancer a year later at only fifty-five years of age, leaving behind a legacy of advertising giants who had blossomed under his distinctive tutelage, and an unforgettable lesson—that **a leader is one who recognizes the leaders in all those he is privileged to lead, who brings out the champions that live inside each and every one of them, and in doing so becomes a true friend, a term never to be used idly.**

'Trikaya' is a Sanskrit term that refers to the Buddhist doctrine of three bodies—the Truth body or the enlightened one; the Created body, manifested in time and space; and the body of Mutual Enjoyment. Ravi Gupta used this analogy to denote the three pillars of advertising—strategy, creatives and media. **He took on the biggies of the ad world with a simple belief—that brilliant creative work founded upon precise strategy could bring in unprecedented results with just a fraction of the media spend.** Mediocre creative and/or weak strategy could also deliver results, but would require ten times the media budget. Ravi Gupta was not a fan of research, and made history with the brand name Thums Up, when research suggested naming the drink 'Bistro'.

Peering over the shoulders of creative giants like Chris D'Rozario, Preeti Vyas Giannetti and Vikas Gaitonde at Trikaya opened my eyes and ears to the power of all that is simple and minimalistic on the one hand, and the persuasiveness of asymmetry, colour and music on the other. Trikaya's signature use of 'white space' in print advertising was to take on a deeper meaning in my life's journey. As for media, well, Ravi Gupta showed me that media planning, in its most useful avatar, is an art and not a science. In doing so, he led me to understand, and indeed pioneer, the growth of media services as a standalone business in the exploding world of media channels over the past two decades.

'There's so much more to flying than just flapping around from place to place. A...a...a...a mosquito does that!'

A RIDE ON THE TRAIN

Mr G, as Ravi Gupta was affectionately called, was not, however, the reason I began a career in advertising and media. That decision was made much earlier, as a gangly teenager in business school. I was one of five girls in the graduating class of forty-five students at the Jamnalal Bajaj Institute of Management Studies in Mumbai at a time when the total strength of business students in the country was less than a thousand, with the proportion of women being less than 5 per cent. (So much has changed in the past decade or so, and for the better. Today, I am told that women management graduates alone number more than a thousand each year!)

The five of us stood out. **We were the mad ones, the bold ones, the intelligent and ambitious ones; the ones who were foolhardy enough to want to make it big in a masculine world.** We were arrogant enough to look down on teachers and nurses and housewives, and most of us were willing to give up marriage and motherhood for a leg up the corporate ladder. Eventually, though, many opted out of full-time careers, while those who chose the finance stream managed to combine their domestic and professional lives well. However, most of my peers in marketing have ended up single, either by choice or because their marriages couldn't withstand the added responsibilities of highly demanding jobs.

Ten years after that walk in the hills, **I discovered that being a teacher and a nurse was actually what would give my life meaning and purpose, and that adding value to another being's existence was far greater than the value of one more well-delivered presentation, one more award, one more promotion.** I'll speak more about that later, but for now, suffice it to say that this was a realization that had silently taken seed during the lectures of our head professor of marketing and strategy at Bajaj, incidentally another Mr G, universally called 'TG'.

Tarun Gupta was feared and revered in equal measure for his unorthodox teaching methods. As our marketing 'text' for the year, he eschewed Kotler and instructed us instead to read and memorize the iconic *Jonathan Livingston Seagull*, a short illustrated inspirational fable by pilot and author Richard Bach. Our class was dominated by IITians (graduates of an Indian Institute of Technology) and other engineers, many of whom also had work experience and were left-brained enough to look upon the exercise as one of futility and foolishness. Some of us younger arts and commerce scholars, however, offered up more open minds.

While the Indian Institutes of Management (IIMs) are residential campuses, Bajaj is not, and I rode the suburban trains every day from home to college and back. JLS, as we called Bach's book, became a text I thoroughly enjoyed, reading it over and over to the rhythm of the wheels on the tracks. I did not enjoy the finance and operations sessions at all, overwhelmed by their complexity and my lack of prior knowledge, and had to rely on my older, more experienced buddies to help me with the assignments. When boredom and frustration took over, JLS became a much-loved companion. I would lose myself in the monochromatic illustrations of the flying gulls, the deceptively simple sentences and the invaluable lessons in self-belief.

'I don't mind being bones and feathers, Mom. I just want to know what I can do in the air and what I can't, that's all. I just want to know.'

A TREK UP THE MOUNTAIN

I came in contact with two women at Bajaj who fascinated me, and I wanted to be like them. First, the petite powerhouse, Vinita Bali, who assisted TG during the marketing lectures and was to play a major role in introducing me to the world of media planning. She has gone on to become a highly acclaimed leader of international repute, while remaining true to our Indian ethos. The second was Roda Mehta, whose one guest lecture was enough to convince me to spend nearly five years at the start of my career under her wing at Ogilvy, Benson & Mather. A pioneer with the guts and gumption to dominate several boardrooms of men, she laid the ground for professional media planning based on data in this country, and introduced many women to the profession.

Ogilvy, or OBM as it was called then, was the ideal place to start one's career in advertising. Its disciplined yet compassionate culture, led by stalwarts like Mani Ayer, Suresh Mullick and Roda, produced many of today's leaders. We also had the good fortune to work with India's foremost advertisers like Hindustan Lever, Johnson & Johnson and Asian Paints, and launch hugely successful brands like Titan.

I once told a journalist that Trikaya was the place to find yourself, while OBM was the place to find your friends. Josy, Kalpu, Bharat, Subhash, Neville, Piyush, Vijay and Lamba, some of whom are now household names, were all just a bunch of eager learners then. **The legendary founder of the agency, David Ogilvy himself, visited the India office twice. Perhaps my most cherished memory is that of sitting by his side at dinner at the Yacht Club, and then taking the sporting octogenarian on a Victoria carriage ride down the waterfront. Back then, I was not aware of the cruelty I was perpetrating on the horses, so the evening was filled purely with inspiration and awe.**

In the winter of 1986, eleven of us were sent to Srinagar for a global leadership training programme, the first of its kind to be held in India. Among other things, we were indoctrinated into David Ogilvy's celebrated Magic Lanterns—principles of good advertising that outlive the test of time, media proliferation and multi-screen complexities. It was there that I was made aware of my 'superior' and 'natural' presentation skills, which I have used to fairly good advantage along the way. We sailed among the lotuses in Dal Lake, climbed up to Pahalgam, sat around the rocks in white waters, observed mountain goats manoeuvre the hillsides with astounding nimbleness and sowed the seeds of friendships that are still always just a phone call away.

'Where is everybody, Sullivan?...Why aren't there more of us?'

A TRIP TO THE STADIUM

Most of my career, however, was spent at Lintas. In fact, people often asked me whether I had ownership of the agency because of my name! I did not. Lintas, however, did own me, as it does everyone who crosses its threshold and works there for a substantial period of time. During the Lintas years of 1995 to 2012, my career spanned dimensions as wide-ranging as media services, consumer research and health-care, event management, knowledge management, direct response and digital media, postgraduate training and corporate governance.

I was recruited by Prem Mehta to launch Initiative Media, the country's first media service outfit. It was a challenging assignment, with the agency having just lost its enormous and prestigious sixty-year-old Hindustan Lever media relationship. I was tasked with building a new service and a new brand from scratch out of the embers of the old.

To a group of people who had once fed easily on a regular client for decades, hunger did not come easy. So I went about changing systems to reflect the flexibility I had known at Trikaya, and replaced some of the diehards with people who had worked with me earlier. The new team and I then recruited people with skill sets in new business development and client management, rather than media operations. We approached large and long-standing clients of the agency and told them to centralize all their media duties with us, even those whose brands were being handled by other agencies. We coined the term 'Central Media Agency' and, within a year, clients like Maruti Udyog, Bajaj Auto and Cadbury had come on board.

It was a heady time, with the media environment itself changing as cable and satellite channels tested the hegemony of Doordarshan, and regional print media began to add editions and reach down the line. **I coined the phrase 'A little initiative goes a long way' to encourage people to take small actions that could result in big things.** Perhaps one of the best examples of this came from Punitha Arumugam, who led the Bangalore team at the time. As cricket began to gain popularity as a televised sport, she came up with the 'third umpire', and Britannia 50-50 biscuits will forever be remembered for its appearances during those few seconds when the chances of the batsman being out or not out were fifty-fifty!

With success came fierce competition as other agencies soon began to catch on to the increasing opportunities in advertising and new media. Large international media agencies began to look at India as a growing market, and we naturally became the main hunting ground for talent and clients. In many ways, it suited the fragmenting media space to support competition among agencies. In fact, one of the biggest game changers in response to this was the consolidation of the media service units of all the WPP agencies into Group M.

Around that time, by sheer coincidence or perhaps by God-given design, the first week of September 1997 brought tumultuous change into my life. A religion-related incident at the workplace led me to reassess my personal goals. I began volunteering with an animal hospital and shelter, the Bombay Society for the Prevention of Cruelty to Animals (SPCA), and, a few months later, in a move that shocked the entire advertising fraternity, went on a sabbatical to Australia.

A DIP IN THE OCEAN

Brisbane was a quiet picturesque town without an Indian in sight. I lived in a wooden Queenslander and walked up a gentle slope past a creek every morning to my classes in the college of veterinary nursing. During the evenings, I spent my time at the Chelmsford Veterinary Hospital where I was to complete my practical competencies, and weekends were spent alternately volunteering with the Royal Society for the Prevention of Cruelty to Animals (RSPCA), the Guide Dog Centre, the Lone Pine Koala Sanctuary and Sea World. I spent holidays trekking in the bush, meeting kangaroos and koalas. One weekend, I took a boat out from Harvey Bay and witnessed a humpback whale and her calf breach and blow, and listened to her mesmeric song on the hydrophone. Another time, I dipped into the ocean at Tangalooma Bay and swam among wild dolphins.

A few months after my return to India, I was introduced to the third significant 'G' of my life. Her impetuous and imperious personality aside, her commitment to the protection of animals and indeed her unfailing and unusual friendship with me, make Maneka Gandhi a woman I both admire and adore. Under her guidance, I donated my ancestral land in Goa and built an animal shelter there. I learnt all the nuances of animal rights and about the abuse of animals for food, experiments, clothing, sacrifice and entertainment. I became a master trainer, and wrote columns, conducted workshops and even authored a book about the life of a street dog.

As the world hurtles though crisis upon crisis—some natural, some man-made—a true leader can no longer afford to ignore the totality of human and natural existence. The interconnectivity of life must be preserved for the earth to be able to survive. I am fortunate that my association with animals has helped me realize this, and that my relationships with the world of media help me propagate the same.

'*Overcome space, and all we have left is Here. Overcome time, and all we have left is Now.*'

A PLEDGE IN THE VILLAGE

In 2007, the Interpublic Group (IPG) announced its acquisition of Lintas. We were now part of a mega global network, and international travel became a quarterly occurrence. **Interacting with people from different cultures adds a dimension of knowledge to leadership in much the same way as does interacting with people from different communities and demographic backgrounds within India itself. The mind opens, and learns to accept the immensity of possibilities.**

That year I was promoted to chairman and CEO of Lintas Media Group, and also assumed chairmanship of the Aaren Initiative board when Lintas acquired the OOH (out of home) advertising agency. We held the first in a series of annual off-site conferences in a village outside Jaipur. At midnight in 2 degrees Celsius, **we committed ourselves to a new motto: 'Reach. Touch.' This attempted to capture the new essence of media engagement in a digitally connected society, shifting the focus away from just delivering reach, to actually touching the minds and hearts of consumers. It also encapsulated our own character and culture by moving away from the clinical and calculating to the more collaborative and compassionate.** We encouraged our employees to volunteer for causes, and supported charities under the Lintas Media Group Humanity Drive. We invested in employee engagement programmes, and I found myself winning an Asia-Pacific award for being the CEO with the best human resources (HR) orientation.

In 2010, IPG requested me to set up the IPG Women's Leadership Network in India, tasked with devising ways to recruit and retain the female workforce. Initially I resisted, believing that any form of differentiated treatment as a woman was something I had personally never asked for and didn't want to encourage. However, they then sent me enough material to make me question that premise, and I embarked on another new journey. I now firmly believe that **this century will be made or broken by the three Ws—the web, the weather and women.** The future of our planet is completely dependent on the survival and growth of the feminine gene and its traits. Every form of engagement—corporate, social, military, legal or governmental—will benefit from having women at the helm.

There comes a time when all that one learns in a memorable career, all the experiences good and bad, all the relationships, all the achievements, cry out to be put to a more selfless purpose. I quit Lintas in October 2012 and, along with media baroness Meenakshi Menon, started Social Access Communications in June 2013, a first-of-its-kind communications firm that works purely to fuel social change and foster social impact. We are now doing what we know best: using the power of communications and the media to deliver what we want most—genuine connections between profit and non-profit sectors that promote beneficial social change. Along the way, we still put a lot of faith in the power of 'Reach. Touch.' and 'a little initiative goes a long way'.

'You will begin to touch Heaven, Jonathan, in the moment that you touch perfect speed. And that isn't flying thousand miles an hour, or a million, or flying at the speed of light. Because any number is a limit and perfection doesn't have limits. Perfect speed, my son, is being there.'

(All quotes in italics are reproduced from *Jonathan Livingston Seagull* by Richard Bach.)

◆

- Never equate your identity with your job. Only then can you become a true leader—one who can encourage those being led to be the best version of themselves.
- Always keep an open mind. You never know what or who might end up changing your life for the better.
- Take the time to hone your communication skills. In today's times, this is vital for improving your personal as well as professional life.
- Interacting with people from different geographies and demographies adds to leadership skills, and should be encouraged in all organizations.
- Stay connected to the world of nature and respect the earth's limited resources in all that you do.

MALLIKA SRINIVASAN, the chairman and chief executive officer (CEO) of Tractors and Farm Equipment Ltd (TAFE), has transformed the organization from a ₹80 crore company to a ₹9,800 crore market leader, from a profit-generating enterprise to one of the most profitable tractor companies, from an Indian player to the third-largest volume player in the world.

Along the way, Mallika has overcome each professional obstacle owing to her strong work ethic, abiding interest in technology, thirst for learning and adherence to a clearly articulated set of personal and business values. Consequently, this Padma Shri awardee has been recognized as one of the most powerful women in India (*Fortune*, 2014). While at home she is mother to her two children, Lakshmi and Sudarshan, and wife of the chairman of TVS Motors, Venu Srinivasan, Mallika admits that she is her father's daughter; even as she successfully juggles her home and career, work is never far from her mind. Today, her daughter laughs and asks her, 'Mom, has everything got to lead to tractors and TAFE?' It is such passion that defines Mallika's success story.

◆

The Tractor Empress
MALLIKA SRINIVASAN

I was no older than twenty-six, fresh out of The Wharton School, armed with one of the most reputed business degrees in the world, and brimming over with giant dreams for the future. When I returned to India to join my family's Amalgamations Group, I found myself in a job with no job description, with a pay package that I believe was perhaps not commensurate with what my Wharton classmates were offered. I was asked to carve out a niche for myself, ensuring that I integrated well with the team that had worked in the organization for many years and had contributed richly to the company's progress. My suggestion that it was perhaps better to be in one of the smaller companies in the Amalgamations Group—on the grounds that this would give me independence for achievement—was spurned. I was asked to work for the flagship TAFE—Appa's explanation being that the canvas here would be vast. I felt the first stirrings of discontent, and burst into the office my father, A. Sivasailam—who was the group chairman—occupied. I announced, 'Sir, I feel that I am not getting my due!' What followed was a litany of complaints—an unclear job description and a lack of clearly identified authority—unacceptable to a Wharton graduate. My father heard me out and then said, **'Sit down, young lady, you might be a Wharton graduate, but I do not need one to run my business.'** With that cutting remark, he put me in my place. I could have airs and graces as a B-school graduate, but I was talking to a man who had nurtured the company and the group; had held his family, group and all the professionals together post the early demise of his father; and had earned the respect of the business community. Here, there was no room for conceit.

The lesson stayed with me and kept me grounded. Years later, in 2010, when TAFE joined the billion-dollar club—remarkably, in the middle of the global economic downturn—and I was presented my twenty five-years' service award, I teasingly addressed my father, 'I hope, at least now, you feel that a Wharton graduate can offer value to your company!' Appa relished the comment and chuckled with pride while the rest of the audience laughed.

I believe that one can't rely on a surname to forge ahead in one's career. In my own family, each of us has earned our stripes. Yes, we are offered an opening; yes, we do have a right to shares and dividends. But the onus is on us to make full use of early opportunities, prove ourselves and earn the right to manage. Besides, in a family business, we have to view ourselves as trustees for a larger group of family shareholders; therefore, we are responsible to them and owe them our full support.

My father was a great believer in building and sustaining relationships of trust. A core value that, when institutionalized, has the power to deliver rich dividends is building long-term relationships with all stakeholders, whether they are business partners, shareholders, suppliers, dealers or bankers. I am proud of the long partnership that we have had with AGCO Corporation— over fifty years—perhaps the longest in our industry. 'Win-win', 'trust and transparency' are the pillars on which long-term partnerships are nurtured and this explains why our partnerships span generations

The fact is that my father had been a strong presence through my childhood years, and even later. As young girls, my sister Jayshree and I absorbed the nuances of managing a business by osmosis, by watching him and all the family elders run enterprises in trading, auto components and tea plantations with integrity and respect for all colleagues. We observed our father resolve the trickiest of impasses—including a long phase of financial instability and labour unrest—by responding with a rare combination of empathy and firmness, and by being a keen listener at all times. **Appa would talk to us about his professional life, and we were encouraged to express our views, even our dissent—the only caveat being that we had to speak politely.**

My childhood, consequently, comes with memories of self-reliance and empowerment, be it when I was encouraged to win the president's award for girl guides, or later, when Amma pushed my sister and me to take an interest in the working lives of the family patriarchs. She did not view us as 'mere girls'; she wanted us to emulate my father in carrying forward the vision of my grandfather, S. Anantharamakrishnan—or 'J' as he was so fondly called—a man who dared to challenge all impediments in the path of India's industrial future and embrace the finest of technologies.

As I grew older, while my father hoped that I would pursue literature, my mother believed in a business education. However, both were united in their belief that a holistic upbringing, an appreciation of the finer things in life, like music, art and Sanskrit, and traditional values were intrinsic to complete character-building.

Amma had a captivating voice, an undying passion for Carnatic music and viewed singing as the ultimate expression of bhakti. She instilled in us an unwavering faith in the divine and made us recognize the value of respecting traditions, organizing traditional poojas and observing festivals.

Appa ensured that all these were followed with strict discipline. In addition, he encouraged us to master driving vehicles, delve deep into the world of technology and acquire skills not meant for girls at that time, such as horse riding and rifle shooting. From my father's perspective, the choice of career was entirely mine. However, my dreams had already been chiselled during dinner-table conversations and breakfast discussions—I had to carve a space for myself in the world of business. And the first step, I believed, was a degree from Wharton.

◆

In 1986, on returning from B-school, and in consultation with senior executives, I set out to outline for myself the areas of focus in keeping with the market context and the needs of the organization. **While some were enormously welcoming, others were fairly sceptical. 'Let's see how long she lasts,' was perhaps their approach. Far from being demotivated, my resolve to succeed only strengthened.** Over the next two years, I held discussions with several employees—especially those who had been with the group for decades, and had remained by our side through thick and thin; they willingly and generously shared decades of knowledge with me. Through them, I not only learnt the nuts and bolts of the business of tractors and farm equipment, but also built strong relationships governed by mutual respect.

Equally, I had the steady support of my father, my boss, who insisted on offering me this 'wide canvas'. It was a dare of sorts—one that I met by chalking out a definite strategic plan, identifying technology as the differentiator and nurturing leadership. I hit the ground running.

In the mid-1980s, when I started work, the tractor industry was transforming. It was the end of the Licence Raj, of an era when the government dictated the number of tractors a company could produce, the way they were distributed and the prices at which they could be sold. In the emerging liberalized era, demand and supply could be in step, and customers began to dictate industry trends. Indian farmers were demanding, and our tractors not only needed to have the relevant technology for India's small farms but also to meet exacting expectations regarding the overall cost of ownership. To fulfil these requirements, we had extensive interactions with our customers—be it in rural tea shops, homes or farms—and I enjoyed listening to their needs and aspirations (and still do). After all, **while it is commonly stated that the devil is in the details, for me God is in the details.**

In the new millennium, after a decade-long period of growth, the tractor industry slumped within a three-year period by a whopping 50 per cent! Sure, it was time to think strategically and out-of-the-box within boardrooms, but it was also vital to remain connected with our customers in the hinterlands. We sent our sales teams cross-country to walk the villages of India. We shifted focus to an intensive personal selling initiative. Simultaneously, even while cutting back on production and working capital, we continued to invest aggressively in research and development. Consequently, when the markets recovered, we had new products to launch—tractors for farmers across the spectrum, whether they were working in orchards or toiling in paddy fields. **The business of tractors tends to be cyclical, with a potential downturn every decade—and I maintain, the only thing that can de-risk us in the lean times (and earn us returns during good times) is an allegiance to advancement and new products that meet new needs.**

Our philosophy has been to offer farmers more than just equipment. Over the years, we have gone beyond traditional product support to offer customers support with increasing their production and prosperity through new farming practices, crop varieties, and water and soil management. We are committed to offering innovative equipment, today as well as for the future, to meet a whole host of farming requirements—plucking fruits, harvesting grain or planting saplings with speed and accuracy— vital for a country where the employment-to-GDP ratio is skewed, and mechanization is of the essence. This not-for-profit exercise has enabled us to build close bonds spanning generations with our customers and helped us understand their emerging needs faster and better. This approach is reflective of one of our core values that is our hallmark—a long-term relationship with all our stakeholders.

Then came 2005. TAFE acquired Eicher's tractor business. This headline-grabbing initiative was far from easy to realize. There was a fair degree of scepticism—after all, the market was yet to become robust, sales figures across the nation were dropping and an acquisition would be fraught with risk as a large percentage of acquisitions are prone to fail. **But I believe that every business is a gamble, and after assessing the risks and evaluating the pros and cons, informed decisions must be made.** And I made them in a bid to grow, aware that such a step, if made intelligently, would offer us an entry into low horsepower tractors, lead us to markets where we had no presence, grant us a ready manufacturing unit in North India and catapult us to the position close on the heels of the market leader. To make the deal a success, I held on to the early business fundamentals instilled in me by my father—taking the TAFE team into confidence and instilling faith in the Eicher team by being transparent about our strategy. The acquisition was more than merely a financial success. Admittedly the profits increased strongly, market shares grew robustly and new product introduction brought in sustainability, with payback earlier than industry standards. But for me the greatest satisfaction has been that the very same team delivered these extraordinary results post-acquisition.

The journey has been long, but riveting. I still feel like I am a student at Wharton preparing for the next day's class. I go to all meetings with heaps of notes, and a long list of questions to analyse projects threadbare; I do this even if I receive research documents late at night for an early-morning meeting. Being well prepared is a part of my work ethic; besides, I have a keen desire to learn more. A senior colleague often reminds me of the time when there was to be a minor change in an act related to accounting. I asked him how TAFE would respond. He said, 'Don't worry, my team will take care of it.' I smiled and said, 'I am not worried about that—I'm confident you will do your job. I just asked because I needed to learn.' And learn, I did.

◆

My professional journey would have been brief or littered with obstacles had I not had the full support of my family. The fact is, **it is only when you're at peace within yourself and with the world around you that you can go out there, build enterprises, dream big.**

In 1982, after graduating in mathematics (which taught me logical thinking) and econometrics (which honed my analytical skills), I married Venu Srinivasan, the grandson of T.V. Sundaram Iyengar, the TVS group's founder. Venu had a demanding career as the then managing director of Sundaram-Clayton Limited and TVS Motors.

Deep within me was the desire to study further and then engage with the world of business. I requested The Wharton School of Business to defer my admission so I could tend to my newborn before pursuing my ambitions, and I am thankful for their sensitive empathy.

Therefore, in 1984, accompanied by my nine-month-old daughter and my wholly supportive mother, and with the strong backing and encouragement of my husband, I travelled to the US to acquire that degree from Wharton. Amma, my daughter and I stayed in a rented apartment off-campus; I'd attend classes through the day, and huddle in the basement laundry room of the apartment block in the evenings to focus on those piles of notes and allow the washing machines' steady hum to drown out all distractions. Every day was a challenge and a lot of fun in its own way, and it would have been so much harder without my mother's active cooperation. Amma, on her part, had done something unheard of back then—she had left her husband for months on end to foster the formative relationship between a mother and her infant daughter.

Later, when my parents fell ill, my family helped me pull through. In keeping with our cultural ethos, my parents required my personal care and involvement—I had to meet this alongside my business and other family commitments. My cousins, aunts and dear friends shared their time generously, helping me balance my commitments. **Throughout that phase, one had to push oneself, multitask, abandon sleep, balance multiple obligations—personal and professional—and I doubt I would have emerged had I not had the unquestioning help of those closest to me.**

Of course, even on the best of days, my work schedule and my passion to live a holistic life have left me with less time than I desire to pursue many other interests, such as reading and travelling. I recall my father grappling with the same issue and leaving, for much later in life, some of those little things that he always wanted to do but had no time for—including learning new languages and studying English literature and Indian philosophy. This has been inspiring to me.

I am my father's daughter.

◆

People often comment on my zest for life and living. To this I say that each of us faces impairments and obstacles, but we should avoid becoming cynical or bitter. Focus on the big picture, move onwards with an open mind and remember that life is multi-dimensional. **Joy has a ripple-effect, filters downwards and ensures that everyone is enthused.**

Spirituality offers our family a firm anchor, balances emotions and lets me take life in my stride. I recall a conversation my son had with our family's spiritual guide years ago. He was asked to pose any question of his choice to our guru. Like most little boys, his world revolved around cars, so his obvious query was, 'Swami, which is your favourite car?' We despaired; clearly this conversation was going nowhere! But our guru chuckled, played along and said, 'A Morris Minor.' Then our guru, rather unexpectedly, added, 'I will give you a big car. Will you take it? You mustn't say no!' The boy was only too thrilled. Then came a caveat, 'Will you give me your car in exchange?' Prompt came my son's answer: 'Sure!' 'Shall I drive it?' the guru asked. Again, without missing a beat, the boy said 'Sure!' The guru smiled and said, 'Your heart is the car and I am the driver.'

To me, there hasn't been a more profound lesson in devotion. I do think that God, a higher power—call him what you will—is the charioteer. And once we learn to surrender to his divine will, we are free of professional and personal fears.

Equally, we should do our duty without expecting rewards. Today's generation is preoccupied with remuneration and designations. Work satisfaction is measured merely in terms of concrete rewards and the career progress of peers and colleagues. Along the way, they lose something vital— inner peace. On the other hand, **if we were to immerse ourselves in our respective occupations, go beyond the 'call of duty' and do our very best with dedication—most importantly, if we were to enjoy our work—we'd have a sense of contentment—and believe me, the rewards would naturally follow. They always do.**

◆

Within our family, my sister, too, occupied a top management position and today, my daughter, Lakshmi, and my son, Sudarshan, are part of the management team of group companies and hold key responsibilities. **Ours is a household that has equal faith in both genders, and believes strongly in a woman's ability to lead with courage.**

However, I realize this isn't necessarily the story across India—far from it. A lot of women struggle to embrace professional challenges on account of domestic responsibilities, and several give up mid-way. The situation with those women who are disadvantaged in some way and are struggling for an opportunity to improve the quality of their lives is even more challenging. Among the initiatives run by our company to empower women, there is the J Rehab Centre—set up well before the age of corporate social responsibility—that assists differently abled women and helps them become financially independent. These orthopedically challenged women are trained to assemble wiring harnesses for our tractors and this provides them a sustainable livelihood. Interestingly, while the aim is to make these women economically self-sufficient, many have gone on to obtain for themselves medical help to overcome their disabilities and become breadwinners for entire families! **That's why I say, success at work is much too limited a parameter to measure a woman's value; she has the power to change the destiny of an entire family.**

I also think that it is incumbent on organizations to offer a congenial environment to women employees. In today's context, safety is an important criterion and organizations have to go the extra mile to ensure this. Given the current low participation rate of women in the workforce in India, we need to create a milieu that is nurturing, one that leverages their skills and diverse perspectives to create strong success stories. Creating successes and showcasing them is the best way of enhancing women's participation. I think organizations have a responsibility to leverage and retain this invaluable talent pool.

However, once an appropriate environment is in place, a woman must be recruited, retained and promoted not on account of her gender, but purely on the basis of her performance. Capable, proficient women pave the way for future women leaders. **Offering a woman a job only on account of her sex is doing an injustice to the cause of all women.**

◆

There are three Ds to success: discipline, determination and the power of discrimination. History provides valuable lessons: Japan was decimated during the Second World War and Korea sank into economic distress after the Korean War. It was discipline, and discipline alone, in professional habits, that ensured that both Japan and South Korea resurfaced. Individual discipline translates into societal discipline, and this in turn ensures success. In organizations, there's much to be gained if each individual displays discipline while fulfilling commitments and delivering assigned tasks as per schedule.

Beyond talent, beyond even education, what leads one to success is determination. By this I do not mean obstinacy—which signifies an unwillingness to correct stances or consider advice. **We all know of unproductive people with aptitude, or unrewarded geniuses, or educated drifters. But can you name one person who is truly persistent, yet wholly unsuccessful? I know I cannot.**

◆

I remember J.R.D. Tata's visit to our house when I was but a young girl. He was the first recipient of an award instituted in my grandfather's memory, and spent time with us after the function. While I do not recall the details of his conversation with my family, I remember how he commanded a sense of respect, even awe—he had the manner and import of a true leader.

Without any bias, I'd say the same thing about my father and my husband—the two biggest influences in my life, and in their own unique ways, consummate leaders. **My father gave me a security net and an opportunity to build a business, sustaining it with solid values. My husband, on the other hand, taught me to fly by encouraging me to take risks and remain intrepid.** Both qualities define great leadership.

A successful leader displays a strong sense of fair play and discrimination. Discrimination is the ability to distinguish between what is morally correct and incorrect, and take educated decisions, in keeping with the role that you are playing, while abiding by fortitude and truth. For instance, a father may also be the boss at work; the factors that he will take into account when dealing with his son as one of his children should be different from those that he is compelled to take into account while determining his son's performance in his professional life—in the latter instance, he will have to consider the greater common good.

A leader's primary responsibility is acknowledging and appreciating the contribution of colleagues and recognizing each individual's strengths. After all, the leader is not the only expert in the room, and extraordinary ideas can come from the most unexpected co-workers. While listening closely to each of them, and sifting out valuable inputs from the noise, a leader must keep colleagues motivated and encourage them to innovate. In short, she must inspire with her crystal-clear vision and her ability to communicate her dreams.

I cannot emphasize the significance of communication enough. In small organizations, leaders can have one-to-one discussions with everyone in a team. As organizations grow in size, expand geographically and pursue scale, such direct communication becomes virtually impossible. A leader, however, must still find ways of reaching out, if not directly then indirectly—through technology or large meetings—and ensure that everyone is on board with the organization's vision, direction and plans. **It is only when each employee, down to the last person, is inspired by the leader's vision, aligns with it and sees a key role for himself or herself, that performances will be exemplary.**

◆

- Have an insatiable hunger for knowledge.
- Do your duty, without expecting rewards.
- Remain optimistic.
- Earn your stripes.
- There are three Ds to success: discipline, determination and the power of discrimination.
- A successful leader displays a strong sense of fair play and discrimination.
- Nurture relationships.
- Embrace spirituality.

MEHER PUDUMJEE is the chairperson and director of Thermax Ltd, a role she took over after her mother, Anu Aga, announced her retirement in 2004. She is also a member of the Confederation of Indian Industry's (CII) Family Business Forum. Over the years, Meher has regularly featured in the *Forbes* 'India's Most Powerful Women in Business' lists. She has a postgraduate degree in chemical engineering from the Imperial College of Science, Technology and Medicine, London.

Meher joined Thermax as a trainee engineer in August 1990. A year later, along with her husband, Pheroz Pudumjee, and a small team, she took over the responsibility of turning around a Thermax subsidiary company in the UK. After her return to India in September 1996, Meher was appointed on the board of directors. Over the years, she grew close to her mother and looked to her for emotional support; her father was her mentor and, from her early childhood, instilled in her the drive to do her best. Outside the world of work, Meher is personally involved with the NGOs Teach For India, Akanksha and Shakti Sustainable Energy Foundation, and has a keen interest in music.

The Powerhouse of India
MEHER PUDUMJEE

My maternal grandfather, Adi Bhathena, was an entrepreneur and started a family business, making sterilizers and hospital equipment. He encouraged his two sons to join the business, but the message my mother got was 'to marry and have children'. In 1966, dissatisfied with his comfortable multinational job which allowed him little opportunity to make a difference, Rohinton Aga joined my grandfather and set up Wanson (India) to manufacture coil-type industrial boilers. He later married my mother, Anu, the daughter of the founder. After the collaboration with Wanson ended, the company changed its name to Thermax. All that followed is history.

◆

Let me take you back to my childhood days. **My parents did not have a separate set of messages for me and my brother, Kurush, who was five years my junior. We were both encouraged to study hard, keep our room tidy and clear the table after dinner.** While my parents expected us to do well at studies, they also encouraged us to pursue other interests. Rare, possibly for those times, gender didn't impact our upbringing by and large (though I must confess that my paternal grandmother who lived with us was partial to my brother, a fact that did bother me). If Kurush showed interest for a while in cooking and knitting, that was fine. The fact that I grew up with absolutely no knowledge of cooking or sewing was fine, too.

I recall that our house was always full of people—colleagues from the company, friends and musicians—many of whom stayed with us.

Did my parents push us to join the family business? Overtly, there was no direct pressure, but I am sure there was the subtle message that it would be good if we did. The fact that both my brother and I decided to study engineering suggests that the subtle message was indeed powerful! Be that as it may, the emphasis was always on putting our best foot forward; on working hard at whatever profession we chose—artist, musician, teacher or engineer.

Looking back, my reason for pursuing engineering was possibly influenced more by my science teacher than by my parents' desire. Not only was my science teacher a radiating personality, she was a good human being who made every child in her class feel special. For her, no question was ever stupid, nor did she ever make any child feel small.

I went to the UK for high school and then joined Imperial College to study chemical engineering—one of fifteen girls in a class of sixty, not a bad ratio for those times. During my long vacations, I interned in Switzerland and in the US, which helped me understand different cultures, while learning discipline and hard work.

◆

As a woman, I have never been discriminated against, and when I was in the UK, I never experienced any racial prejudice. I sometimes wonder how much of our attitude brings about negative responses! Having said that, whenever I answered the telephone in the UK and the person asked to speak to the sales representative, and I said that was me, they asked again; I guess presuming that an engineering manufacturing company would have a 'male' salesman! Gender stereotypes are present world over.

After completing my masters in chemical engineering, I was keen to get back to Pune, more so as I had fallen in love with a wonderful man named Pheroz, who later became my husband. I joined Thermax as a trainee engineer. Along with about a hundred other such trainees who were being inducted, I spent the subsequent few months being inducted into the company workflow and processes, through each division and department of the company.

I remember a very meaningful experience from that period. My mother and her boss, who looked after human resources within the company, did a three-day workshop for us. One of the exercises was to earn ₹10 within two hours by performing any task but without letting on that we were from Thermax. I remember walking from house to house for an hour offering to do any household chore, without any success. **I realized there was a direct correlation between the size of a house and the trust factor: the larger the house, the less its occupants trusted strangers!** Disheartened, and with just a few minutes to go, I spotted a gardener. Very hopeful, I asked him if I could help him in return for ₹10—I was hugely embarrassed about having to ask the poor man for this favour, but then that was the set task. The gardener agreed. I helped him in the garden, after which he took me into his little hut, gave me a cup of tea and, with a lot of dignity, handed over ₹10.

At the end of the workshop, each of us had a different story, every one more powerful than the other. This experience helped all of us understand the power and value of humility; it helped us shed our arrogance, intellectual or otherwise, and understand that respect is not linked to one's economic or social strata. This was a strong lesson, for work as well as for life.

◆

Emotionally I was, and am, very close to my mother, but I looked up to my father as my mentor: for his passion for excellence, his ability to motivate and empower people with his vision and his focus on hard work. Dad was a workaholic and routinely came home late from office. I missed his presence at many of my school events because he was often travelling. But every year he would take a few weeks off and we would all go on a vacation though, at times, his work would come along with him!

With his busy schedule, I was amazed at how much patience he had to teach me maths and English. **On a Sunday, Dad would be willing to sit with me for hours. He taught me that my essay might start like a piece of cloth, but I ought to work towards making it the perfect dress—groping for that exact word that would convey what I wanted to say.**

Dad was a perfectionist. Preparing me for a piano concert in the UK, he made me practise every day for a few hours. When it was time to walk onto the stage, he whispered, 'Darling, play to express, rather than impress.' These words have helped me through life—whenever I have done anything with the desire to express myself, it has always been very fulfilling.

Dad had a massive heart attack when he was in his late forties. This made me realize how important it is to have a balanced life—focus on work, but not at the expense of your health and family and friends.

◆

My husband Pheroz joined Thermax and, in 1992, both of us were sent to the UK to turn around a small subsidiary which was not doing well. Most Thermax employees had a great sense of loyalty to the company, and this was demonstrated when our research and development (R&D) director, Dr Joshi, willingly agreed to accompany us to the UK for a year to help and mentor us, leaving his family behind. Our people at Thermax have been our greatest asset. **Neither my grandfather nor my father or mother were engineers, and yet, they built a very successful engineering company. This was only possible because they trusted people and developed them as intrapreneurs who felt like the company truly belonged to each of them.**

The four years we spent in the UK taught us the most valuable lessons in management. We learnt to play multiple roles and understood the meaning of cash flow as against profit and its criticality for a viable business. We also learnt the value of teamwork. Added to that, I discovered the art of running my own home; in Pune, I was lucky that I was staying with my in-laws and didn't have the responsibility of looking after the household.

Those were challenging times, but also very rewarding. We never thought of work as a chore; there was so much to learn and achieve. Often succeeding, sometimes failing; and when the latter would happen, we would move on and try something different.

We had decided to be hands-on and proactive, particularly since we were establishing ourselves in a new marketplace. We were a team of five who had to manage everything—from understanding the dynamics of the market and choosing the products to manufacture and sell, to managing finances, the shop floor, vendors and administration. We learnt how to negotiate a loan with the bank when we had very little to offer as collateral. Such experiences contributed to great learning, and we came to handle stress and celebrate the little gains with the team!

There were times when we would be summoned to customer sites even on a Sunday to service breakdowns, and we would oblige. In fact, I remember one such Sunday call when Pheroz and I had to take our six-month-old baby along to the site. And that was fine. So was the fact that, in an effort to manage costs and spending, Pheroz routinely chose to travel by car to a site in the then East Germany rather than fly.

It was in the UK that I learned the art of time management—we were in the office from 9 a.m. to 9 p.m. many days. However, when in the fourth year our son was born, and could be left with the babysitter only until 3 p.m., I would have to leave for home—I managed fine thanks to prioritizing my time and work. I developed the knack of focusing on what was critical to complete that day, saying no and delegating what I thought someone else could do better. It made me a lot more efficient and I learnt to enjoy the time with my son without feeling too guilty.

As women, we have learnt to feel guilty, especially if we are working mums. After coming to India, I have shamelessly taken help from my in-laws, my mother, friends and domestic help. I do not believe that to be a good mother you have to be with your child twenty-four hours a day. I have two children and they have become independent, responsible, caring young adults without their mum being with them a lot of the time.

◆

Unfortunately, my father passed away due to a heart attack when he turned sixty, and the task of leading the company fell on my mother. The board decided that my mother should become executive chairperson. Though she was hesitant to assume this responsibility, she managed her role extremely well.

As I have said earlier, while growing up, my father was my role model, but as I grew older, I enjoyed my mother's company and I would say she is my closest friend, my mentor (at times, my tormentor), my philosopher and guide. She is a strong person with enormous wisdom, commitment, discipline, humility and genuine concern for those less privileged. She is a go-getter and displays the remarkable ability to learn.

My brother, Kurush, who also decided to join Thermax as a trainee engineer, suddenly passed away in a car accident when he was only twenty-five. This occurred only fourteen months after my father had passed away. It was a traumatic time, and I found it very difficult to deal with the deaths of two precious people in my life. I kept doubting there was a god—kept asking: if there is a God why should two people I love be taken away from me so suddenly? It was my mother who was my pillar of strength during this time. I learnt from her that after a loss, pain is inevitable but suffering is optional. Suffering happens when you keep asking questions which have no answers—a wasted exercise which only leaves one miserable.

My mother taught me the importance of feeling grateful for all that there was rather than mulling over what wasn't.

Indian society is very male-centric and **I remember when my brother died, one major newspaper mentioned 'Thermax loses its future CEO', the clear assumption being that, as the male offspring, my brother would head the company. Most women are not groomed to take over family businesses and they get leadership positions by default, that is, when there is no male to take over.** Unfortunately, I don't see a huge change in this mindset. I am very active in the Family Business Network (FBN) of the Confederation of Indian Industry (CII) and I have seen the secondary status women are often accorded in family businesses.

◆

Coming back to our company's story. The Indian economy went through a downturn, and Thermax's performance started deteriorating—a broad idea of the deterioration can be discerned from the drop in share prices, from ₹420 at one point to ₹36 by the end of the 1990s. Realizing that we were out of our depth, we as a family decided to seek external help from a consulting company. We had to take some tough decisions. We moved out of non-core businesses and brought operational efficiencies into those we were intent on pursuing. We also trimmed our workforce in an effort to establish organizational efficiency. This wasn't easy since we always looked upon our business as generating employment and had only ever asked people to leave on grounds of integrity. With this rationalization, thanks to the hard work of our people, and of course the turn in the economic environment, the company turned around.

It was at this time that we decided to reconstitute the board which till then had nine executive directors, including four independent directors and three family members. It was difficult for us executive directors to objectively evaluate our own performance when we sat on the board, especially when the company was not doing well. Hence, we decided that the new board would have five independent directors and only one executive director—the managing director. The family had to decide whether it wanted to pursue the role of a director or be executives and manage the business. **Pheroz and I were used to rolling up our sleeves and doing work as part of a team and later were overseeing independent divisions. However, we decided to remain on the board** and take non-executive roles—this way, we could step back and view the business from 30,000 feet and give an overview of risk, values, governance, long-term strategy and succession through the board.

It was a very difficult transition at the time, since we had to get used to allowing executives to take decisions; we had to rely on trust and empowerment. We had to refrain from giving advice or making any decision down the line. As a family, we could, and always will, influence values within the organization. Though challenging, this is one of the best decisions the family has taken. I believe that we should allow 'professionals' to run the business, whether these are family members (as in the case of my father) or non-family persons (as in the case of our current chief executive officer or CEO), in the overall interest of the company.

When my mother turned sixty-two, she decided to retire, and the board appointed me as chairperson. **I admire the way my mother has genuinely retired and does not do any backseat driving. Maybe women find it relatively easier to let go!** I am sure it was a struggle for her but she worked on it. I have seen many youngsters in family businesses getting frustrated by their fathers or uncles who, despite being late into their eighties or having officially retired, refuse to let go. In my case, luckily, my mother was incredibly disciplined. She had faith in our capabilities and genuinely wanted to see me and the company succeed.

Having seen both my parents achieve great heights, I was very nervous and unsure of myself when I took over as chairperson. To help me deal with my anxiety, I decided to go for 'Vipassana' meditation which helped me tremendously at the time. I also had a personal coach who mentored me for eighteen months and supported me as I understood my new role. I have learnt over the years (especially while seeing my mother at the helm of the organization) that asking for help and openly showing your vulnerability is not a weakness. What also helped me was the realization that I have to focus on my strengths and not keep looking at my limitations—as my mum has taught me, an apple tree cannot give oranges, and therefore I should not keep comparing myself to my parents. I am who I am and should exploit my strengths.

I consider myself very lucky because throughout my life I have had several options and choices. I am aware that in India, a majority of people, especially women, do not enjoy that luxury. Having decided to be a non-executive, I have time for pursuing other interests which I enjoy. I am closely connected with our company's Foundation, two other NGOs that focus on education for the economically underprivileged, as well as one that focuses on energy sustainability. I love music and am actively involved with a choir based out of Pune. I am available to my two children and my husband, though my husband's constant complaint is that I have no time for him. Has any wife found a way of meeting all the expectations of her husband? Having said that, I feel it is important to emphasize that it certainly helps to have a husband who is supportive and self-confident— who doesn't feel threatened by his wife's work. I am very lucky to have married such a person.

◆

Life has taught me many lessons—a deep sense of gratitude for the love of my precious family, as also every day that I am healthy and alive; the importance of being true to myself; giving out my best in whatever I do; an understanding of being a trustee of wealth—and the responsibility that goes with it; playing multiple roles as a daughter, mother, wife, in-law, friend and colleague—being comfortable doing so and enjoying every aspect...

◆

- Learn to live a life of humility.
- 'Play to express, rather than to impress'—these are words that I hold on to.
- Prioritizing is vital if you plan to juggle personal and professional responsibilities.
- Make time for yourself and the things you love.
- There is no shame in being vulnerable.

With a first degree in history and science from Harvard University and a master's from Johns Hopkins Bloomberg School of Public Health, USA, **MIRAI CHATTERJEE** could have pursued a lucrative career abroad. But inspired by her parents' Nehruvian ideals and her meeting with Ela Bhatt, she returned to India to work for the Self Employed Women's Association of India (SEWA). Since then, for the past thirty years, Mirai has been at the forefront of improving the health and financial security of women in India's informal sector, and highlighting the importance of gender equity, education and sanitation. She says, 'The daily inspiration from the women I work with—who have so little materially, but are full of courage and good cheer—keeps me going.'

For her commendable work as the director of SEWA Social Security, Mirai has been presented the Global Achievement Award by Johns Hopkins University. When she's not at work, Mirai loves reading, gardening and unwinding with her friends, her three daughters and her 'jeevan sathi', her husband.

◆

The Working Woman's Champion
MIRAI CHATTERJEE

Thirty years is a good vantage point from which to view one's life as a working woman. I have been especially fortunate to be part of a sisterhood of working women—SEWA—a national union dedicated to ensuring that its members have access to work, food and social security, to ultimately move out of poverty and towards self-reliance.

When I look back, I distinctly recall the day I was drawn to this kind of work. I was fourteen, and from the balcony of our Mumbai home, I saw an old man shuffling along, singing for a living. The neighbours threw some coins at him. As he stooped to gather the loose change, it struck me how unfair his circumstances were.

These budding sensibilities were nurtured both at home and school. My parents were young and idealistic when India became independent. They followed Pandit Nehru's call and involved themselves with nation building. They hosted meetings with young scientists, discussed and debated the role of science, especially atomic energy, and tried promoting the spirit of enquiry. **My mother immersed herself in the Congress party—back then, the party that had given us our freedom—and formed a circle of like-minded friends, ready to serve the fledging nation. It was an invigorating environment to grow up in.**

My father's untimely death from cancer at the young age of twenty-eight changed our lives. My mother lost her partner who shared her values and ideals. With two toddlers to provide for—my sister and me—she had to join the workforce. I watched my mother slowly rebuild her life with courage, good humour and positive energy, supported by friends, many of them women of resilience. Some had been widowed early, others had left marriages that had not worked (in an era when separations and divorces were uncommon), and still others were breaking new ground with brave career choices. I recall being privy to their conversations and struggles, especially with male colleagues who resisted their leadership. They did not seem to agonize much over a work-life balance, and rose to executive positions in their chosen careers. **My mother herself, employed with a German company, was the only female executive there in the whole of Asia in the 1970s!**

In my growing years, I lived in an open house. I remember, some of my mother's friends would come for dinner and stay for months! Then there were couples—old, steadfast friends of my mother—who adopted me as their additional daughter. In London and later, in America, family friends were my home away from home. At a young age, my sister and I learnt to share with and care for those beyond blood ties, and to open our hearts and homes to all who crossed our paths.

As a young girl, the other major influence was school. I had the benefit of a solid education at the Cathedral and John Connon School, Mumbai, which exposed me to a world beyond our circle of family friends. As a member of the Interact Club, a social work group, I was taken to corners of the city that were tucked away and encouraged to play with the children of construction workers at Nariman Point; I learnt of the concerns of mothers who did not have the wherewithal to send their children to school or buy medicines. With the gentle guidance of teachers, I became increasingly aware that we lived in an unequal world and this needed to be changed.

I remember an incident at school which opened my eyes to the particularly disadvantageous position of women. **Students were about to elect the president of the Interact Club. As the frontrunner, I was quite keen to take charge. However, our teacher, an Australian, told me to turn down my nomination, because with a girl at the helm, boys would not join.** I was surprised. But I did not question his decision. A close male friend became the president, and I was offered the position of the secretary. We worked well together, but the incident brought home the pervasiveness of the glass ceiling. This awareness only intensified as I started reading *Manushi*, then the only feminist journal in India, attended my first protest march against domestic violence and got exposed to women, young and old, who felt strongly about women's rights and equality. Thereafter, there was no looking back.

◆

By the time I reached Harvard University, via the United World College of the Atlantic in Wales, I had resolved to use my education to serve others, especially women. My inclinations had been refined at Atlantic College, where classmates from across the world debated the deep divides that persisted in their respective home countries. My views were further chiselled at university, where I was drawn to political action. I involved myself with the anti-apartheid movement (at that point, aimed at getting Harvard's investments out of South Africa), and protested against America's support of the military juntas in Central America. I was also active in the Phillips Brooks House, Harvard's social service and action institution, and was elected its first non-American president. Later, as a part of Education for Action (a small group dedicated to doing exactly what the name suggests), I helped organize a boycott of grapes in the campus dining halls in support of the United Farm Workers' campaign for minimum wages. I even got to meet Cesar Chavez, the legendary union leader of migrant Latino farm workers, and was introduced to union organizing. **As I got to see, first-hand, the underbelly of the richest society in the world, I realized that injustice and inequality were not restricted to India alone.**

I also realized that women were not safe anywhere. This realization hit me when my roommate was molested on campus and a friend was raped near Harvard Yard. We organized 'Take Back the Night' candlelight marches against violence, and I helped as part of the organizing committee in the Women's Clearinghouse on campus.

It was here that **I heard of SEWA and its founder, Elaben Bhatt. When I met her after my graduation, she said, 'Why don't you finish your studies and join us? We need young women like you.' Her gentle ways left a deep impression.**

I had been all set to become a doctor, but I switched to public health as my senior thesis made me realize that health care was what India really needed. The professors at the School of Public Health at Johns Hopkins, who had done path-breaking work in Punjab on nutrition and infection in young children, assisted me with my graduate degree, but also reminded me of the need to make my way home and work in the midst of the poor.

I joined SEWA in 1984 to develop a community-based health programme for our members. Elaben Bhatt served as a role model and a mentor. She advised me to be with our members, to listen and to learn. She put me in the safe hands of Sumanben, a herbal toothbrush or datun vendor and a founder of the SEWA Bank. Sumanben took me under her wing and led me to Shankar Bhuvan, a lively community of street vendors on the banks of the Sabarmati. **The vendors quickly put me in my place: 'Oh-ho! What will this young thing teach us? She won't last even five minutes here!' But with their candidness and good humour, they wove their magic around me.** And so I stuck around.

For the first six months, I attempted understanding the vendors' world. They taught me garba and Gujarati, and introduced me to gunpowder-hot lasan ni chatni with bajra rotlas. I became involved with their everyday problems. Shardaben, a young garlic vendor, had been labelled a witch; she had been divorced by her husband, separated from her daughter and left heartbroken. Mangiben had tuberculosis and needed treatment. A four-year-old at SEWA's childcare centre had been raped by her uncle and had had to be rushed to hospital. These were just some of the stories I encountered. Yet, what amazed me was that despite adversity, **my Shankar Bhuvan sisters displayed a philosophical acceptance of the ebbs and flows of life. Even today when I need recharging, I turn to my friends by the riverfront slum, who set me right with their worldview.**

◆

Some vendors from Shankar Bhuvan became SEWA's first health workers, providing primary health care to their community, health education, referral linkages to public and private hospitals and much-needed tuberculosis care. This small band of enthusiastic health workers expanded to include more women from the slums and chaalis of Ahmedabad; with time, we trained health workers in the villages of Ahmedabad district.

In one of these villages, Sumanben and I were working hard to save a baby girl. Her young mother had no childcare access, and had tried to keep the baby quiet by giving her some opium. The child was critical, and the grandmother saw little value in saving her granddaughter's life. 'She is only a girl,' the grandmother said, 'and we don't have the money.' Once again, the community came to the rescue and between us, we scraped together some cash, rushed the baby to a hospital and helped her recover. That was a turning point. Women joined our union, started their savings group and began to trust SEWA.

I witnessed the power of sisterhood and solidarity on several occasions. One such occasion was during the communal violence in Gujarat in 2002. SEWA members supported each other, hid each other's children in their homes and crossed 'front lines' to provide food to one another. We worked in teams in relief camps. On one occasion, **we rushed to a**

particularly devastated neighbourhood to check on a friend and colleague, Rahimaben. When we found her well, we stood in those deserted and curfewed streets, a tight circle of women, and wept with relief at having found one another, and sorrow at what had befallen our city. Slowly, a ring of men emerged around us, observing the scene incredulously—Muslim and Hindu women falling into each other's arms like long-lost sisters. We felt safe and protected in an atmosphere that otherwise was anything but.

◆

After some years, I became a part of SEWA's core team. When Elaben stepped aside to make way for younger women's leadership, I became the general secretary. Then the baton was passed on to others, and now rests with Jyotiben, a close colleague and the daughter of a tobacco worker.

It has been a privilege to be a part of this SEWA sisterhood, working jointly for social change, and with women in the lead. I have associated closely with Sumanben, Ayeshaben, Chandaben and others, who never take 'no' for an answer. Their enthusiasm and courage is infectious. Together we have developed many membership-based democratic organizations, like our health and insurance cooperatives. I became responsible for SEWA's Social Security Team, and also its health care, childcare and insurance programmes.

One of the important contributions of SEWA has been to help develop grass-roots-level women, so they become powerful and effective leaders. Thousands of local women leaders now run their own organizations and the SEWA movement across the country. Elected from among SEWA members, these leaders are often unschooled, but have home-grown wisdom and intelligence. They have taught women like me about collective or shared leadership. This kind of management requires trust and a deep commitment to working collectively. It is still a work in progress. It is not easy to shed traditional notions of power and leadership. And human nature, with all its frailties, plays its part, whether we are male or female.

Nurturing working-class women's leadership is particularly important if they are to lead their own organizations and movements. **Educated middle-class men and women may have much more exposure, better networks and connections, but they also come with class, caste and gender prejudices, and the belief that those with fewer**

degrees are unskilled and incapable of leadership. We know that at SEWA we are swimming against the tide, but that is what the SEWA movement is all about.

◆

In my journey, the role of family and friends has been critical. My mother has been a staunch supporter and role model; our beliefs and values happily coincide. Then, there are close family members—uncles, two maternal aunts, some of my mother's cousins and my sister—who have been sources of solid support.

At SEWA, too, I was fortunate to have colleagues who became friends and mentors, and from them I learnt how to organize workers and combine grass-roots action and policy change.

I have also found strength and some answers in Gandhiji's thoughts and actions. To begin with, I knew little of his life beyond the usual biographical sketches one learns at school. However, through our work at SEWA, I have begun to comprehend his message, and the fact that he understood our people and this country as few others have. I have turned to his writings and have read all that I can lay my hands on. **Gandhiji has been a presence—a sort of guide. Often, when in doubt, I remember his path and all that he overcame.** It is both humbling and inspiring, and I find the strength to go ahead.

◆

Our choice of spouse is crucial to the path we finally embrace. In my case, this certainly holds true. Binoy and I ran into each other at a meeting and became firm friends on account of our shared beliefs. **Once we married, my husband moved to Ahmedabad—a city where he knew nobody—since he respected my work at SEWA. To date, he jokes that he knows what a new bride in India must feel!**

I believe that Binoy's approach to me and my work has a lot to do with his upbringing. Born in a small village in Odisha, he witnessed his mother and other women toiling from dawn to dusk, with little recognition and respite. He also saw injustice and exploitation first-hand, with the Dalit children in his class being blatantly discriminated against. People in his village were determined to seek a better future for their children, and built the local school brick by brick. Binoy became a champion of women's rights and of those who were downtrodden, drawing from his own life experiences.

I could not have asked for a better 'jeevan sathi'. Quiet yet firm in his beliefs, deeply committed to working for the poor and the vulnerable, critical but a solid source of support, Binoy has always been by my side. I'm sure it hasn't been easy for him—we both work full time, and have had to raise three daughters, a joy but also a handful. **Our twins were ten months old when I was to be made SEWA's general secretary. Binoy's simple (and characteristic) response when I solicited his opinion was, 'Please go ahead. I am with you.'**

In hindsight, I would perhaps do things somewhat differently in relation to maintaining a work-life balance. I think parents need to enjoy time with their children, especially in the early, formative years. **When my eldest daughter got sick, I put it down to my being busy at work or with the younger ones. I have struggled with that guilt for years,** even though my eldest daughter and her doctor have endlessly explained that there is no reason to blame myself. What was painful was that some of those close to me gave subtle and not-so-subtle messages that my being work-centred caused the problem. I took comfort in the stories of other women and how they dealt with similar situations.

I am often asked why I have continued in the same organization. 'Don't you get burned out or fed up?' people question. I do get tired and frustrated sometimes. But never burned-out or fed up. I think **the daily inspiration from the women I work with—who have so little materially, but are full of courage and good cheer—keeps me going.** Besides, I am fortunate to have colleagues, friends and family with whom I can blow off steam.

◆

- Follow your heart. Find work that you enjoy and believe in as far as possible.
- Keep healthy. Eat well, exercise and do what you love to take care of your soul—be it reading, listening to music, tending to plants or enjoying the company of friends. These are what keep body, heart, mind and spirit together.
- Visit a nearby park, walk in a forest, sit by the sea, or trek through mountains. Nature keeps us humble, fills us with wonder, and reminds us of our small place in this beautiful world.

- Listen to the stories of others. We are all a part of the human family and can draw inspiration from the lives of those around us. Besides, it is strengthening to know that we are not alone. Others have struggled and persevered. We must draw courage from them.
- Explore books on spirituality. Such books nurture and heal the soul.
- Choose a partner carefully. Money and glamour are skin-deep; the love between two people is sustained through common interests, values, beliefs and mutual respect. If your future spouse refuses to acknowledge your individual desires and lays down far too many boundaries—like asking you to give up your work—think long and hard about accepting him into your life.
- Choosing to be a homemaker or a full-time mother is a perfectly valid decision. The women's rights movement is all about giving choices, options and opportunities. Each of us is different and has to make individual selections.
- It is true that you can't have it all. But then, no one can have it all! Each of us has to make choices—often hard choices. Sometimes you will make the wrong choices; this is fine, as long as you learn from your mistakes. Do not be afraid to take risks or change your mind.
- Find one or more mentors. Older women and men who have been through the ups and downs of life are wise and care for you.
- Read about the lives of other inspiring human beings, especially women. There are many unsung heroes and heroines in our world.
- Children make life worth living, whether you have your own or not. Love them, learn with them, but give them the space to be and find their own paths. You are their role model, whether you like it or not. Tell them that we are all human. Share your trials and tribulations, but celebrate your small victories and achievements, too. The key is to live a life of compassion and gratitude for the world and the people around you.

NAINA LAL KIDWAI is executive director on the board of the Hong Kong and Shanghai Banking Corporation (HSBC) Asia-Pacific and the chairman of HSBC India which employs 32,000 people. She is also a non-executive director of Nestlé SA and former president of the Federation of Indian Chambers of Commerce and Industry (FICCI).

Interestingly, Naina says, 'My sense of equanimity comes from continuously working in areas of social interest both within my office and outside.' In line with her concern for women's empowerment through livelihoods, the environment, water conservation and energy efficiency, she is vice chair of the World Economic Forum's Global Agenda Council on Water and on the boards of not-for-profit organizations such as The Energy and Resources Institute (TERI) and the Shakti Sustainable Energy Foundation.

A master in business administration (MBA) from Harvard Business School and a Padma Shri awardee, Naina has made regular appearances in *Fortune* and other magazines in listings of powerful women in business globally and in India. When not at work, Naina spends time with her husband, Rashid, her daughter, Kemaya and stepson, Rumaan, and makes short escapes to nature reserves in India.

◆

The 'First' Lady
NAINA LAL KIDWAI

'To know what we do not know is the beginning of wisdom.'
—Maha Sthavira Sangharakshita

As a ten-year-old, I'd occasionally visit my father's wood-panelled office. He was the chief executive officer (CEO) of one of the largest insurance companies in India and his room was a source of endless fascination. I recall perching myself on his leather swivel chair in the late evenings while waiting for him to finish his work. **I do believe that the seeds of my later decision to work in the corporate sector were sown right there—in that room, as I whirled in the chair, in awe of the respect and love my father received from those around him.** I yearned to be a part of that world. Years later, as a young twenty-five-year-old executive at Grindlays Bank, when I sat in a little cabin shared with a colleague, I had a quiet sense of satisfaction while looking out across Mumbai's busy Mahatma Gandhi Road at the resplendent old buildings of the Fort area and at my father's office, which had been such a source of inspiration.

My father's interests honed my sister's professional inclinations and my own. Dinners at home—always lively affairs—were marked by conversations on either the economy or golf. It's no surprise then that while I veered towards finance, my sister embraced golf to become India's leading golfer of her time, playing for the country and winning many prizes, including the prestigious Arjuna Award. My mother's deep-rooted spiritualism and visits to her guru's ashram helped us understand our Hindu traditions and respect each other's beliefs. Our home saw people from all walks of life and from all parts of the world, as my parents welcomed them—always perfect hosts, and generous with their time and support for those who sought it.

My memories of my early childhood are of a charmed life in Mumbai. School was always something to look forward to, and the success I tasted early by topping my class boosted my confidence, honed a spirit of competitiveness and made me realize that I could achieve and excel. My parents made it a point to instill in me the need to remain grounded and considerate. **They taught me the value of 'saving' through a strict regimen of pocket money**—I learnt that the twenty rupees I was handed each week could go a long way and buy my books and music and chocolates, if I used what I had saved wisely.

At the age of eleven, I joined a boarding school, Loreto Convent in Simla—a school that placed an emphasis on not only academic achievement but also the pursuit of extracurricular activities. This is when I developed an interest in team sports, especially basketball and badminton. It wasn't all fun and games; rather, it was hard work to wake up at 5.00 a.m. in the bitter cold of the Himalayas, follow a strict regimen, even while ensuring that grades and other extracurricular pursuits didn't suffer. All the toil and diligence paid off—I entered the school team in the eighth grade and we won many of the inter-school and state-level championships. **The lessons I learnt back then stayed with me—the importance of teamwork, the need to surround myself with achievers, the value of building a team with members who complement each other's skills and weaknesses and the art of losing graciously in a sportsmanlike manner.**

Early experiences in debating competitions and school plays helped me gain in self-confidence. This period was defined by my keen interest in Western classical music—I sat the Trinity College of Music exams till grade seven, and played the piano. Yet, a part of me felt embarrassed that while well-versed in Western music, I knew little about Indian classical music. I began going to the music concerts of our great masters—Vilayat Khan, Hariprasad Chaurasia, Ravi Shankar—with knowledgeable friends patiently explaining the nuances. My interest in Indian classical music and especially the sitar and the flute has only deepened over time.

As I struggled to wear a saree to work, I began to appreciate our rich tradition of handlooms and fabrics—from the Patola to the Baluchari and Kanjivaram—each so distinct from different parts of India. I read about our leaders and those who were defining the economy. I travelled through our forests, appreciating our immense natural heritage and biodiversity.

Those early years defined my relationship with the India I so love, and persuaded me to build my roots here.

◆

In the years to come, as I graduated from class captain to house captain and head girl and, still later, to secretary and then president of Lady Sri Ram College's (LSR) student union, I came to realize that I sought and enjoyed leadership roles. As I graduated with a bachelor's degree in economics, my father suggested that I pursue chartered accountancy.

I then faced my first frustration as a girl. On applying to Price Waterhouse and Coopers (PwC), I was told that while I had all the qualifications they needed, they didn't hire women. **Back then, I didn't have many Indian female career role models to choose from; so I looked at the men occupying top and mid-level posts and asked myself, 'How am I less capable? Why can't I do what they do?' Perhaps, the more one is discriminated against, the stronger one becomes.** Therefore, exasperated as I was, I persisted. Finally, in 1977, PwC chose to take the first three women (including me) as articled clerks. Today, when I see that 40 per cent of PwC's employees are women, I can say with some satisfaction and joy that change comes surely and steadily with the right catalysts and when good sense finally prevails!

While at PwC, I decided to pursue my dream of going to Harvard Business School (HBS). My parents, while progressive, were concerned about my living in the US at the 'young' age of twenty-three years. I finally prevailed and spent two magical years at HBS. **I suspect my canvas would have been more limited, my outlook more parochial, had I not had the benefit of those years in Boston. In 1982, I became the first Indian woman to graduate from HBS—a sad social comment as Indian men had been going to Harvard for over thirty years!**

Even while at HBS, I was certain I wanted to return to India—not only because it is home but also because I knew I could contribute more to India's progress than to America's. The impact of a US$100 million deal in this country is probably greater than that of a US$1 billion deal in the USA. Therefore, upon graduation, despite receiving lucrative offers in the USA, I chose to embark on my career in investment banking in India at Grindlays Bank—then the largest foreign bank in the country.

◆

None of the women in my extended family worked. My mother, on her part, decided it was just as well that I had chosen a vocation in banking since I couldn't cook to save my life! I think my male relatives' utter disbelief at my decision only spurred me on. **I refused to be perceived as a 'pushover' or overlooked when I delivered results.** This, of course, meant that I had to work much harder than my male colleagues to prove that I was as, if not more, competent than them.

The first seven of my thirteen years in Grindlays Bank took me from being the head of the regional offices of the investment bank to the head of the investment bank. Then came a critical move into retail banking— this was something I actually asked for, much to the surprise of the top management of the bank. **I have not merely relied on the organizations I work for to make career choices for me; rather, I've discussed my concerns and persuaded them to understand my areas of interest.**

For Grindlays, the decision to appoint me as the head of NRI (non-resident Indian) services in retail banking was a leap of faith. I was aware of this and wanted to prove myself. However, just the day before the bank's CEO, Bob Edgar, called to offer me the job, I discovered I was pregnant! Here was a career opportunity I had always wanted. But could I accept the offer, given the hectic travel schedule it came with and the responsibility of setting up offices around the world? Pregnancy was a new experience, an 'unknown', and I didn't know if I would be able to cope with the travel or the pressures of a new demanding role.

Therefore, I simply asked for time. It was Bob's turn to be surprised as he thought I'd jump at the opportunity, especially as I had asked for it. After a chat with my husband, I explained the situation to Bob the next day, prepared for the likely eventuality that the offer would be withdrawn. Instead, although a little taken aback, he asked, 'Naina, what would *you* like to do?' I said, 'I'd like to give this a try.'

And I got the job.

I have to say, I have never worked harder in my life. The faith the organization had placed in me propelled me to attend to every matter, even from my hospital bed! I was travelling right until my eighth month—even on the day Rajiv Gandhi was assassinated. That night, I had a flight to catch from Mumbai to Dubai. When news of Rajiv Gandhi's death trickled in, there were cases of sporadic rioting, incidents of stone-throwing, rasta-rokos. My husband urged me to stay home, but I couldn't—my heads of NRI banking were assembling in Dubai, I had all the important papers and documents, and I felt accountable to the organization that had entrusted me with the new role. I chose to go, and my husband drove me through riot-hit areas and barricades. He still kids that I didn't give a thought to his having to drive back through those troubled areas! I made it to the meeting—just about. Interestingly, not long after, my boss banned me from travelling, as the flight he was on had an emergency landing and he had to slide down the chute, shoes in hand.

Back then, and in the years that followed, I made it a point to push myself hard so that no one could point a finger. **As a woman in a top job, I believed I was always under a magnifying glass and that people were watching me closely. Every false step could be used as an advantage by others. In a man's world, I knew I had to perform better than *all* men to get what I deserved.**

Moreover, the 'firsts' in my career brought the additional burden and responsibility of delivering; after all, any failure on my part would make it difficult for organizations to consider *other* women.

◆

The timing of my entry into retail banking proved to be fortuitous since the Gulf War happened and NRIs poured money into India. My experience in retail banking proved useful later when I was considered for the position of the CEO of HSBC.

In 1994, I was headhunted by Morgan Stanley. My desire to work for a bulge bracket investment bank in India and my love for deal-making led me to the difficult decision of leaving Grindlays after twelve years. It took me four months to make up my mind before I finally accepted the offer! The next eight years proved to be exhilarating as I worked on key government disinvestments in India, the M&A (mergers and acquisitions) transactions that shaped the future of industries like telecom and banking, and the first listings of Indian companies on the New York Stock Exchange (NYSE). Beyond heading the investment banking operations of Morgan Stanley, I took Morgan Stanley into a successful joint venture with JM Financial, which enabled JM Morgan Stanley to become the leading investment bank in the country. We were now able to do smaller deals and not just wait for the handful of US$500 million-sized deals that Morgan Stanley otherwise restricted itself to.

I had no desire to work abroad, and as I was considering the question 'What next?' I was fortunate to get headhunted in 2002 by HSBC as the head of their investment bank and capital markets. As I had hoped, I moved to become deputy CEO of the bank in India, and then the CEO—becoming the first woman to head a foreign or private bank in India and the second to head a bank in the country. (Ranjana Kumar had just taken over as the head of Indian Bank, which she successfully turned around.)

Then, as the chairman of HSBC, I have overseen the India operations comprising HSBC's 32,000 employees and its businesses in asset management, insurance, banking and software development and BPO (business process outsourcing). Exposure to a wide range of issues across the financial services space has been a great learning experience, as indeed has been my appointment to the board of HSBC Asia-Pacific. This provided me with key insights into markets like China, Singapore, Indonesia, Malaysia, Japan and South Asia, and a bird's eye view of the region.

◆

I am often asked how I manage both family and home.

I think that **it's easier for us to succeed as working women in India than it is for many of our female counterparts in other parts of the world. After all, in India we have the distinct advantage of an extended family of mothers, sisters and in-laws, and house help.** I have to admit, in those critical early stages of motherhood when relying on any and every manner of support becomes a survival strategy, I had assistance close at hand. My mother-in-law would come join us at short notice and my mother and sister, even friends, would pitch in. And then, there was support and care from that great institution in India—the ayah. I was fortunate to have Janki—who had brought up my sister and me as kids—come back to keep an eye on our daughter, Kemaya, as she grew up.

Most importantly, I have Rashid. **I always say, choose your husband with care! Rashid is my soulmate, the friend who keeps me grounded and whose advice I always seek and treasure.** He gave up a lucrative job in Delhi to be with me in Mumbai, and continued to make adjustments and compromises along the way. He shared the duties of parenting, was deeply involved with bringing up Kemaya and my stepson, Rumaan, and was there for all the parent-teacher meetings, with or without me.

There were times when I wondered if I was doing all that I needed to as a mother—questions often asked of me by *my* mother, reflecting my own doubts about managing a home and a career successfully. But with my own desire to make it work and Rashid, always understanding and supportive, I managed. Besides, I believed that if I stepped away, it would be a sorry reflection on all women. I wanted to prove to myself and the world that a woman could embrace both worlds.

This desire for the dual pleasures of a family and a profession, though, comes with its compromises. I was half a world away on our first wedding anniversary, and missed a number of Rashid's (and my own) birthdays. But when I *knew* I was needed, I made it a point to be around. When Rashid had lung cancer and I had a number of important board meetings, I prioritized and juggled every commitment during the six months of his operation and chemotherapy. I didn't expect my employer to understand, so I pushed myself, relying on my organizational and time management skills and Rashid's complete understanding while fulfilling my responsibilities.

Other than the crystal balls of family and home, there is a third ball though that we, as perennial jugglers, forget—that third ball is 'me time'. I treat this as a rubber ball—allow it to drop and bounce back when I can afford to attend to it. Often, 'me time' covers those stolen moments when I listen to music and watch films during long flights, or the short escapes with my family to nature reserves in India. I would love to get back to reading the books I enjoy rather than just the pink papers and business magazines that I go through from cover to cover.

At the end of the day, every woman is challenged by the work-life balance issue and tries finding her own unique solutions—some do not marry, some never have children, a few marry late. It is a journey that every woman must define for herself.

To this end, I believe, it is incumbent on organizations to make a woman's passage easier. In my own career at HSBC in India, when I was the deputy CEO, I asked to head the 'diversity initiative'—enhance diversity in the workplace, and encourage women to join us and rise to senior positions. We set up task forces across the country—groups of ten to fifteen people, mostly women but headed by men who at that juncture were my direct reports. They made recommendations on how to make the workplace more diversity-friendly—be it through a five-day week, flexi-hours or paternity leave. Some of these initiatives resulted in HSBC winning 'best employer' awards. As CEOs, we need to create an enabling environment for all talent to progress.

Today, it brings me some satisfaction knowing that **we've come a long way from the time I entered the workforce—when we, as women, did not have the luxury of flexible hours or even washrooms on**

the same floor! I have often said that you know the importance of women in an organization by the size, quality and location of the ladies' washrooms.

◆

I value George Bernard Shaw's statement: 'You see things; and you say, "Why?" But I dream things that never were; and I say, "Why not?"' **Even the most unrealistic dreams can be turned into reality through sheer effort, dedication and most importantly, passion.** As professionals, and equally as leaders, we need to be enthusiastic about achieving our goals and committed to improving our performance at all times. The accolades that may come our way are only endorsements that we are on the right path.

A hallmark of a leader is that she believes in herself, takes risks and challenges the status quo. Believing in yourself does not amount to believing you'll *always* succeed. You must have the courage to take risks, knowing that if you fall, you will get back up again on your feet and move on, having learnt from your mistakes.

As you take risks and chase dreams, you will encounter cynics and naysayers. Believe in yourself and stay with your convictions. I like quoting the example of Sam Pitroda who brought a telecommunications revolution to India's villages with public call office (PCO) booths and rural exchanges. It is said that in the early days, he encountered many who gave him multiple reasons why he could not achieve his goal of creating a telecommunications network across India. He heard them but forged right ahead, giving India its first wave of connectivity across the length and breadth of the country.

Most importantly, leaders—and indeed, all professionals— keep learning. Do not be nervous about admitting ignorance, for such an admission is synonymous with searching for knowledge. Equally, do not hesitate to seek the advice of others. To grow intellectually and professionally, I always urge colleagues to attend new training programmes, learn fresh skills and techniques and gather up-to-date information.

While a leader, I believe, must lead from the front, there are times and also situations when this leadership style has to embrace being part of the team and empowering people so they assume responsibility. When I was the CEO of HSBC, thirty-two of our employees were stuck in the Taj and the Oberoi hotels in Mumbai during the terrorist strike of 26/11 in 2008. We set up a 'war room' within minutes of receiving the news and monitored all activities through that hideous period. We had strong external relationships with the police force and the chief minister's office, and continuous contact was managed by our expert office team that sacrificed sleep, worked through the night and guided our colleagues, holed up in the hotels, to safety. **It is during such situations that you realize how important it is to hire your teams on the basis of the principles they hold dear; you also learn how vital it is for you, as the leader, to imbue in your colleagues the right values, so you can trust them to do the right thing.** As the 26/11 attacks unfolded in all their gruesomeness, no one in our team needed to be told what to do; no one had to be reminded to man those phones round the clock. Their inner moral compass guided them. I am proud to say, my colleagues have always supported me and often are a source of inspiration.

◆

No matter what the pressures of my profession, **my sense of equanimity comes from continuously working in areas of social interest both within my office and outside.**

I was able to guide HSBC into championing the cause of financial inclusion for women. For example, we sponsored the HSBC Manndeshi Udyogini—a business school for rural women in Satara, Maharashtra, which gives women practical education in financial literacy and running a business, so they can start up small ventures such as vegetable vending, tailoring, etc. Also, HSBC lends to Manndeshi Bank and other microfinance institutions, who go on to lend to other women members. Over time, I became very interested in microfinance and set up and chaired the Financial Inclusion Committee of FICCI in order to work at the policy level in this space.

When Sheryl Sandberg reached out to me to do the introduction for her book *Lean In*, a point she made that resonated very strongly with me is the need for women to help one another. I have witnessed the power of women working collectively first-hand at an undergarment manufacturing factory in Tamil Nadu that had a largely female workforce drawn from the local rural community. In just a few years, these women changed the social norms of the area. Instead of women moving to their husbands' villages, husbands began shifting to their wives' home since they came to recognize women's earning power! It is such empowerment of women— through livelihoods and by reminding them of their economic power—that increases the respect they earn from the joint family and community.

I've also gained similar insights by participating in my husband's work; he has been associated with the not-for-profit sector for the last fifteen years and his association with the Self Employed Women's Association (SEWA) and the Grassroots Trading Network for Women has shown me how livelihood creation can change the lives of women. Tiny interventions of this kind not only transform a family's aspirations but also shape the future of a country—after all, if women make educated choices and vote intelligently, they will lay the foundation for a strong democracy.

Apart from a keen interest in the corporate social responsibility (CSR) initiatives of the organizations I have worked for, my interest in women's empowerment and the environment has led to engagements with not-for-profit organizations like TERI, the Shakti Sustainable Energy Foundation and SEWA. I founded and chair the Water Mission at FICCI, which draws the attention of industry stalwarts to the important matter of water conservation and access. I also founded and chair the Inclusive Governance Council at FICCI which has brought together corporates, NGOs and the government, and has sought to institute best practices for women at the workplace, a code of conduct for companies, and legal intervention through the Anti-Corruption Bill. From members of these committees, I have gained rich perspectives that I might not have had the opportunity of gaining at work. I have been forced to study issues in-depth and form views on matters of importance for the development of our capital markets and banking. **I advocate external assignments and roles for senior executives as it opens one's mind to new learnings and also widens one's networks.**

It never stops to amaze me how the most obvious things, if implemented properly, can have a huge impact. I am inspired by the concept of 'Creating Shared Value' that my professor at HBS, Michael Porter, espouses. He says:

> Now more than ever—in the midst of a global economic crisis that has strained the capacity of governments and NGOs to address complex societal challenges—it is time to restore public trust through a redefined vision of capitalism with the full potential to meet social needs[*]

Like him, I believe that **it's possible to create win-win situations for corporates working with the communities they serve.**

---

[*]In HBS, <http://www.isc.hbs.edu>.

To this end, I am reminded of my visit to the Nestlé factory in Moga, Punjab, as a member of the Nestlé Global Board during their first ever board meeting in India. Moga is an excellent example of a mutually beneficial collaboration between a corporate and a local community. Nestlé has taught Moga's farmers how to enhance the milk productivity of their cattle; has encouraged them to grow from being the owners of a couple of cows to a few hundred; and has provided them veterinary care and other extension services with no obligations (the farmers don't have to sell their milk to Nestlé). Nestlé, on its part, has benefited immensely. Even through the worst crises in Punjab, the Nestlé factory remained open since its functioning was vital to farmers. The insights I gain as a non-executive board member of Nestlé and as a board member of HSBC Asia-Pacific are as good as those I've gained in the classrooms of HBS.

As I retire from HSBC at the end of 2015—having reached the retirement age of fifty-eight—I will now be able to devote more time to working in the areas of women's empowerment, water conservation, energy efficiency and the environment. So begins a new chapter in my life as I engage with areas where I hope to make a difference.

◆

- Put people first and respect team diversity and inclusiveness.
- Remain passionate about your work and excel in what you do.
- Believe in yourself, take considered risks and stay with your convictions.
- Influence policy and thought leadership through membership of external committees, and expand your networks.
- Be fair, ethical and socially responsible.
- Keep learning and do not hesitate to ask.

In her prolific career as an Indian Foreign Service (IFS) officer, **NIRUPAMA RAO** has served as the Indian ambassador to the United States as well as the foreign secretary of India—only the second woman to hold the post. She was also the first woman to be appointed spokesperson of the ministry of external affairs and was the first woman high commissioner to Sri Lanka.

Born in Malappuram, Kerala, Nirupama and her two sisters grew up in various cities across India as her father was an army officer. Listening to her uncle's stories of his experiences as a foreign service officer inspired her to take the civil services exam in 1973. After her training, she was posted in Vienna, from where she began her illustrious career. After her retirement from public service, she dove into the world of academics and was appointed the Meera and Vikram Gandhi fellow at Brown University. In 2014, she received the prestigious Jawaharlal Nehru Fellowship to complete her book on Indo-China relations. She is also widely followed on Twitter, with *Foreign Policy* naming her one of the 100 most influential women in the world on the social networking site.

The Exemplary Ambassador
NIRUPAMA RAO

Well, life has been a baffled vehicle
And baffling. But she fights, and
Has fought, according to her lights and
The lenience of her whirling place.

She fights with semi-folded arms,
Her strong bag, and the stiff
Frost in her face (that challenges 'When'and 'If.')
And altogether she does Rather Well.

—Weaponed Woman, Gwendolyn Brooks

I start with this poem as it represents the radical yet non-violent struggles of women against patriarchal patterns of power, whether familial, political, economic or cultural, the world over.

My life has been a struggle, too—a struggle to build an identity for myself as an independent professional woman who has wanted to break free of the stereotypes that define feminine lives, especially in societies such as ours. My life has been defined substantially by the years I spent in India's foreign service, as a civil servant and diplomat; it was here that my personality developed and I pushed at the limits of the definitions of what a woman could achieve.

I entered the service at the age of twenty-two, and was catapulted into a world very different from the sheltered environment I had grown up in. It was essentially a world dominated by men, and patriarchal attitudes prevailed in the foreign service as they did in every sphere of life at that time.

I was born into a matrilineal family in Malappuram in north-central Kerala. The green, verdant surroundings of my ancestral house are what I remember from my childhood days, for we spent our school holidays there every year. My father was an army officer, and through my growing-up years we lived in various cantonment towns across India. My two sisters and I were given the best education possible, and life at home was simple and modest. My parents had friends—basically army families—and outings mainly included children's parties, treats at the tennis club where my father played, picnics and trips to the regimental cinema to see both Indian and Hollywood movies. We, my sisters and I, had a fun childhood. We were seriously into music, and Nirmala, my middle sister and I, played the guitar and sang at many college and university functions. I was an avid fan of Joan Baez in my late teens and early twenties.

I was a voracious reader. History fascinated me, particularly modern Indian history. My father nurtured my thirst for knowledge and constantly encouraged me to read as also to keep abreast of current affairs through newspapers and radio broadcasts on current affairs. Equally, I was strongly influenced by my mother. She was a woman of remarkable intelligence, with great dreams for her three daughters. She was the first university graduate in her family, and a perfectionist who paid meticulous attention to detail. She had a great sense of duty and morality, setting the highest standards, particularly for me, her first born. **Both my parents were forward-looking and wanted their daughters to do as well as the sons of their friends and colleagues. Such aspiration and confidence no doubt made me what I am.**

I had an uncle, my mother's brother, who was a diplomat, and listening to him tell me about his experiences in the foreign service inspired my childhood dream to join the IFS. One of my formative experiences was meeting His Holiness the Dalai Lama in February 1960, when I was just nine years old—I still have his signature in my schoolgirl's autograph book!

I sat for the civil services examination as soon as I was eligible to do so—at the age of twenty-one. I will never forget the day, in May 1973, when a telegram was delivered to our home, informing me that I had stood first in the all-India list of successful IFS and Indian Administrative Service (IAS) aspirants that year.

◆

I became a diplomat because of my curiosity about the world around me, about history and the manner in which I was impacted by the spirit of a newly independent India, and what she stood for. In my youth, I questioned, I was a seeker, I sought answers to so much I saw around me. I did not follow the crowd, preferring to set out on my own, always. I was very clear about what I wanted in life. There was so much to see and learn and so little time in which to accomplish it all. I believed that there was no field of activity or realm of thought that is not within a woman's reach.

A recent book on women diplomats called them women of the world. Indeed, the world is the oyster for diplomats and they operate in the oceanic depths of the corridors for power. But women are recent entrants to the field of diplomacy. Diplomacy, the field to which I belong, was for long the exclusive preserve of men. The very thought that statecraft, the conduct of relations between sovereign countries, could involve women was anathema, even up to a few decades ago. The question asked, for instance, was: can women deal with drunken sailors seeking consular assistance? Of course, the answer given by men was always, no. Prime Minister Jawaharlal Nehru, who always said that India has a feminine, not masculine soul, wished to see women in the diplomatic service, but even he could not remove such constraints as the marriage bar, which compelled women to leave the service once they were married. Many bright careers were extinguished in this manner. The struggles of C.B. Muthamma—the first woman to write the civil services exam and join the IFS—to improve the system created extraordinary opportunities for those who have succeeded her. Today, the IFS can proudly count in its ranks a growing number of women ambassadors and high commissioners, not to mention all its other women diplomats, who represent India abroad, and also those who handle complex assignments at headquarters. But all this has not been accomplished without the pioneering efforts made by the first generation of our women diplomats to ensure fairness and equality of treatment.

I have no regrets about choosing the foreign service as a career. Diplomacy is a profession that is full of life's lessons—how wars are created or prevented; how negotiations succeed or fail; how, just as in our personal lives, so too in affairs of state, we should be far-sighted, firm without being overbearing, conscious of our interests, not allowing them to be eroded, and determined to defend them, while acting with responsibility. Looking back on my years in diplomacy, I realize that I never for a moment thought of myself as a woman in a man's world. I just felt I was like the rest, that nothing could stop me from achieving what the men could. There was no glass ceiling inside my head.

This is not to say that I didn't face formidable challenges. My marriage to an IAS officer meant that I had two choices before me. If I wanted to lead a conventional married life I would have to quit my career because there was no possibility of both my husband and me living and working in the same place, except in New Delhi. The other option was to accept that there would be periods of separation when my husband would be on his various postings in Karnataka (the state cadre to which he was allotted) while I served in various Indian embassies abroad. We chose the second option and lived apart at times—when I served abroad and he served in Karnataka—and together at others—when both of us were in New Delhi on central government postings. This meant that we had to be reconciled to having separate establishments, meeting briefly during leave periods, and that our two children had also to adjust to a life where they rarely saw their parents together. It was a most unconventional marriage and one that defied popular definitions. But survive we did, as a family, and I believe we did because of a sense of mutual commitment, trust and belief in our relationship and in each other.

My constant effort was to integrate and create a viable balance between my professional and personal life. I now look back on those decades, grateful for a life full of discovery, for the love that I received from family and friends, and the intellectual richness of a profession where one constantly sharpened and broadened one's vision and deepened one's understanding. **I am of the view that a professional woman can live a well-rounded life if she is able to harness her innate strength and resilience. However, she needs to understand that whatever the circumstances, life will always be bittersweet, with its ups and downs.**

I took each day as it came in the spirit of the Vedic hymn:

Look to this day,
For it is life,
The very life of life.
In its brief course lie all
The realities and verities of existence...
Today well lived,
Makes every yesterday
A dream of happiness, and

Every tomorrow
A vision of hope.
Look well, therefore, to this day.

◆

My foreign service career threw me in the midst of kings and kingmakers, presidents and prime ministers, and also simple folk. I will never forget the latter, particularly. I remember the days I spent more than three decades ago in Sri Lanka as a young officer addressing the problems of tea estate labourers of Indian origin in the Lankan plantations. I still feel the thrill of leading a group of pilgrims on a one-month-long high-altitude trek to Kailash and Manasarovar in Tibet in the summer of 1986. I realize I was contributing to a first draft of history, literally, when I helped prepare for Prime Minister Rajiv Gandhi's visit to China in 1988. In more recent times, I recall my meetings with the then US secretary of state, Hillary Clinton, and her warmth and impressive intelligence. Becoming India's first woman foreign office spokesperson was another high point in my career. It made me a true believer in the importance of public diplomacy. Ambassadorships in Sri Lanka and China, followed by my stint as foreign secretary, demonstrated that we as women can handle the most sensitive and demanding assignments.

Throughout my career, I approached my role first as a professional diplomat, and only then as a woman. One has to engage with one's work regardless of gender, and it is thus that I attempted to provide a blend of strategic, directive, team-building and operational leadership in my job. I tried to lead by example, be energetic, build consensus, be responsive to colleagues, remain decisive and quick in dealing with pending issues, be alert and responsive to voices around me and pay attention to public diplomacy and communication issues. The qualities I admire most in people are intellectual honesty and integrity of soul and spirit. The two leaders whose writings and whose lives have impacted me the most are Mahatma Gandhi and Jawaharlal Nehru. Kamaladevi Chattopadhyay is another inspirational figure, because of her independence of spirit and the example she set for our women to break away from the stranglehold of patriarchal tradition.

I am guided by the principles of integrity and meritocracy. I believe that you have to be able to anticipate change and be

willing to deal with it if you are to move ahead. A closed, 'cribbed, cabined and confined' mind is counterproductive to your growth as an individual and the impact you can make on the world around you. It is important to retain a spirit of enthusiasm, avoid cynicism and be eternally questing—questing for knowledge, ideas and genuine meaning in whatever you undertake. You should be prepared to embrace reasonable risk. I attempted to do this particularly when I became the spokesperson of the ministry of external affairs, being the first officer to conduct live television briefings and interviews in real time, with questions thrown at me in all directions, and also introducing the system of transcribing all the spokesperson's briefings on the website of the ministry. The 'Public Diplomacy' imprint of the ministry was vastly expanded in my tenure as foreign secretary, and I was one of the first Government of India senior officials to use social media—Twitter—as a means of outreach to the general public with good effect. My 'following' on Twitter (over 300,000 at the time of writing) has brought me thousands of new friends!

Five years ago in August 2010, PepsiCo head Indra Nooyi, addressing Indian ambassadors and high commissioners, noted that whether 'you look through the lens of diplomacy or the lens of the corporation, the task is the same—to create a world in which we feel safe, settled and happy'. I completely agree with the point that prosperity and security reinforce each other; that safety and security come from economic progress, from innovation, enterprise and technological invention. As the job of a diplomat gets redefined and she is no longer locked into lofty chancelleries, but rather engaging with the world of business and entrepreneurship, her role does not differ very greatly from the one performed by those in a business or entrepreneurial environment. **Public diplomacy has acquired a very important dimension, in which diplomats have to come out into the amphitheatre of civic engagement to explain and enlist public understanding of governmental policies. The corridors of power cannot be self-confining any longer—the world outside will not allow that.**

Can women deal with these challenges I have outlined and come out victorious and smiling? I believe the answer is yes. The fundamental principles you need by your side are belief, determination and focus—belief in the values you have imbibed at home, school and university during your early years; the determination to achieve what you have set out to do; and focus, laser-like, on the goals you have set for yourself. You have to be patient. Don't look for a harvest on the morning after the sowing is finished. Acknowledge your doubts because, as the poet once said, it is only then that you can feel 'less despair about despair'. Added to this you need to be an honest judge of yourself; have a strong sense of integrity, of right and wrong; have compassion for people less privileged than you are; be generous; and have a sense of humility, coupled with sincerity of approach and demeanour. **Very often in our society, people who have achieved success tend to place a premium on being vainglorious and bumptious. It pays, in my view, to be generous and large of heart and mind; bumptiousness never pays.** Lastly, you must be firm about defending your beliefs and your convictions. Also, I have no patience for humbug. I also tend to set very high standards and that is not always easy to implement within the system. I must acknowledge that I have felt frustrated at times!

Madeleine Albright once said, 'For democracy to thrive without women is impossible. If women are undervalued or underdeveloped then that democracy is imperfect and incomplete.' Decision-making and the prioritization of issues that affect human security have to involve women and men, not just men alone. There are key questions of human rights involving half of humanity—whether these are on account of a gang rape in Delhi, or the shooting of a young Malala, or a struggle by women to seek their human rights, to seek freedom from fear, and their security, physical and psychological. Women need access to information, they need education and vocational skill development, reductions in maternal and child mortality and access to health care—all of which are core issues for gender rights.

The mechanisms of decision-making in the world—and democracies are no exception—are essentially male dominated. Decision-making is the preserve of men the world over. But democracy, human rights, development and good governance are of concern to women as much as men. Eleanor Roosevelt once said:

> Too often the great decisions are originated and given form in bodies made up wholly of men, or so completely dominated by them that whatever of special value women have to offer is shunted aside without expression.

This can change only if more and more women enter and occupy positions in public service.

I come from the world of foreign policy, having spent four decades of my life in the practice of diplomacy. As a woman who has been a foreign policy practitioner, I would urge more young women of our country to consider careers in the foreign service. We are under-represented in this space, as in the rest of the bureaucracy. Women need to be more involved in determining the future trajectory of many issues of foreign policy concern in India, whether they are border and territorial questions, neighbourhood policy, trade and connectivity, regional economic cooperation and security, energy security, politico-military issues, or public diplomacy. This will help in the mainstreaming of gender-related issues and bring new perspectives to bear on our policy concerning our neighbours, in particular. **Women can bring courage and resilience of the feminine sort into the public sphere, and a concept of sisterhood that is focused on long-term solutions to problems.** They can help with the building of common ground, and the creation of cross-border synergies for peace and reconciliation. Preparing our women, equipping them with the art of negotiation and empowering them to build peace is key. I believe, like many of our sisters, that history can and must be pushed in a positive direction. We can do it.

◆

- Remain curious about the world you inhabit and engage with it. Be eternally questing.
- Professional women can achieve some work-life balance if they remain resilient and intellectually honest.
- Anticipate change and learn to deal with it.
- Life's many experiences are meant to teach you humility.
- Integrity and meritocracy are principles we need to imbibe.
- Democracy, human rights, development and good governance are some areas that need the active participation of women.

A senior partner and head of litigation and competition law practices at Amarchand & Mangaldas & Suresh A. Shroff & Co., India's leading corporate law firm, **PALLAVI SHROFF** is referred to as one of India's most powerful and influential women (*Verve*, 2009; *Business Today*, 2013, 2014), and as 'a legal luminary with the brilliant acumen necessary to crack the most complex legal cases' (Chambers & Partners).

The daughter of the former chief justice of India, P.N. Bhagwati, Pallavi has been a litigator with a track record of successfully representing corporate giants, a key member of the high-powered SVS Raghavan Committee and principal advisor to the Federation of Indian Chambers of Commerce & Industry (FICCI). Besides, she has been actively associated with competition policy and law in India.

With the entire family married to law—from her husband, Shardul, to her two daughters and her son-in-law—Pallavi admits, 'The question of completely switching off from work did not arise when I was a new mother, and still remains an impossibility.'

The Queen of Courts
PALLAVI SHROFF

Koi lautade mere beete hue din (if only someone could return those bygone days). The song echoes at the back of my mind, even as images from my childhood flash before my eyes.

I remember, for instance, how my sister and I would jump into a car with absolute delight for family holidays; we'd drive to different parts of India and, over time, we covered the length and breadth of this diverse country. **Growing up in Amdavad (as Ahmedabad was then known), I recall a childhood that was not only happy and carefree, but also filled with immense possibility and exposure—both my sister and I would get regularly introduced by our parents to the dignitaries who would frequent our home.** We learnt how to meet, talk to and present ourselves before a range of prominent entities—from the governor of Gujarat, to leading judges and lawyers, to charismatic politicians.

I also remember my enlightening interactions with my father—and of these, one stands out. My sister Parul and I—still schoolgoing girls—were in Porbandar with him. It was late afternoon, and my father wanted to sleep. However, Parul and I kept squabbling in the background, fighting over something inane, as sisters are wont to do. We wanted to read the same book, at the exact same time, and neither of us was willing to concede defeat. Suddenly, my father appeared out of nowhere. Quietly, without a word of reprobation, he took the book from our hands. Swiftly, he tore it in two; he gave one segment to Parul, another to me. That was it. He went back to sleep. My sister and I, silenced, looked askance at the now-ragged book. My father's one act had spoken more emphatically than an hour-long sermon. We got the message, loud and clear: we learnt to build our lives around the principle he abided by—equanimity.

While my father would go on to become the seventeenth chief justice of India, my mother was the chief justice of our family and home. I still recall how she'd hold my hand, firmly tugging me along as we'd visit distant flood-stricken towns or villages reeling under famine. My mother would volunteer help to the distressed, the starving or the ailing, and I, as a little girl, would absorb the care she'd administer to everyone she'd meet. Few images hold as much value to me as this one—my mother with me in tow working to support grief-ridden people. And few lessons are as valuable as those early ones in compassion. It's a value I've held on to, and have tried passing on, as the single-most important bequest, to my own daughters, Shwetambara and Natashaa.

◆

Most people find it hard to believe that law wasn't my first career choice—business was!
Even as childhood passed by in the blink of an eye, and I completed my school education and (what was then known as) pre-university, I was ready to begin a new, exciting chapter—college. My father had just moved to Delhi to take up his responsibilities as a judge of the Supreme Court of India and I had to choose the subject to major in at a college in the city. My uncle, Professor Jagdish Bhagwati, a world-renowned economist, who had been keenly following my academic graph, was convinced that I'd be an ideal student for economics and mathematics. I decided to follow my uncle's advice, and in the years ahead secured an honours degree in economics from Lady Shri Ram College or LSR (at Delhi University), and a master's in business administration (MBA) from Jamnalal Bajaj Institute of Management (Mumbai). A dedicated student of management, I hoped to secure a decent job, like all my classmates, after my degree.
This is when **law decided to pursue me! I got engaged to Shardul Shroff, an aspiring lawyer, who was working as a trainee with his father Suresh Shroff, the managing partner of Mumbai's leading law firm, Amarchand & Mangaldas. My fiancé kept unusually late hours at the office—they *do* call law a jealous mistress! So I thought, I may as well join him; it was our best shot at spending time together!**
The truth also is that in Shardul's company, I found my latent interest in law gaining definition. Just as I completed my MBA exam, I was asked by Shardul to read a bunch of papers, attend a conference and consider

a simple issue—the imposition of fees by a university. Accompanied by the late Firdaus Talyarkahan, a superb lawyer in his own right, I attended my very first conference with the legendary jurist, H.M. Seervai, as a raw beginner, not knowing what to expect. Talyarkahan patiently trained me in the art of thinking law, thinking laterally and planning a matter. Even before the matter I had been handed was finished, I was asked to attend to another one and work with senior counsel J.J. Bhatt, who would, in so many ways, be my first teacher in law.

In the meantime, even while I was gaining experience at a furious pace, I needed a formal law degree. So **I applied to the Government Law College in Mumbai. The college, on its part, didn't know how to process my application—it had never received a request for admission from a postgraduate student, that too with an MBA—so its instinctive reaction was to reject my submission. I had to personally visit the principal and persuade her.** It took some convincing, but finally, I secured a seat and was on my way to becoming a lawyer. My father wasn't in the least bit surprised! In fact, he was very happy.

A year-and-a-half later, I was married to Shardul. From here, my journey as Pallavi Shroff began, as also my entry into one of the most illustrious legal families of India. I started working at Amarchand & Mangaldas even as I was studying law.

You'd think the way forward would be predictable—but this was not the case. Barely a month after Shardul got registered as a lawyer, Indravandan Shroff, the sole proprietor of Shroff & Co., passed away in Delhi. The firm decided to open an office in the capital and Shardul was asked to 'go, run the Delhi branch!' **In 1980, both of us, complete novices— Shardul, two months old at the bar; me, yet to secure a formal law degree—found ourselves in a new city, without a legacy to rely on.** To make matters worse, of the three lawyers at the branch, two left in the second month. It was a baptism by fire. Shardul and I had to literally start from scratch! I doubt we would have managed without the direction of friends like Murlidhar C. Bhandare—then a practising senior counsel who would guide us, sit next to Shardul and me and mentor us through our trials—and those truly helpful judges, so encouraging of young talent.

Together, Shardul and I nurtured and grew the firm—from the two of us to around three hundred lawyers in New Delhi, Gurgaon, Amdavad and Kolkata—while maintaining the highest ethical standards.

◆

My professional journey has spanned over three decades. During this time, I have represented a number of giants. One of my career highs has been the four months of exhaustive work that put the Satyam–Tech Mahindra deal together. Most had written off the IT firm, but with the intervention of the newly appointed board and our assistance (and the help of a few others), it managed to recover under a new leadership. While these landmark moments have been deeply satisfying, the frustrations and triumphs of those early years as a practising woman lawyer hold special nostalgic value.

I had begun work at a time when only a handful of women practised law. The assumption was that women would dabble in the field, then quit, get married, run their homes and tend to children. Consequently, the real challenge in this male-dominated profession was to be taken seriously as a female lawyer. I had no choice but to work extra hard—much harder than my male colleagues. There was no room for erratic behaviour. One slip, one day of absence and colleagues and clients would be quick to say, 'Oh, her kid must be sick,' with a dismissive shrug and a let's-write-her-off grimace.

In this environment, I had to block out the noise of sceptics, critics and naysayers. This was easier said than done. There were occasions, too numerous to count, when clients, on encountering me, would tersely say, 'We will wait for Mr Shroff.' True to their word, they'd actually linger for hours in court corridors and in the office, more inclined to kill precious time than trust a woman with their case. During such moments, Shardul would come and tell them firmly, 'Pallavi has been assigned this case and only *she* will handle it.' The clients would have to take heed.

In court, the situation was no different. **I would often be asked if I was just holding place for Shardul to come and argue the matter. When I'd inform the judges that I was, in fact, ready to present my own arguments, they would invariably look surprised.**

At such times, I'd cling to a few gratifying episodes—one, in particular, comes to mind. A week after I qualified, I happened to be doing a witness action before the remarkable Justice Leila Seth. Justice Seth, in her own way, was guiding me with the processes. When my husband, having finished his matter, happened to walk into the courtroom, Justice Seth politely asked him to leave the court; she told him I was doing well, I could manage, I didn't need help. That little pat on the back offered me just the encouragement I needed!

Over time, slowly but steadily, as I continued doing good work, giving solid advice and offering all deliverables on time, clients started acknowledging my work. The big breakthrough came a few years into my profession. I had to argue a bank-related case in court because my senior could not make it for the hearing. I represented the bank as best as I could, backing every statement with solid fact; at the end of the hearing, the judge ordered the defendant to pay a crore of rupees to the bank—a huge amount of money back then! **The day the bank got its money, its chairman called to ask, 'Who exactly got me this crore?' For me, it was a moment of vindication when he was told that the counsel representing the bank was Pallavi Shroff, a woman.**

However, it was in 1991 that I really knew I had come a long way. After undergoing a back surgery, I found myself unable to travel to Allahabad for a matter by train. I told my client to take somebody else from the firm. Instead, the client arranged for a chartered flight and insisted on having me handle the matter.

From being eschewed to becoming a trusted advisor to clients—it has been a long journey as a woman lawyer!

◆

If I've had a fulfilling career as a lawyer, I have two towering figures to thank—my father and my father-in-law. Indeed, today, when I am felicitated with titles like 'one of the most powerful women in Indian business' or 'doyenne of Indian competition law', I silently dedicate every award to them.

My father, Prafullachandra Natwarlal Bhagwati, is my role model and inspiration. Apart from that early lesson in equanimity, he has taught me the value of simplicity, impartiality and compassion—he sees the entire world with an equal eye, the eye of humanity.

While my father has chiselled my personality, my early professional life was steered by my father-in-law, Suresh Shroff, who treated me as his third son. He was a human computer with a razor-sharp memory. It wouldn't be an exaggeration to say that he could write the firm's balance sheet on the reverse of a Bombay-Delhi air ticket—he knew the firm's finances by heart, the details of every account, right down to the date, bill and matter.

Not surprisingly, he expected the same degree of attentiveness from those he worked with. He taught me how to think both ahead and laterally, and reminded me, 'You are as good as your last mistake.' Each evening, as a young lawyer, when I'd return home from court, I would excitedly share with him what I had done in each matter. After hearing me out patiently, he'd ask: 'What next steps have you considered?' The seemingly simple question would keep me on my toes!

◆

What are the qualities that define a leader in the legal space? Apart from dedication, I'd say determination; the ability to maintain client relationships by relating to them, understanding their needs and providing legal business solutions; a strategic vision; an eye for detail; and a tireless quest for perfection are essential.

As a leader, I know it is my responsibility to inspire my team and lead the way. I cannot have expectations of my colleagues if I do not impose the same expectations on myself. Therefore, if a teammate is working on a Sunday or clocking out later than usual, she can see that I work long hours and attend to projects on holidays, too. If I demand integrity from my teammates, they can see that I practise it in my everyday life—by emphasizing that my ethics are among my greatest lifetime achievement awards, and also by letting my values dictate my professional decisions. In my career, there have been a few occasions when, while defending people, I've spotted false affidavits. I have refused to file them, no matter how prominent the defendant is or who risks being vexed!

If a firm remains small, it could well be because the founding partners have focused on themselves instead of letting the team grow with them. This goes against the grain of leadership—a leader gives people responsibility, empowers them, while also making them accountable. This is how institutions are built. **In my view, the biggest task confronting any leader is people management and resource allocation.** I consider people our best assets—hence it becomes all the more important to manage their aspirations and expectations by providing support. At Amarchand & Mangaldas, I sit with the partners, lawyers and professional managers, share my vision with them and let them develop every idea further under my guidance. The aim is to make every retainer feel a sense of ownership.

As you can see, **I place a huge emphasis on communication. By communicating, I do not mean shouting; nothing comes of that except acrimony!** By communicating, I mean something quite simple—if you're happy with the way a job has been done, convey your satisfaction; if you're unhappy, make your displeasure known politely but firmly. At Amarchand & Mangaldas, we largely have an open floor layout. I can stop and talk to the associates on my way to meetings, or walk up to partners for a quick tête-à-tête. **Instead of waiting for others to approach me, I make it a point to reach out—remember, it is always intimidating for team members to come to leaders. If you're the boss, make the first move.**

The flipside of communicating is granting people space. In my own life, this ideal becomes especially relevant, since Shardul and I work for the same firm; my husband is also my colleague! It's inevitable that we will disagree, not see eye to eye on some matters. The only way to navigate such an impasse is by respecting each other's space. While Shardul does non-contentious work, I do contentious work—this is our way of ensuring that we grow together, yet independently.

Beyond the business of law, a leader has to remember her duties towards society at large. At Amarchand & Mangaldas, we have a corporate social responsibility (CSR) forum, 'Pankh'—led by one of our partners—which engages in several socially relevant activities. Everyone is encouraged to participate. On my part, besides associating with NGOs like Save the Children and the Society for Energy, Environment and Development (SEED), I try fulfilling my social commitments by being a part of government committees and assisting with policymaking. Since I'm beholden to this nation for the remarkable opportunities it has offered me, I feel obligated to render any service I can to the government pro bono.

But what gives me special satisfaction is contributing to the future of Indian legal education. To this end, I am a board member with the Institute of Law, Nirma University. Few things make me happier than seeing a young generation of idealistic, committed lawyers emerge.

Fulfilling social responsibilities can be time-intensive. But if each of us could, in some small measure, give back to the world, the world will be an infinitely better place for our children.

◆

The beauty of being a woman is that you get to play different roles—wife, mother, grandmother, professional and leader. But this is also where the challenge lies. As a working woman, how do you establish a work-life balance?

In response, all I can say is: what work-life balance? **If a lawyer claims, 'I manage beautifully, I set aside my evenings for my family,' I suspect she's not being entirely honest. In a demanding profession like ours, long hours are a given.** For three decades (and counting) as a lawyer, I have been consistently at work. I rarely take a Saturday or Sunday off. I go on vacations perhaps once in two years. And I do not hesitate to cancel holidays, no matter how meticulously planned, if a professional matter unexpectedly comes up.

Back in the day, I worked till the nth hour before both my daughters were born. Due to professional exigencies, I did not have the luxury of a long maternity leave; **I returned to my office barely forty days after giving birth. My fellow colleagues joked that it was as though the birth of my children happened between two matters!**

The times that followed were equally frenetic; the line between work and life grew dim. I remember how I carried an ailing little Natashaa in one arm and simultaneously flipped the pages of my files with the other hand; how I took the girls to counsel conferences where, even as I presented, they would sit in waiting rooms; how we celebrated their birthdays not in restaurants, but at the office while I worked. I recall how they'd spend their short breaks in court literally hanging on to my coat-tails; how they'd sit in the office on Saturdays and school holidays and make register entries; and how they would good-naturedly sacrifice holidays because they knew, 'Ma has a new matter to attend to.' Today, with the entire family (including my son-in-law) in the same profession, shop talk is inevitable at our dinner table, either because we wish to celebrate a good order or rejoice at closing a big deal. The question of completely switching off from work did not arise when I was a new mother, and still remains an impossibility.

Given the pressures that come with this profession, a support system is vital. I was fortunate—I had the unstinted support of my both my mother and mother-in-law. While my mother happily took my girls under her wing and taught them religion and values, as well as how to independently keep home, my mother-in-law would stay up with my children till 3 a.m. and assist them with their exams—all this, while I'd toil at the office. **The question of abandoning my career never arose—my mother-in-law treated me as the daughter she never had and encouraged me to pursue my dreams!**

The biggest sources of support, though, have always been my husband and children. While Shweta and Natashaa have been amazing daughters—never complaining about my long hours of work or travel and, in fact, revelling in the awards I win or the appearance of my name in newspapers—my husband has encouraged me to have my own career and an independent personality. He has boosted my ambition and has been wholly supportive of my travel schedules and hours of work. Indeed, **Shardul has chipped in every step of the way—from dividing responsibilities equally, to travelling such that one of us was always around for the girls when they were growing up.** Both of us, in the early days, forfeited our social life. With full-time careers and two little children, we decided we would rather nurture them, make them feel wanted, than meet friends or colleagues.

However, of all that I've surrendered to build a strong firm, what I miss most, perhaps, is kathak. **Not many know that apart from law, my passion in life used to be classical dance.** I have learnt kathak from two great gurus—from Smt. Kumudini Lakhia in Ahmedabad for a decade, and then from Pandit Birju Maharaj for three years. While in college, I used to perform in their dance troupes. But the demands of the legal profession did not leave me with time for riyaaz; I finally had to relinquish my second love to devote myself to my first. Today, cooking and spending time in the garden help me unwind, as also those stolen moments with my grandson, Yohann—but if ever I catch a kathak performance, or hear the call of music, I am overcome with a kind of homesickness for what was.

◆

Times have changed, but women still hesitate to embrace the legal profession. One reason is social pressure—women are expected to attend to families and are not encouraged to spend long hours working.

How then do we attract and retain the best female talent in Amarchand & Mangaldas, and maintain a 45–55 per cent female-male ratio? There's no easy answer to this question, but I can say that we have worked very hard to institute systems that empower women and grant them an enabling environment—from flexi-time on a one-on-one basis, to a concierge facility to assist with day-to-day chores, a safe-cab service, amenities like a well-quipped gym and medical care with homeopaths, general physicians and a lady doctor in attendance. The ecosystem is one of absolute equality. (I've never held back a woman's progress because she happened to be pregnant, and never will!) While we treat both sexes on a par, and there is no distinction in the allocation of work or the quality we expect, we are aware of the difficulties women face juggling work and home, a career and children. So, as firms, the onus is on us, too, to make their journey a little easier.

To this end, **we decided to open a day-care centre at the office where young mothers can bring their six-month-olds (and those older!). The firm's babies and toddlers are looked after by caregivers, taught by teachers who train them for pre-school (and beyond) and sometimes, even entertained with puppet shows!** The CCTV cameras in the crèche are connected to the laptops of our working mothers, so they can pursue their careers while keeping one eye on their infants.

Besides, unlike some leaders, **I do not view children as impediments at the office.** I recall, one late evening, I had a meeting with a female colleague; the crèche had closed for the day. She asked if I would mind if she came with her child. I said, 'No! Bring him along!' The mother was relieved. We had an excellent discussion while the child sat at my table and busied himself with a paper and a few crayons.

It reminded me of the time when my own children were little, and my legal briefs were filled with colourful scrawls and crayon marks. How fleeting those moments are...

◆

- Equanimity, true compassion, humility and faith in humanity—these are the cornerstones of success.
- As a leader, the onus is on you to set an example through words and deeds.
- Remain inclusive and keep communication channels open.
- Dedication, determination, the ability to build and nurture client relationships, a strategic vision, an eye for detail and a desire for perfection are a few hallmarks of professionals.
- Do not forget to give back to the world.

Above and beyond a distinguished academic career—with a master's in public administration from Madras University, and an honorary PhD from Dr MGR Medical University, Chennai—**PREETHA REDDY**'s professional career as a second-generation entrepreneur has been illustrious. She is the present executive vice chairperson of Apollo Hospitals.

Preetha is acknowledged for her skilled leadership, getting JCI Accreditation for Apollo Hospitals, and initiating partnerships with telecom providers to establish mobile-health solutions in India. She has also helmed various health-care initiatives for the underprivileged, including SACHi (Saving A Child's Heart Initiative).

Ranked among the fifty most powerful women in business (*Fortune*, 2010, 2011), Preetha interestingly says, 'We are more than working entities. We need avenues for expression beyond the corporate arena.' Therefore, Preetha makes time for photography and painting; in fact, many of her canvases can be seen in the corridors of Apollo Hospitals.

◆

The Patron of Health
PREETHA REDDY

When Apollo started in 1983, its purpose was clear to all of us—to generate a huge transformation within the Indian health-care landscape and bring good health to Indians. In more ways than one, my journey as a professional is linked to that of Apollo.

When I joined Apollo, I was extremely young; I was asked to 'just help out'. Having been married when in college, I had no work experience. To make matters worse, I was thrown into the deep end, right in the midst of a staff strike! Tensions were running high, slogans were being shouted and there were protests everywhere. As a precautionary measure, the canteens and other administrative facilities were temporarily closed.

When I heard of the impasse, oddly enough, my first instinct wasn't to engage in talks or negotiate a compromise. My primary concern was that with the canteens closed, the protestors would be hungry. Much against the administration's wishes, **I asked the canteen staff to serve food to the dissenting employees. What followed was remarkable— stomachs full, satiated, the demonstrators calmed down.** They went right back to work.

This incident shaped my approach to my profession; I learnt to put people first. My epiphany was in keeping with Apollo's innate vision— today, it is not only the largest integrated health-care provider in Asia, but also a space where people are treated as equals, and where all individuals, rich and poor, are viewed with respect.

That early incident at my workplace taught me a second, equally valuable lesson—that I had to, at all times, trust my instincts. Indeed, I'd go so far as to say that **it is this remarkable (and often, unerring) 'gut feeling' that makes women such valuable assets to organizations.**

Apollo wasn't just an organization for us—it was my father's dream, his vision to transform Indian health care. From the very beginning this vision galvanized us; it became our collective goal. It was hard work. Almost every brick in Apollo signifies a struggle we went through to move it from dream to reality. Even after we started operations, the challenges never stopped; they just multiplied. In those early days, as well as today, our response was to work harder. We continuously tried to answer my father's—our chairman's—call: 'Have we done enough?'

◆

We all need mentors while working. I was fortunate to find a role model in my father, Dr Prathap Chandra Reddy, the founder of Apollo. He has shaped my work ethics and has inspired me with his constant refrain, 'Whatever we do is not enough to meet the nation's needs.'

As young girls, whenever we'd visit the hospital, my father would say, 'Tell me anything that's not good. We will change it.' We'd ask, 'What about the good things, Daddy?' And he'd reply, 'The good things are for people to enjoy; they'll help them heal. The bad things, on the other hand, help us change and improve.'

If I have come to learn through personal experience that individuals count, my father has always known this intuitively. To date, **whenever we present a new proposal, my father asks, 'Is this a plan for people or for a building? Give me a plan for people. Give me a plan for those who are under-served.'** Therefore, while several private hospitals have come up since Daddy started Apollo, we remain distinctive—not only because we have introduced clinical excellence or leveraged technology to amplify the reach and effectiveness of medical delivery, but also because our care recognizes each person's uniqueness. This is especially relevant since healing is a humane process. **Without empathy and understanding, one cannot mend completely; without 'health care with a smile', there can be no well-being.**

When I look back at Daddy's life, I see the immense influence of the Vedas and the Mahabharata. Both my mother and he would relate excerpts from the epics and sacred texts to us. For me, Daddy's focus on his personal and professional goals is akin to Arjuna's single-mindedness. It's said Arjuna secured the hand of Draupadi by winning a seemingly impossible archery challenge—he had to shoot the eye of a fish that had been placed on a rotating wooden wheel. When asked how he did it, Arjuna replied, 'I saw only the eye.' Daddy has this precise, rare ability—to concentrate on his objectives. When his aim was to provide superior health care to India, he achieved it. **Daddy's ability to pursue a dream with full commitment—to be, at once, a visionary, a humanitarian and a karma-yogi—is inspirational for me.**

Apollo Hospitals has been nurtured by our father over the past three decades. We are led and will always be led by our chairman. Irrespective of who is at the helm, my sisters and I will continue to drive Daddy's agenda of health care for all, and health care that is affordable to all.

◆

As a full-time professional, I have often grappled with questions regarding leadership. For me, as for my father, **leadership is not an attribute we are necessarily born with; it's not an inherent trait. Rather, it constitutes the willingness to embark on a journey, and take responsibility for all things that the journey brings.**

In my view, a leader isn't rigid is her approach—least of all about her definition of success and satisfaction. Rather, she is able to zoom out, look beyond set targets and goals, focus on the big picture and visualize opportunities despite obstacles. An emphasis on success alone can make one both complacent and myopic.

Leadership should also be linked to a democratic approach. **Today's leader cannot be autocratic; she has to nurture the voice of her people.** Equality and fairness have to be her cornerstones.

I believe leadership is all about tapping human resources and unlocking the hidden strengths of employees. This is only possible if we work towards building genuine and insightful relationships with the team. The Apollo story stands testimony to this kind of relationship-building. In 1983, twenty-five people came together to change the Indian health-care landscape. Their commitment to a cause and their sincere respect for one another led to several other associations and linkages. The Apollo family grew, and today, continues to flourish. Out here, **we don't merely provide jobs, but build careers.** Consequently, in May 2014, Apollo Hospitals was ranked amongst the top organizations to work in by Gallup Great Places to Work (GGWA); it is the only group to have won the honour during the first wave of engagement. This means that Apollo is now amongst globally recognized organizations for mastering how best to engage with a large workforce to deliver sustainable growth. This has reinforced our belief in treating 'employees' as family members.

◆

As women, we have specific challenges. We have to juggle the family at home and the family at work. While my sisters and I are passionate about our professions and view Apollo Hospitals as extensions of our lives, we never compromise on the time we wish to spend with our families at home. As in the case of millions of working women, the question of choosing one over the other never arises. Each has its own importance and its own role.

I have to say, **I don't fret about time management—I just take things as they come.** I don't suffer from stress. Perhaps this stems from the deep core of spirituality I have inherited from my father. One of my biggest driving forces is my faith in god. I express this faith by praying at the temple at the start of each day. I visit Tirupati regularly and go to Tiruvannamalai every Shivratri. But more significant than these overt gestures and rituals is my practice of meditation.

You may well ask why I place such emphasis on meditation. It is because, **while I am a working woman, I also need time for myself, my soul and my mind. For me, nothing is healthier and more satisfying than the tranquillity I find through meditative practice.** No day is complete till I find some time to connect with myself.

The truth is that **we are more than working entities. We need avenues for expression beyond the corporate arena.** For me, art and dance are ways of communicating with myself and the world outside. I make sure I keep this magical connection strong. Equally, I try capturing the moments that pass through painting and photography. Trapping a perfect instant teaches me about patience, focus and the humbling beauty of the world!

And yes, **I believe in miracles. I have seen so many miracles at the hospital that my faith in the universe's kindness is reaffirmed.**

◆

- Ask, listen and implement.
- Our principles define who we are. While goals are specific locations on a map, values are like directions on a compass. Establishing a goal based on one's values infuses the former with deeper meaning,

and ensures that even if the goal shifts, the moral compass remains unchanged.

- A leader isn't an autocrat, but receptive to the voices of those around her.
- Employees are an extension of one's family.
- Relax and smile. We take ourselves too seriously. And this takes a definite toll on our life and health. Smile more often and life becomes easier, the journey more joyous and success a lot more rewarding!

After taking over as the chief executive officer (CEO) of CRISIL in 2007, **ROOPA KUDVA** more than tripled the firm's revenues, grew its market capitalization four-fold, expanded its customer base to encompass some of the world's largest investment banks as well as tens of thousands of small firms criss-crossing India, and led CRISIL's evolution from a leading Indian rating agency to a diversified global analytical company. She has featured as one of India's most powerful women in business (*Fortune India*, 2011 to 2014), and is a recipient of several prestigious awards including 'Outstanding Woman Business Leader of the Year' (CNBC-TV18 India Business Leader Awards [IBLA] 2012).

As part of her job at CRISIL, Roopa always adapted—from learning French during a secondment to Paris at Standard & Poor's, to wearing an abaya while visiting Saudi Arabia on an assignment! Despite a hectic workday, Roopa keeps time for her passion for books, her fitness regime and her family. She says, 'While discussing the need to balance professional and personal commitments, the implication tends to be that women must choose between the two. However, I enjoy both.'

In April 2015, after a twenty-two-year innings, Roopa moved on from CRISIL to take up a new assignment as an Omidyar Network (ON) partner and managing director of Omidyar Network India Advisors. Established by eBay founder Pierre Omidyar, ON is a philanthropic investment firm dedicated to harnessing the power of markets to create opportunities for people to improve their lives.

◆

The High Priestess of Ratings
ROOPA KUDVA

They say that if you really reach for something with dedication and hard work, nature will conspire to give it to you. The adage certainly holds for my three-decade-long career, the bulk of which has been spent at CRISIL. Even as I worked with absolute commitment, opportunities arrived, as did bigger responsibilities. The universe gave, and how! I found myself assuming the role of a chief executive officer (CEO).

Come to think of it, it has been quite a journey from the small towns in Assam where I grew up. My father was an Indian Administrative Service (IAS) officer and my mother was a homemaker for several years, before she trained as a teacher and started working at a school. **Even as a ten-year-old, I noticed a change in the way people related to my mother once she became a teacher in Guwahati. The impression stayed with me and was reinforced when I perceived the respect and status enjoyed by my father's colleagues, the women bureaucrats.** Besides, my parents, in a couple of conversations, asserted that it was important for a woman to be financially independent.

Compared to the life I now lead, my years in Assam in the 1970s and early 1980s were very different—gentle, slow, caught in a time warp. Over weekends or holidays, it was customary to wake up in the morning, eat breakfast and run into a nearby forest to play; we returned only when we felt hungry. It was a life without worry, without concerns about where we were or what we were doing.

Not surprisingly, **I did not grow up as a terribly ambitious person. Nor did I have any inkling about the world of business. I hadn't so much as heard of Hindustan Lever until a kind classmate told me that it was the company that made Lux and Dalda!** I let life lead me by the hand. When I graduated in statistics and confronted the question, 'What next?', a cousin told me that the best college to attend was the Indian Institute of Management, Ahmedabad (IIM-A). And so, IIM became a goal.

Even then, I did not have a Plan B. The first time I secured admission to an IIM, I was not allowed to join—Assam was in the throes of anti-foreigner agitations and I could not complete my graduation exams on time. I had to reappear for the common admission test (CAT) a year later, and I spent the intervening period teaching kindergarten students, among other things. I was lucky that it was fun, especially since I had no backup strategy!

The thread running through everything—the spontaneous decisions and the serendipitous ones—was that I enjoyed what I did. Therefore, for over a decade—which saw me graduating from IIM-A in 1986, starting my career with the Industrial Development Bank of India's (IDBI) project finance division, and moving to CRISIL in 1992—I primarily pursued job satisfaction. Additionally, I did whatever was given to me very well.

◆

When I started working, women in India's financial sector were quite a rarity; if they held positions, they'd be tellers at banks or operate from customer service counters. Therefore, when I assumed the role of a project finance officer at IDBI, I was the exception rather than the rule. I remember, **I used to inspect sugar factories in Uttar Pradesh—a feudal and utterly male-dominated territory. To those I interacted with, I was an oddity; they must have wondered, 'Who is this woman, what does she understand about finance?'** I also remember that facilities for women were practically non-existent. Despite these challenges, each time I proved myself, I was treated with utmost professionalism. So if you ask me whether being a woman comes in the way of work, I'd say no—as long as you are competent.

Today, while we hear of the prevalence of violence against women, there has been a simultaneous and antithetical shift in the world of business—working women have carved a space for themselves. The past decade has been most conducive for women seeking careers in finance, technology and the media. Indeed, women constitute a third of business school graduates, and there are many who head businesses (including a few who are in charge of the largest banks in the country).

The fact is that those of us who entered the Indian workforce in the late 1980s and early 1990s benefited significantly from the huge uplift after economic reforms were unleashed. No other generation has seen this kind of growth trajectory.

While recent history has been kind, there is no doubt that in a country of 1.2 billion people, I am among the very privileged. I am a part of a company that is not only a trusted voice in the market for policymakers and regulators, but is also recognized for fair play, meritocracy and gender-neutral practices. At no stage in my career of twenty-two years at CRISIL have I perceived being treated differently just because I am a woman. What also gratifies me is that these days, **many women in CRISIL come to me and say, 'My mother and mother-in-law tell me: "Focus on your job, we'll take care of things at home."' That's a big change!**

What's even better news is that more conversations in Indian boardrooms are about building women leaders. At one of our recent board meets at CRISIL, we discussed diversity and how we could increase the participation of women within the company. Thirty per cent of CRISIL's employees are women; we have seen a sharp increase in senior women leading businesses; we are proud that the largest business vertical in the company is run by a woman and two women oversee half the employees. But we'd like these numbers to increase rapidly over the next three to four years. The sky is not the limit.

Of course, the countrywide picture isn't entirely optimistic. We have a long way to go. Of all the CEOs in India, only 1 per cent happen to be women, and barely 4.7 per cent of the seats on company boards are dominated by our gender. Why do we not see more women in the higher echelons of the corporate world? When I consider the question, it strikes me that the biggest barrier is that women underestimate their capabilities and achievements. They hesitate to ask for what they think they deserve. Typically, women presume: 'If I am doing a job well, someone will notice it and I will be recognized and rewarded.' This might be true in the early stages of our careers, but at senior levels, the onus of demanding a seat at the table is entirely ours.

In the case of women, specifically, the first challenge in the early stages of their careers is staying the course—in other words, not dropping out of the workforce for personal reasons like wanting to start a family. I believe that employers and leaders play a very big role at this stage; they need to be encouraging and help women stay invested in their careers. The second challenge comes at a later stage—when **women**

need to begin *thinking* **of themselves as leaders, position themselves for it, and, if needed, ask for the top jobs or major challenges!**

My own experiences stand testimony to this. In 1998, I found myself in Paris on a secondment to Standard & Poor's. When I returned to CRISIL at the turn of the millennium, I got to know that the position of the chief rating officer (CRO) had become vacant. I asked the then CEO of CRISIL about the vacancy, but he told me that he did not wish to find a replacement; those directly subordinate to the CRO were running their respective verticals quite well.

For the first time, I felt the stirrings of ambition. Soon after, at a company conference in Goa, I prepared a three-slide PowerPoint presentation—an amateurish effort by today's standards, I must add—on why CRISIL needed a CRO and why I was the best person for the job. As I completed my presentation, the CEO smiled and said, 'Sounds great, leave the presentation with me.' I did. For a few months, I didn't hear a thing. Then suddenly, one day, the CEO came to me and said, 'Do you remember, a few months ago you had sought the position of CRO? We are happy to offer it to you.' And so it was: I became the CRO of CRISIL, and seven years later, in 2007, I was chosen to lead CRISIL as the managing director and CEO. Sometimes, life presents opportunities. But sometimes, you have to claim them.

◆

I believe that a major impediment in a woman's life is the constant fear that she won't be able to strike a work-life balance. In this context, there are two facts to remember. First, we are all faced with choices at every turn. **What is important is that we accept that there will always be trade-offs, without feeling guilty or thinking of them as 'sacrifices'.** In the long span of a career of thirty to forty years, priorities will keep changing and so will the choices we make. Sometimes, work will assume centre stage, and at other times, our family and personal commitments. I think this is but natural. During the first dozen years of my career, I made a conscious choice to relocate with my husband whenever he was transferred by the bank he worked for. Negotiations of this kind will confront us at every turn, and we should learn to be comfortable with the decisions we make.

Second, **while discussing the need to balance professional and personal commitments, the implication tends to be that women**

must choose between the two. However, I enjoy both. I derive happiness from my work, and believe that nothing compares with the satisfaction of a job well done. CRISIL has offered me a series of challenging, but extremely satisfying, assignments—so no Monday blues. At the same time, on the personal front, I have found immense joy in the time I spend with my husband and family, who offer their unstinted support. Why must we opt for one or the other, when we can have the best of both worlds?

Besides, I keep time aside for myself, too! I read and unwind. My job requires me to keep myself updated with research and analysis, so when I read for pleasure, I look for a complete change—nothing to do with business or management. I love reading biographies, autobiographies and memoirs, and of course, the classics. I enjoy travelling, too. My favourite destinations include the Manas National Park in Assam, Egypt, Prague, Spain and Israel. Additionally, I am a movie buff! As you can see, there is a life one can pursue beyond the corporate arena, even while retaining a high-pressure job.

◆

I draw inspiration from the work I do. At CRISIL, we have rated or assessed more than 75,800 small-and medium-sized enterprises (SMEs) and their entrepreneurs come with motivating stories. How much one can learn from them!

The truth is, I draw inspiration from the lives of successful people—there are so many who have done so much that's remarkable. One example is Katharine Graham, author of the Pulitzer prize-winning *Personal History*. She was born into a privileged family, but was never brought up to run a business. A personal tragedy, however, compelled her to assume responsibility of the Washington Post Company. Instead of resting on past family glories, Graham led the *Post* through some of its biggest successes—including a breaking story on the Watergate scandal that led to the resignation of Richard Nixon. Here was a woman who, for the longest time, had a piece of paper under her glass table that said, 'Assets on the left, liabilities on the right'! When the *Post* went public in 1971, the share price was US$6.50. When Graham stepped down in 1991, the price was US$222. Katherine Graham, almost single-handedly, made the *Post* a huge financial success.

◆

I believe leadership is a complex term demanding straightforward processes. For one, **a leader asks simple questions.** This has probably been the most important lesson drawn from B-school, and it has held me in good stead throughout my career—especially today, as the CEO, when I have to process information, views and analyses. I have learnt to approach all problems by beginning with first principles and posing the most basic of queries. This helps me identify key issues, structure my thinking and take a holistic approach.

Besides, **I believe that a leader is not necessarily the sharpest person in the team; rather, a leader has the humility to learn from her peers.** Surrounding yourself with people who are better and brighter not only helps you identify your unique strengths, but also allows you to raise your game. This was true for me in B-school, and remains true at CRISIL. At work, I never really was the best analyst. But I did acknowledge the strength in others and harnessed this. Even today, I am surrounded by people who are much quicker than me; I bring my unique strengths and simultaneously tap into their capabilities.

Interestingly, as I rose to more senior positions in CRISIL, I realized that it was not enough to have a good idea and the capacity to execute it. I also had to develop the patience to work with many different kinds of stakeholders, and pilot, chisel and fine-tune my ideas based on their feedback and perspectives. Often, this is the hardest part of getting things done—and it takes time!

Finally, a leader has the capacity to see the big picture from an outside-in perspective. **At work, I always look at a problem from the stakeholder's point of view—from the customer's perspective, the board's standpoint or from a regulatory angle. This is in direct opposition to a bottom-up approach,** and what it brings to the table is invaluable.

At the end of the day, there are no quick fixes. To this end, I must quote Hesiod, the Greek poet, who said, 'Before the gates of excellence, the high gods have placed sweat; long is the road thereto and rough and steep at first; but when the heights are reached, then there is ease, though grievously hard in the winning.'

◆

- There's much to be gained by staying the course and remaining with an organization for a long period of time. In an age of instant fixes—

when it is altogether common to find people who have changed five jobs in the first twelve years of their career—the rewards of holding on can be immense.

- There are no shortcuts or quick fixes.
- The ability to connect with people across the world is vital for career success. Simplify your communication to heighten its effectiveness. And learn how to paint the big picture. This is especially vital if you're dealing with boards and very senior stakeholders like policymakers and regulators, or even while communicating with large and global teams.
- Know your strengths and use them well. Make an honest assessment of your weaknesses and stumbling blocks, even while revelling in what makes you different in a positive way. Great organizations look for a diversity of skills and competencies, and not for people who are clones.
- The people at the top may not necessarily be the best in key areas—only the most receptive to new ideas.
- If you enjoy your work and relax, you have a better chance of being successful. By this, I mean, take your work very, very seriously, but don't take yourself too seriously.
- Always try having a Plan B that is likely to bring you fulfilment.
- People talk of 'giving back' by offering money to charities and volunteering temporarily within the social sector. But you can also 'give back' through your core job—by taking responsible business decisions; keeping the vision of the business alive (and not just the goal of making money); creating opportunities for small enterprises and those from less-privileged backgrounds; and ensuring that your organization creates value for all stakeholders.
- If the commitment to a greater common good drives your day-to-day professional life, you will, more often than not, also see career success. It's a richer and more satisfying approach than focusing solely on pay, promotion and a swift ascent up the ladder.

SANGEETA PENDURKAR is the managing director of Kellogg India. With over twenty-six years of marketing, sales and general management experience, spanning across three sectors—packaged goods, pharmaceuticals and financial services—Sangeeta has been listed among *Fortune's* most powerful women in business for four consecutive years from 2011 to 2014. She has also been featured on *Impact's* list of the '50 Most Influential Women in Media, Marketing and Advertising' from 2012 to 2015.

Over the years, Sangeeta has worked for several multinational corporations, including Novartis, Unilever, HSBC and Coca Cola, both in India and abroad. She is currently the chairperson of the FICCI Food Processing Committee, the first woman to hold this position. She was the co-chair of the committee in 2013–2014.

As the youngest of five children, her ambition was to pursue her father's profession and secure admission into a medical college. When that didn't quite work out, she chose a different path which played to her strengths. She took a journey across sectors which required her to adapt to different organizational cultures; she displayed a strong willingness to adjust. Her parents and siblings had a great influence on her as a child and she owes a lot of her success to them and the unwavering support of her husband and close friends.

Married to Sandeep Pendurkar, Sangeeta enjoys reading and music, besides being an avid art and antiques collector.

The 'Cereal' Winner
SANGEETA PENDURKAR

Building winning teams, driving a consumer-centric agenda and excellence in execution is what I am passionate about. I give my best to everything I do and believe in a 'never give up' attitude. There have been several bends and curves during my journey. Each one has been a learning experience and has given me stronger focus and the determination to achieve more.

Born and educated in the suburbs of Mumbai, as a child I was quite shy and a bit of an introvert. I was an academically oriented student and consistently ranked amongst the top three in class. With my father being a trained Hindustani classical singer, I grew up listening to such music. Indeed, it was my father's penchant for music that gave me my name. Under his influence, all of us at home pursued Indian art forms in one way or the other. While one of my sisters and I were interested in Indian dance, the other played the sitar. I pursued rigorous training in Kathak, Bharatnatyam and Indian folk dances, so much so that at one point I even considered pursuing dance as a career. This training in dance had a lasting impact on my life. To excel in the art, one needed to practise until perfect, especially whilst performing as a team. Getting to a stage of complete harmony with everyone else, without missing a single movement or a beat, required persistent efforts and days and months of practice. **Dance taught me the importance of rigour, perseverance and helped me develop my planning and organizing skills.**

My parents have been among my greatest influences. They inculcated in me the habit of giving my best to every task. They always encouraged me to make an extra effort and taught me to believe that nothing was impossible. **My father was my first mentor and role model, and**

also perhaps my biggest critic. His constant push, to raise the bar and strive harder to achieve greater heights, instilled in me the passion to do things right and give my 100 per cent to everything. My father's own story—beginning his medical education in Karachi and moving to Mumbai after Partition, with no financial support and without a passing acquaintance with anyone in the country—has been a source of inspiration.

My mother was one of the most content and caring individuals I have come across in my life. Her ability to be happy with what she had, to accept what life had to offer without ever complaining, and to care selflessly for people around her and make a difference to their lives, was something that I saw every day while growing up. She truly was the epitome of selfless giving and in many ways lived a saintly life. **She taught us to build strong, lasting relationships and to care deeply about people. Watching the way my mother led her life, I learnt to count my blessings and give what I had to others.**

As the youngest of five siblings, and with none of them carrying forward the so-called 'family profession', I was the last hope in the family to do so. I did believe that I was destined to practise medicine, just like my father and grandfather, and I worked towards it. However, I missed securing admission to a medical school by a narrow margin. Therefore, I decided to pursue a bachelor's degree in science with a specialization in microbiology from Ruia College, Mumbai. Surprisingly, a few weeks into the course, I learnt that a seat for the bachelor's degree in pharmacy (B Pharm) at the KMK College of Pharmacy, University of Mumbai, had just opened up. By then, I was well-settled in my class at Ruia College and I was keen to continue there. My father made me rethink my decision; he convinced me that it was a great para-medical course and I should not let the opportunity pass.

Moving from an extremely protected environment to a tough professional course, amongst people who had a ruthlessly competitive outlook, required significant reconditioning. It was also extremely challenging to settle into the programme as a late entrant. I began looking for a quick way of catching up on what I had missed out. On asking my classmates for direction, everyone pointed me to the most academically proficient girl in class. I walked up to her and asked if she would share her notes with me. She was brutally honest and replied candidly, 'I've worked very hard to assimilate these notes. I see no reason why I should part with them and why you should benefit from my work.' That was my eureka moment; it was when I realized what the world outside was like. Whilst the girl's response caused immense hurt initially, over a period of time it helped me realize how tough the world was, and that I needed to step up and become strong mentally and emotionally.

During the entire tenure of my undergraduate and graduate programme, I had long commutes in Mumbai's suburban trains. I would spend more than three hours each day travelling. While these weren't the most comfortable of journeys, they were great learning experiences in terms of meeting people from all walks of life. They also tested my patience and my ability to adapt and adjust. **My commutes, coupled with the strong influence my mother had on me, made me resilient and flexible. These qualities have helped me both personally and professionally as I moved across sectors and organizations, working with diverse teams.**

My train travels also gave me the chance to make some great acquaintances, including my closest friend Shilpa, who currently resides in Canada. She influenced the course of my life in many ways. As teenagers, we shared our closest secrets and biggest joys. She was far more confident than I was, and always articulated her thinking perfectly. I admired her (and continue to do so), not just for these reasons but also for her knack of influencing people around her. In the final year of my graduation, it was Shilpa who spoke to my parents and suggested that I move to a girls' hostel close to my college along with her so as to make more time for studies. To my parents' credit, they changed with changing times and have always been accepting of new ideas. The year I spent in the hostel exposed me to peers from different states and countries. It resulted in a huge boost to my self-confidence.

◆

Though serendipity played some role in my life, both with respect to my education and career choices, **my focus, determination, strong sense of commitment, being self-driven and my passion to succeed contributed hugely to my progress.** As we were finishing our final year examinations, Shilpa talked me into appearing for a master's in business administration (MBA) entrance exam. I appeared for both the exams (MPharm and MBA) and passed each with flying colours. I was at a crossroads and finally decided to opt for the MBA. Based on my conversations with a few industry captains, I realized that I was more suited for a career in business strategy and marketing rather than research and development.

◆

To leverage the two professional degrees I had, I decided to start my career in the space of pharmaceutical marketing. In 1988, I joined Hindustan Ciba-Geigy (HCG; now Novartis) as a management trainee. I was amongst the first women managers to join the business and ended up being the only woman in marketing for the first few years. I often get asked if it was tough being the only woman in the team. My simple answer is that I never felt the difference. **The challenges I faced were no different from those faced by my male colleagues. I was focused on giving my best shot to everything and my gender never stopped me from taking on new challenges or from being successful at a task or role.** Of course, I was also fortunate to have colleagues who were welcoming and didn't discriminate. Subsequently, it was great to see more women come on board. Those were the formative years of my career and it was wonderful to be working with colleagues and bosses who contributed significantly to my learning curve.

It is critical to plan one's career and perhaps even important for women to do so, given the multiple roles they play, and their strong desire to balance their personal and professional responsibilities. Choosing the right partner for the journey is one of the most important decisions for women. I was quite clear that I wanted to marry someone who respected my ambitions and was supportive of my career. I found such encouragement in my husband, Sandeep, whom I met a few months into my first job. We decided to get married after a short period of courtship. Being a marketer himself, he has always understood the pressures of my job and has been a great supporter all through my career. I owe a lot of my success to him; with his backing, I had the confidence to raise my hand and explore possibilities in my career as and when they arose.

My first experience in the corporate world was fascinating and I had the opportunity to run different portfolios as a brand manager—from gynaecological drugs to antidepressants and cardiovascular medicines. I was also fortunate to get the opportunity to successfully launch some breakthrough products which were being introduced in India for the first time, such as the first drug for obsessive compulsive disorders (OCDs) and a transdermal patch for menopause. Each of these projects involved a lot of hard work and one needed to ensure that one delivered at par with the other male colleagues.

One of the most challenging assignments that I worked on during my tenure at HCG involved a strategic project with McKinsey to draft the ten-year blueprint for the organization. I put up my hand for this assignment and was chosen as one of the four members (and the only woman) of the core team that led the project. This was a full-time commitment and the expectation was that this would get done over and above our day job! It was a huge ask and the project spanned a year. **There were days when I couldn't go home (given the long commute) and would have to check into a hotel across the office. But the experience of working with a top-class team on a strategic assignment of significant importance to the organization, early in my career, made the effort seem worthwhile!** It is during times like these that the family's encouragement and a support system at home become critical. This is what helped me sail through this difficult period.

A few years into the job, I realized that the pharmaceutical industry was highly controlled; it was difficult to influence several of the marketing levers. Secondly, it was, and continues to remain, a very technical industry. One constantly needs to stay abreast of new developments in the space of diseases, its prognosis and treatment. Hence, after spending seven years in the industry, I chose to shift to the fast-moving consumer goods (FMCG) sector.

◆

Unilever was a fantastic training ground, and between two assignments spread over eight years, I gained strong and diverse business and marketing experience. As soon as I joined, I had to move to Pune to be part of the Kimberly-Clark Lever joint venture start-up as the brand manager for its feminine care range, which was to be launched within a fortnight of my arrival. The thrill of being part of a new brand launch was exciting. However, within two weeks of the launch, an unfortunate situation arose and the product had to be recalled. Here I was, in a new industry, in a new organization, in a new city all by myself, trying to manage a disaster that I didn't know enough about! It was a testing time and I was under immense pressure to solve the issue at hand, despite having only a limited understanding of the business. It was baptism by fire! While stressful, in hindsight, it proved to be a great experience on two counts—learning to manage a disaster and putting my resilience to test! The rigorous and relentless efforts that followed over the next eighteen months to ensure a successful relaunch while working with a cross-functional team resulted in an extremely gratifying experience. This also sharpened my focus on consumer-centricity and equipped me to deal with ambiguity better, besides teaching me several other valuable lessons.

My next assignment within Unilever four years later took me back to Mumbai as the marketing manager for the skincare business. The experience of managing strong flagship brands such as Fair & Lovely, Pond's, Pears, Vaseline and Lakmé proved to be invaluable. It gave me the opportunity to do some remarkable work with a great team of people. Amongst various marketing initiatives, one very close to my heart is the launch of the Fair & Lovely Foundation in 2002. The brand platform of women's economic empowerment was brought to life with the projects that the foundation supported. The ability to influence the lives of many girls by opening the doors for them through the platform of education resonated strongly with my own purpose and leadership compass. It is an initiative that I am truly proud of and is a great example of how brands can make a difference to lives of consumers and people, beyond the product.

A key milestone event during this assignment was a 360-degree feedback session, which contributed significantly to my leadership journey. The session was facilitated by a coach and included the entire business team—my peers, subordinates and boss. During the session, it dawned on me that I needed to change my leadership style and empower my team a lot more. The feedback I received from the rest of the team acted as a mirror and made me realize that at times my passion to achieve perfection was an impediment; it impacted the people reporting to me and restricted their ability to learn and grow. That was a turning point in my professional life. I made a very deliberate attempt from then on to change my leadership style. It took a lot of effort, but I persisted. Soon, **I realized that the joy of creating a winning and an empowered team was far greater than doing things yourself in the pursuit of perfection.**

◆

I debated moving from Unilever, the most celebrated and well-known organization for marketing, to Hong Kong and Shanghai Banking Corporation (HSBC), which was in a completely different and unfamiliar sector. Finally, based on the counsel of my husband and a few close friends, I decided to take the risk. It was totally out of my comfort zone. My new role as the chief marketing officer gave me the opportunity to be a part of the leadership team of the organization. My mandate was to set up the product and marketing function and make a positive impact on business growth. I was excited about the challenges and with the possibility of creating something new. **Using my experience in the FMCG sector, I was able to successfully demonstrate that it was possible to differentiate products in the banking sector, if the consumer was at the heart of all decision-making.** Indeed, the sixty-odd member team that I created delivered spectacular results. The role at HSBC India was seminal to my leadership journey; it granted me the opportunity to create and lead a strong functional team by adopting a consumer-centric approach and sound organizational principles.

◆

On the back of the success in India, I moved to Dubai to take up the role of chief marketing officer (CMO) for all of Middle East. I had to recreate what I had done in India for nine other markets and it was a great opportunity to gain experience outside the country. Sandeep was running his own software company out of Pune and it was not possible for him to move along with me. Therefore, to accept the role or not was the question. As they say, the youngest in the family never grows up for the parents! **My father was quite reticent about my moving and living in another country by myself, but Sandeep believed that it was the best thing that could have happened to me. He felt that making the move was important for my career, since I had never worked internationally.** I still recall the day when both my husband and my father were trying to convince each other about their respective views on my accepting this assignment. After a couple of hours of intense debate, my father took me aside and asked me if everything was okay between Sandeep and me! He just couldn't fathom why my husband was so keen that I take up an assignment that would have us living in two different countries, miles away from each other!

The experience I gained in the Middle East was exceptional. Making the bank relevant to a diverse set of consumers was a phenomenal challenge and gave me a completely different perspective on managing complexity. It was not only a great leadership experience, but also gave me the chance to work with cross-cultural teams. I led a team that had people from twenty different nationalities. It was extremely fulfilling to see a winning team being created once again.

◆

After five years in banking, I was keen to get back to the FMCG sector. I realized that having spent twenty-odd years in marketing, it was time for me to shift gears and work actively towards moving to a general management role.

My next position at Coca-Cola India as the head of strategic planning allowed me to do just that. This was another great organization, with an unmatchable passion for its brands and a strong competitive spirit. My short stint there, working closely with the chief executive officer (CEO), allowed me to get a bird's-eye view of the business. Being in a staff role for the very first time was quite different from being in strong operating, profit-and-loss-led roles, which is what I had done through most of my career. It took me a while to come to terms with the situation, but I knew it was important for me to gain this experience if I was to become a general manager in the future. I was soon given the additional responsibility of running the Georgia tea and coffee vending business independently, alongside my strategy role at Coca-Cola. This was my first business head role and offered me a great perspective into running an end-to-end business.

◆

In October 2010, I joined Kellogg as the managing director for India and South Asia. The journey at Kellogg has been fantastic. It is an organization with which I share my own values and beliefs. My role began with the mandate of defining a sound growth strategy and building a team capable of executing the plan. The challenges associated with transforming the organization and delivering strong business results have been exhilarating. Talent and leadership development have been the key business priorities. I feel privileged to be a part of a high-performing team of professionals in India and in the Asia-Pacific region. Having come from different organizations, they bring with them cultural diversity, besides diversity of thought and gender, a key ingredient for balanced decision-making and success.

At Kellogg, globally and in India, gender diversity is an important

agenda. It is not viewed as something that is 'nice-to-have' but as a key enabler of success. The belief is that women represent our consumers and also bring in a different perspective to business; hence, it is important to dip into this talent pool and include them in the workforce. Globally, the Women of Kellogg (WOK)—an employee resource group to help women with career development—is a key initiative. This is now being rolled out in the Asia-Pacific region, and I am honoured to be its sponsor.

Much has been said and written about gender diversity. Establishing such diversity is vital, not because one gender is superior to the other, but because we hope to create a world where both men and women can coexist. They are like the yin and the yang, complementing each other. Secondly, success is gender-agnostic; it is linked to your skill sets and leadership abilities. Your performance determines your growth trajectory. And, finally, as a woman I believe that all women who are successful today need to pay forward and help other women climb up the ladder.

I am truly excited by the future growth possibilities for Kellogg India. **The legacy I would like to leave behind is a team that is capable of continuously winning in the future; a team with leaders bigger than me, leaders who will take this business to even greater heights.**

◆

- **Define your purpose**
  Have a strong goal, and define what success means to you. Choose something that you are passionate about, so that you can sustain your enthusiasm for work for the rest of your life.
- **Be authentic**
  Be yourself and be genuine in your interactions with people. Guided by your inner voice, always do and say what you mean.
- **Give people what you have**
  Help people recognize their potential and make a difference to others by sharing what you have.
- **Seek your own balance**
  Create support groups, strong relationships and networks that you can rely on to help you balance your family, career, friends and yourself, effectively.
- **'Me time'**
  Ensure you find quality time every week to engage in activities that help you reconnect with yourself.

A social crusader for over twenty years, **SHAHEEN MISTRI** is the founder and chief executive officer (CEO) of Teach For India and the founder and chairperson of the Akanksha Foundation, a non-profit organization that aims to uplift the lives of less-privileged children. She is an Ashoka fellow (2001) and was named a 'Global Leader for Tomorrow' at the World Economic Forum in 2002. Shaheen also serves on the boards of Ummeed, The Thermax Social Initiative Foundation and is an advisor to the Latika Roy Foundation. She also serves as a committee member for the National Council for Teacher Education.

Despite growing up in the midst of wealth and privilege, Shaheen was interested in making a difference in the world from a very young age. When she was eighteen, she decided to move to Mumbai from the US and enrolled in St Xavier's College in order to understand the city and its people. It was in Ambedkar Nagar that she started Akanksha, an NGO to educate children from poor families so that they could fulfil their potential. Five years ago, in collaboration with McKinsey, Shaheen and her team adapted the Teach for America model for India and changed how education was imparted for low-income households across the country.

◆

The Dreamcatcher
SHAHEEN MISTRI

I look handsome, I look smart,
I am a walking work of art;
Such a dazzling coat of many colours,
How I love my coat of many colours!
It was red and yellow and green and brown
And scarlet and black and ochre and peach
And ruby and olive and violet and fawn
And lilac and gold and chocolate and mauve
And cream and crimson and silver and rose
And azure and lemon and russet and grey
And purple and white and pink and orange
And red and yellow and green and brown and
Scarlet and black and ochre and peach
And ruby and olive and violet and fawn
And lilac and gold and chocolate and mauve
And cream and crimson and silver and rose
And azure and lemon and russet and grey
And purple and white and pink and orange
And blue.

—*Joseph and the Amazing Technicolor Dreamcoat,*
lyrics by Tim Rice

The patchwork tails of Latif's kurta whirled in a flurry of brilliant hues, flying ever higher, rising up around him as he twirled effortlessly across the stage, singing his beautiful song, the melody of a dream, replete with all the colours of what could be.

It was two years later, and I was in my car driving to Pune when I received a call informing me that Latif had been hospitalized. It was dark, and I turned around on the highway and headed straight back to Mumbai, but by the time I reached the hospital, Latif had died. Akanksha's star would no longer sing or dance; the other children would no longer grab hold of his spinning coloured kurta. I started to comprehend how his dreams of earning enough money to pull his family from the open mouth of poverty, of educating his two-year-old nephew who followed him around so adoringly, of winning the vocal competition in which he was a contestant and of finishing college, would never be realized.

The day after he passed away, I went to visit his grandfather in the 10x10 shanty where they had lived together. The old man was bent, arthritic, and just gazed at me silently for a long while. His eyes were empty wells and were shrouded with the questioning look of defeat. He finally spoke to tell me that he had pressed ₹14,000 into Latif's hand, pleading with his grandson to take the money and go to a private hospital to receive the medical attention he so urgently needed. Knowing well the hard labour his grandfather had endured for years in order to save this money for retirement, and not wishing to send him back to work, Latif secretly slipped the money back into his grandfather's trunk. He chose instead to go to a free municipal hospital, where he died of an acute respiratory infection less than twelve hours later.

Now I remember Latif as a living star, more dazzling than any of us could even have imagined. **I remember the many colours that Latif left us—the gentle shades of his kindness, the brilliant hues of his limitless potential, the light swathes of joy inherent in his laugh, and the deep and true intensity that shone through even as he gave his all.**

◆

My childhood was filled with wonderful colours. We stayed at the Little Governors' Camp on a Kenyan safari; we learnt to ride horses on a farm in Australia; and saddled donkeys towards an Indonesian volcano at sunrise. We sailed down the lush line of the Nile, heard stories of the pharaohs, snorkelled in turquoise waters, visited European museums, heard great concerts in grand halls and went to all of my favourite Broadway shows. Dad would come back from frequent business trips with a suitcase of gifts we'd excitedly unpack; we'd wake up on Sundays to Chopin and Mozart;

and Mum would make sure each and every meal was special. I remember laughing as our spaniel raced around the garden pool in Jakarta, barking as my brother and I jumped in and gleefully splashed around. I would hide my hamster in my pocket so he could come to school. Once, I overheard a chef at the Hilton say he was going to cook the little rabbits in an Easter display, and surprised my mother by bringing a cardboard carton filled with eleven rabbits home with me. **I went to ten schools in six countries and lived in pink and blue bedrooms in mansions of different sizes. For the entirety of my childhood, I felt safe, happy and loved.**

This was a world of make-believe. I'd put all my toy animals to bed after making them pyjamas from paper napkins. I believed in Santa with my whole heart, leaving milk out for him and carrots for Rudolph for maybe a few too many years. With Rosa, our caretaker and friend, we built a wood-and-wire cage the size of a little house around a garden tree for a slow loris that we rescued from a crowded illegal Indonesian market. My brother and I had countless adventures. We set up a little room with a 'no adults allowed' sign on the door in a corner of our garden, where we brought a fruit bat with a broken wing, various stray cats and other wounded insects and animals until we could nurse them back to health, and then set them free. At night, we would play cassettes of scary stories that our nani would make up and record in her scariest voice and send to us wherever we happened to be in the world. After reading the book *Harriet the Spy*, we fancied ourselves as young detectives, looked everywhere for suspicious behaviour and eventually kept a minute-by-minute diary that tracked our driver's every move.

Perhaps it was the flux of colours that saturated my childhood, and the beauty that stemmed from experiencing a wide and wonderful world of possibilities open to my imagination, that made me a dreamer and a believer.

When I was made aware of the less idealized side of the world, I saw at the same time the people around me doing something to make a positive difference where it mattered. Mum was a speech therapist with a smile that immediately put everyone at ease, and would often have children with speech and other challenges come to our home; she would patiently correct their lisps and take them through exercises that would give them the confidence to emerge from their shells. Kids who had once been silent spoke. She read to us, and fostered a love for visual art. She loved people, made friends everywhere and was kind in almost every moment I can remember. Dad worked hard every single weekday, and often worked on Saturdays as well. He had huge responsibilities at Citibank and all the many pressures associated with them. But he always operated with staunch and spotless integrity and attempted to benefit the economies of the countries in which he was posted, as well as drive profit for the bank. Where many of his colleagues seemed distracted around their families, he was affectionate and involved with us. He demanded we both excel, especially in the arts, and consistently gave generously and unconditionally of himself to an extended family and many others who needed his help or sought his advice. There were so many other inspiring people around me. Mr Kachuba, my chemistry teacher, would come to class with stories of caring for Siberian tigers in his free time. Our Bahasa Indonesia teacher, the beautiful and elderly Ibu Malik, would always carry an injection with her to put seriously ill stray animals to sleep.

I started taking my own little steps when, at the age of twelve, I began spending my summers volunteering with children in orphanages and special schools. **We'd travel to India and I'd devote my days to a school for the blind and a school for the hearing-impaired. I'd return to the new academic year feeling disconcerted; something felt wrong with a world that had given children such differing opportunities. From dreaming of how the world could be, I started dreaming of how we could get there.**

At eighteen, an ordinary experience on an ordinary day was the catalyst for a sudden decision to withdraw from Tufts University in Massachusetts and move to Mumbai. **I was stopped at a busy Mumbai traffic light, one that I had been through a hundred times before, when three children ran up to my car window to beg for money. In that moment—for me now suspended forever—I knew that India's children would lead me down the path to discovering the greatest life I could lead.** After a long conversation with my parents, I set out to get myself admission to St Xavier's College. I was told I couldn't meet the principal, and that admissions had long been closed. I somehow still managed to sneak into his office through a side door and fervently blurted out to him in my confused five-country accent that I *had* to stay in India and do something for children. Father Emil D'Cruz was moved just enough to take the gamble and granted me admission to St Xavier's College, despite my average grades and it being three months into the academic year.

I started exploring Mumbai—going to police stations and into jails, walking around train stations and in the red-light district, visiting littered beaches and the sprawling slum communities. The Ambedkar Nagar community was an endless maze of alleyways where I found a girl named Pinky. She must have been six, and wore little white shorts with a dark brown ill-fitting T-shirt. She had bright oval kajal-lined eyes, exquisite and piercing with her potential. I remember wondering if that far-reaching dream I could see there so clearly would one day be realized.

That same day I walked past Sandhya's home in the community, and she stopped me with a smile, welcoming me into the tiny room that was her family's home. She introduced me to her grandmother, who was frail and had a wide toothless smile, and showered me with love. Sandhya taught me how to cook on a small gas burner, and then laughingly showed me how to wear a sari. Sandhya and I were both eighteen and so similar, but our lives could not have been more different. Her tiny home became my first makeshift classroom when a few children trailed in, asking me to teach them a few words of English. I was struck by how little the children seemed to know and how their world had been so completely confined to the community in which they lived. I was struck by their joy, energy and passion to learn. Like Pinky, each one of the children had eyes that were filled with the unmistakable evidence of their limitless potential.

Each day in the community, joy would collapse into despair, and would somehow put itself together only to fall apart again. Most days, I'd be welcomed into the community by smiling children squealing 'Didi! Didi!' when they saw me, but then, one day, as I entered I saw that fourteen-year-old Sunita was on fire and was screaming. She was severely mentally challenged and had been left at home alone. No one had ever taught her how to stay safe. I watched her die from her burns at a hospital fifteen painful days later. Nagesh had a growth the size of an orange on the side of his neck; I spent time with his mother, trying to convince her to take him to a doctor to examine what she was sure was a sign of the devil. I remember the happy delight in Sona's home the day that her little brother was born and then visiting a few days later to find the room dark—the baby had died from dehydration. I remember learning that a mother with fourteen children had incorrectly been giving her husband birth control pills.

After six months, **I went to visit my parents, who were now living in Riyadh, and sat alone in the large stone living room of the house; I asked myself if I could actually commit my life to working for children. The answer came easily for me, and I returned to India a few days later, sure of my choice and with a sense of purpose.**

Akanksha was founded on the simple belief that within India existed all that was necessary to give *all* her children the opportunities to meet their potential. India had over 300 million children eager to learn, millions of young adults who could be mobilized to teach, and all the resources required for coordination and support. There, in Sandhya's home, I had children ready to learn. All I needed was volunteers who wanted to teach, the space for classes and the resources to make this happen.

The start of Akanksha came with a flurry of hand-painted posters that my friends and I carried from room to room down the halls of St Xavier's College; they said in bold letters, 'You can make a difference.' The search for our first classroom led us through twenty schools, all of whom refused us for no good reason. We spent countless hours waiting in the charity commissioner's office to submit the documentation needed for our registration as a trust. We had a friend hand-draw our first sun logo, and remembering our own elementary school instructions, created rudimentary lesson plans. We then raised money from family and friends for our one expense—a bus to bring our new students to school.

On the first day of school, the fifteen children we had selected boarded the green-and-white bus parked outside the community. I was not prepared for the hundred-odd children that followed them—laughing, pushing each other, wanting so badly to get onto the bus. I remember watching a group of them as the bus drove away, standing and waving, some of them even hanging onto the back of the bus, having to hop off as it picked up speed, but still running after it.

Our fifteen children would come to class at Akanksha after a morning of standing in long queues in order to buy a bucket of water. They were responsible for looking after even younger siblings, and doing other labour-intensive housework. Some days were worse than others. Two of our girls, best friends, had their lives drastically interrupted when one of their mothers doused the other in kerosene and burned her to death, and got taken away that night to prison for life. There were many days when I would receive frantic calls from parents saying the bulldozers had come, unannounced, to demolish the illegal structures that were the only homes the children had ever known. **There were those days when our children would show us a painful welt where they had been whipped with a belt, or reveal a malicious burn from a cigarette. Despite all these devastating hardships, they'd come with their hair oiled and tightly pulled back, proudly wearing their bright, brand-new Akanksha T-shirts, smiling watermelon-sized smiles, bouncing with energy, ready to learn.**

My 4,000 children showed me that hope is the colour of transformation in the face of great difficulty. Sameena, whom I had taught when she was three, graduated from Sophia College and enrolled in a bachelor of education (BEd) degree programme for children with special needs. Vanita went from not speaking a word of English to studying in a top university and starting her own non-profit, Rangmanch, whose mission is to encourage the pursuit of the arts among low-income children in the community where she grew up. Renuka, who carried her dead mother to a hospital after her father threw a rock at her, moved to a top boarding school and graduated a confident young woman, ready to face life. Naheeda, whose elder sisters were married at thirteen and fourteen, co-founded Pragati, an NGO that aims to bring joy to children in government hospitals, and today works as an Akanksha teacher. Parveen, although from a conservative family, made her fiancé wait for three years to marry her, so she could complete college, earn enough money to secure a home loan and move her family out of the community.

Seventeen years later, **fuelled by what our children had actually achieved, my dream became bigger. If so much had already proved possible, we had to find a way to secure an excellent education for *all* children living across India.**

My search for the path towards this heady goal began with late-night conversations with friends; led me to Teach For America—whose ambitious vision was to achieve an excellent education for all children in America; and ended with the premise that to solve India's educational crisis we'd need a new generation of leadership committed to ending educational inequity and creating a system under which every child would receive an excellent education. I believed that if we built an army of bright young leaders committed to this vision, India could actually be redrawn for all of our children.

Through an engagement with McKinsey we explored whether a version of the Teach For America model could work in an Indian context. After three months of heated debates, replete with carefully researched and heartfelt exchanges, we had a blueprint and a unanimous hypothesis that Teach For India was indeed feasible. At the time we all felt pretty sure that Teach For India was a crazy idea. Our small starting team included people from Teach For America and Teach First. Together, we had to find schools that would believe in our ability to select, train and support brand-new teachers. We had to find more funding in our first year of operations than I'd ever raised at Akanksha. We were asking India's brightest, most passionate young people to spend two years teaching low-income students full-time, as part of a lifelong commitment to ending educational inequity. To most families, and arguably most of Indian society, this would seem like a poor choice after graduating from a top college or working at a reputed company.

It was like starting again from nothing. Our small team of six stopped to ask children in crowded low-income communities where their schools were. We had endless cups of chai as we explained our mission to their principals. **We made hundreds of presentations at colleges and corporations, asking young people, 'Are you ready for the greatest challenge of your life?' From an applicant pool of 2,000, we selected our first eighty-seven Teach For India fellows and our first thirty-four schools. Our fellows would teach 4,000 children in the first year of Teach For India.**

In our first five years, Teach For India would keep selectivity at between 5 and 7 per cent, growing from 87 to 910 Fellows, from thirty-four schools in two cities to 300 schools in six, from 4,000 to 30,000 children. Many of India's smartest, most driven people applied for the fellowship. Rakesh Mani left J.P. Morgan in the US, Kishan Gopal came from Tata Consultancy Services, Indira Aditi Rawat was a graduate from St Xavier's College, Srini Srinivasan relocated to India, leaving an eight-year-long job with Schlumberger. They all came to teach, but more fundamentally they came for India. Their fellowship began at the Teach For India training institute, where they immersed themselves in sixteen-hour days of learning, rigorously preparing themselves to be the strongest starting teachers for their students that they could possibly be.

Nothing at the institute could have quite prepared them for the world they were about to enter. Their schools had severely leaking roofs, bathrooms were often unusable and all had severely under-resourced classrooms. Their children often came to class after a night of abuse, or after having spent a sleepless night in a tiny room flooded with rainwater, or with a painful rat bite. **Fellows would be challenged to understand why a girl infant had been flung off a balcony, why a parent had put chilli powder in a child's eyes as punishment, why a student of theirs had died of a disease that was so easily curable. They would come with lesson plans only to discover they didn't have a classroom in which to teach, or that they would have to learn how to deal with a teacher in the next class who would beat her students with a stick.**

For two years, these Fellows took the arduous and exhilarating steps of learning how to become the teachers they needed to be to get their children onto a new and better life path. Classrooms were christened with names like 'The Explorers' or 'Champions', peeling wall paint was hidden behind brightly coloured wall displays that set ambitious visions and class goals for the children. Learning was student-driven, and opportunities were created in which students could be leaders. I'd walk into classrooms where children would tell me about the maths olympiad they were a part of, or say that homework 'just helps me get smarter'. I saw fellows give their mobile phone numbers out so their kids could contact them at any time of the day or night. School for our children was now a blend of values, academics, and exposure to a world they had never seen.

We began to see what was possible with *transformational* teaching. Nirali Vashisht's third-grade students grew from not knowing the alphabet to reading *Harry Potter* in just eighteen months. Avantika Thakur's third-grade student Tushar would explain in confident and precise English how excellence was his class value; he'd track his academic progress on a tracker on the wall, and talk to you about how Norah Jones was his favourite singer. Ragini Kashyap's fourth-grade students, who so recently could not speak a single sentence in English, staged a phenomenal production of *James and the Giant Peach*. At the end of two years, Gaurav Singh's grade four student Shazia proudly showed me her progress on the writing tracker from grade two to grade five. She pointed excitedly to the graph, exclaiming, 'I'm off the chart, Didi!' Shazia had bridged her achievement gap; she had surpassed her grade level and now would have the same choices that other children have. This was the colour of transformation.

The fellowship was only Act One. What the Fellows would be able to achieve in their lives after they left the fellowship would really get us to our vision of 'India redrawn'. **I started to visualize the problem of educational inequity as a complex puzzle—each piece could be defined as an area in need of leadership. As with any puzzle, the solution lay in the pieces coming together. Our alumni movement was based on the idea that Fellows would graduate and choose their piece in the puzzle, and then fit in with other alumni; together, they can catalyse a movement for change.**

Teach For India's 700 alumni now span diverse pieces of the puzzle— policy, corporate social responsibility, teaching, school leadership, media and others. They're all fervently determined to have an exponential impact on bettering the lives of children. They are opening schools for the most disadvantaged and starting teacher training institutes and other fellowship programmes. They are aspiring to enter politics, are on a path to joining the Indian Administrative Service (IAS), or are mobilizing resources from the corporate sector and entering consulting companies focusing on reform in education. Surya Pratap and Kanika Saraff have started the community-based school Re:Imagine; Prakhar Mishra has founded a rural fellowship programme called Youth Alliance as a step towards entering politics; Saahil Sood has stayed with Teach For India to spread the fellowship to Hyderabad and Ahmedabad. Arnab Thokder teaches in a school in a remote region of rural Sikkim, convinced that despite intermittent electricity and often freezing weather, his students will still make their way to college.

Across the world, this growing network of national movements spans thirty-five countries. Inspired by the Teach For America model, programmes range from Teach For China to Teach For South Africa. Around 15,000 Fellows and 30,000 alumni are working relentlessly every day all across the globe to achieve an excellent education for all children. The Teach For All network brings these partners together, enabling collective learning so that each of us can accelerate our impact.

Despite this, there remains a sinking awareness of how much more there is to do. The hope of an army of idealistic people charged with building a more equitable future is constantly juxtaposed against the reality of an education system where 61 per cent of standard three children cannot read at standard one level, 46.5 per cent cannot do two-digit subtraction with borrowing, and 90 per cent of children don't go on to college. Rote learning, where the focus is on passing exams and not on building concepts and character, is rampant. Too many classrooms are without a teacher, or with one who views learning through fear and physical abuse as the norm.

Grim demographic statistics tell us that Renuka and Naheeda, Nirali's student Faraz, and Avantika's student Tushar would have been among the 42 per cent of India's children who don't even complete an elementary school education. What does 42 per cent mean for each of those x million children? **What happens to a nation where nine out of ten children are not given the opportunity to meet their potential? What *economic* price does India pay for that? What is the impact on the social fabric of our country when 90 per cent of India's people feel they will never get an equitable opportunity to try to be their best?**

Twenty-four years into this work, I like to flip the equation. I dream about what India will look like when 100 per cent of our children have the opportunity to meet their greatest potential.

In my search for my own potential, I have tried to look into my inward mirror and live my life for a purpose that I know is larger than myself. My children have helped me see that people will, more often than not, live up to your belief in them. My children have shown me that there is immense power in little things. They have pushed me to try and think good thoughts, speak good words and do good deeds. I have seen from them that we, as living beings, are all so closely connected. I have seen that try as I may to focus on the way the world is, **I am by nature a dreamer and will always end up seeing the world that I wish for.**

The world that I wish for is a world where we refer to educational inequity in the past tense, as something that happened once upon a time. It is a world where we're maximizing our collective human potential, and in doing so, changing the world into a better place.

I know that a revolution of 'what is possible' has started because I have seen that the colour of transformation can overcome the shadow of despair, because the colour of hope is stronger than any desperate reality, and each day into the future brings with it a slightly brighter hue. Like Latif, as he spun across the stage in his coat of many colours, this revolution will depend upon each one of us peering deeply into our own inward mirrors to find our truest colours and rising together to a belief as clear as white—with all the tacit grit of brown, the energy inherent in ochre, the cool reflection of blue, the patience and surety of purple, the urgency of orange, the spontaneity of a tickling pink, the soft unrelenting wisdom of grey, the blood of red, the serene order of green, the thick conviction of black and a bright idea, of yellow, a sun-driven vision of India redrawn.

I believe that one day, the little boy you pass on the street outside the restaurant where you've just eaten and the little girl begging at the red light where your car is stopped will both attain an excellent education. *Every* girl and boy across our vast nation, all of them, will have the chance to be who they want to be. As all of them discover their own light, like magic their true colours will come to life. That will be a morning worth waking up for, in a kind, strong and peaceful, a more beautiful India.

◆

- Always ask why.
- See beyond what is visible.
- Think of the world as ours.
- Spot inspiration everywhere.

- Be ordinary and extraordinary.
- Look into the mirror, and ask what you can do about the world.
- Be gentle with yourself and others.
- Know that alone there is little we can do; that we must stay together.
- Dream, but do more than just dream.

SHANTI EKAMBARAM is president, consumer banking, at Kotak Mahindra Bank, leading a team of more than 12,000 people. She has repeatedly featured on *Business Today*'s 'Most Powerful Women in India' list and was awarded 'CA Woman Business Leader for 2014' by the Institute of Chartered Accountants of India; she was also named the 'Woman of the Year 2013–14 in Banking and Financial Services' by the Indian Merchants' Chamber's Ladies' Wing. In 2013–14, when the markets were sluggish, she helped Kotak clinch seventeen crucial deals worth over US$2 billion. Shanti is also a philanthropist at heart and lends her support to several non-governmental organizations (NGOs) working for various social causes.

From very early on, Shanti recalls having a deeply rooted ambition to be successful and financially independent in life. Since her primary interest was finance, she chose to get a bachelor's degree in commerce from Sydenham College followed by a chartered accountancy qualification. Her first job was with the Bank of Nova Scotia (BNS), where she met Uday Kotak, who was the bank's client. He convinced her to join Kotak Mahindra Bank in 1991, and she hasn't looked back since.

◆

Destiny's Child
SHANTI EKAMBARAM

It is said that ambitions start forming early on in life. I clearly recollect how, right from my schooldays, I wanted to be successful and achieve something. I come from a simple, middle-class family. From the beginning, my parents made it clear to my sister and me that a good education was critical and thereafter it was up to us to decide what we wanted to do. I grew up with middle-class values, such as being comfortable with the basics in life. Thus my aspirations were built on this foundation and I wanted to be financially independent. My values are at the core of my being even today.

I also distinctly remember wanting to do something in the space of finance. The memory of appearing for an aptitude test in the ninth grade is still fresh in my mind. On the basis of my results, my teacher suggested that I take up engineering, but I told her that I would prefer commerce. At that time, I had absolutely no idea what I wished to do in the area of finance or what banking meant, but I was convinced I could find success in this space.

Consequently, I finished my bachelor's degree in commerce from Sydenham College and pursued chartered accountancy (CA). Interestingly, **I got my very first job with Bank of Nova Scotia (BNS) by accident—I was standing in for a friend who got the interview call but had already got another job. As it turned out, the interview went off so well that they asked me to join the next day itself.** That is how my journey in the world of finance began—by default rather than design.

Starting your career at a foreign bank, particularly a small one where you can get all-round exposure, is always recommended. This is where you can learn to be a credit analyst as well as a relationship manager, and gain an understanding of treasury and operations. My early days at BNS were spent learning how the banking sector worked and eagerly lapping up all opportunities that came my way. Soon, I started wooing Kotak Mahindra Finance Limited (KMFL) for its bill-discounting business, finally bringing it into BNS as a client. This is when I met Uday Kotak, who preferred dealing with BNS directly at the time. I liaised with Kotak and, of course, Uday, for almost two years, for the most part haggling over interest rates.

When I finally decided that it was time to move on from BNS in 1991, I had offers from two other banks on the table. Confused, I went to Uday for advice. 'Since you deal with so many banks, which one do you think I should join?' I asked him. 'Why go anywhere? Join me,' he replied. He made me an offer on the spot, allaying my fears of working with a non-banking financial company (NBFC) after having worked in a foreign bank for so long. I had seen the passion displayed by the small team at Kotak and thought that, if it didn't work out, I could create a job for myself by becoming an entrepreneur. However, my family and friends were against my joining Kotak as they considered the move incredibly risky. After about four months of serious thought and discussion, I decided to join Uday after all, spurred by the hunger and passion he displayed every day, along with my own risk-taking appetite. I haven't looked back since.

In the rewarding twenty-four years (and counting) at Kotak, I have handled several businesses, many of which I have helped set up and grow. During this time, I have spent roughly an equal amount of time between capital markets and banking, devoting almost ten to twelve years to each. In the early 1990s, the Securities and Exchange Board of India (SEBI) was set up and Indian capital markets opened up to foreign institutional investors (FIIs). Taking advantage of this opportunity, we formed a strategic alliance with the US-based investment banking firm Goldman Sachs. This was my earliest contact with the world of investment banking and I had to quickly learn to deal with investors, equity research, mergers and acquisitions (M&As), private equity and, of course, the successful emergence of debt capital markets. In retrospect, I was very lucky to get that sort of exposure early in my career. I not only learnt the nuts and bolts of outstanding relationship management, client pitches, deal execution and team coordination, but also grasped the global standards of client management and product and execution excellence. This left a deep impact on me. Later, I adapted as many of these standards as I could to meet the requirements of our investment banking business.

During my early days at Kotak, we were the underdogs in the market, and markets usually do not tend to focus on underdogs. Hence, it was easy for us, as outsiders, to bring a differentiated approach to the table, build on it and make it successful. Of course, I cannot say that anymore as KMFL has grown monumentally and things are different now. Through the mid-1990s to the early 2000s, I enjoyed the highs of sealing deals and experienced great despair when deals were lost. My stint in the capital markets in the formative years of my career really helped me understand the complexities associated with doing business, the versatility and volatility of trade, as well as the impact of local and global factors. It also taught me how to handle failure along with success. From a very young age, I hated to lose and it was this competitive spirit that helped me navigate my way through pitches, initial public offerings (IPOs), and M&As, when we at Kotak were trying to build our now strong investment banking franchise. However, along with being hungry for accomplishment, I learnt that I had to accept occasional failure.

In 2003, KMFL received a banking licence, and I was given the opportunity to build the corporate banking business for the company. Capital markets had steadied by then and having spent close to eleven years in that sector, I decided to take up the new challenge offered to me. It turned out to be a completely new and different experience. While investment banking involved small teams working together on deals and a large dependence on individual contributions, banking was about large teams, processes, transactions and volumes. Initially it was difficult to adjust, but as the annuity revenues started building up I recognized the scalability of the business. Given my experience with deal-making, I brought focus to deal-based revenues in addition to the annuities business in the bank. Consequently, in the last eleven years, we have managed to build various business segments, products and, most importantly, an outstanding team.

However, **it seems like my risk-taking nature has not diminished with the passage of time. In April 2014, I was given the opportunity of taking charge of the consumer banking franchise of the bank. I have been an investment and corporate banker all of my life, with very little exposure to retail. Unlike in the past, though, I did not take a lot of time to make up my mind and accepted the offer almost immediately.** This, once again, has been a whole new world to me—particularly the digital phase that banking is moving into and the fascinating kaleidoscope of preferences across varying customer segments. It's early days yet, but I am hoping to make a difference in this sector.

I have often been asked if I have a mentor or someone who has influenced my life greatly. My answer is always the same: while I cannot point to anyone in particular, I am inspired daily by the people around me. I have seen ordinary people come up with extraordinary ideas and then go on to execute them in a spectacular fashion. I have always learnt from the people I work with—whether it is my team, my colleagues, my contemporaries or Uday himself. Many clients, too, have inspired me by showing a great deal of maturity in exacting situations.

I have experienced highs and lows at every stage of my career. The key is to learn from the highs, keep your feet on the ground and move on. What has kept me going, apart from the need to excel and win, are the challenges at every stage, which I have faced head-on. Moving from capital markets to retail banking was a particularly daunting challenge, but was also a completely different experience. Since I looked at the sector from a unique perspective, I brought different learnings to the table. The diversity of the work and the successes and failures I faced along the way have kept things interesting and provided enough fodder for thought during each stage of my career.

In terms of work ethic, integrity is one of the most crucial values I hold on to. I also prize passion, and believe in myself and the people I work with. **I think, if you really trust people and work with them, you can move mountains. I keep telling colleagues—you can do extraordinary things if you believe you can—and that is what drives me.** It is not possible to always succeed, so it is important to learn from your mistakes. You have to be happy with every small success; you must celebrate something every day.

As for leadership, it boils down to the following basic rules:

a) **Hire the best person for the job**
b) **Give people space**
c) **Have the ability to listen to your team**

You need to communicate your goals clearly to the team—what it is that you want to achieve and what you expect—and then give them sufficient space to achieve the set goal. Management books say that it is the ability to get the best out of people that makes you a good manager and I genuinely believe in that. Hence, effective communication, being a team player, a willingness to learn all the time, a commitment to applying the best practices, passion, sharing goals and visions and bonding with the team—these are the qualities that define a leader. You have to be perceived as being humble, involved and understanding, while asking the right questions. Only then can you nurture a team.

As I grew within Kotak, I faced several challenges along the way. However, none of them was because of my gender. I was always part of a team, always thinking, ideating and executing, and no one ever made me feel that I was different. What really mattered were competence, passion, the ability to think differently, teamwork and entrepreneurial skills. In fact, I viewed my gender as an advantage while trying to make a mark in the world; it was an asset rather than a liability. Hence, **I never really faced the glass ceiling. This is not to say that it does not exist. However, in my view, the problem is often exacerbated by women themselves by not having the confidence to push themselves forward, aspire, grab opportunities and take matters into their own hands.** The truth is that there are fewer women than men at senior leadership levels and you will always be working with and competing with men. Therefore, you need to display ambition and confidence.

Where finding a work-life balance is concerned, I think the situation is actually gender-agnostic. **We think that only women have to balance work and life, but men have to as well.** In my view, a work-life balance means different things to different people and each one has to identify what the ideal means for him/her. This is because a work-life balance is not just defined by you but also by the ecosystem and social structure that you live in. Some people have a strong family support system; for instance, I have been very lucky as my parents live with me. They have been my anchors and are there for me while I try to maintain my busy schedule. However, not everyone has such support. The most important thing is to define what a work-life balance means to you. If your definition points towards working five days a week and spending two days with your family, then ensure this happens. If you want to put in more hours at work, then stick to your decision and do not crib. If the circumstances around you change, adapt accordingly. At the end of the day, it is all a state of mind. I have always been very clear about the fact that if I take up something, I must make it a success. I fine-tune the rest of my life to accommodate my interests. For example, I am into fitness, so I dedicate an hour at least four days a week to working out. I spend at least one day a week with my family and I also enjoy watching movies and meeting friends. In fact, work itself is sometimes destressing; instead of running away from an issue, focusing on resolving it can be very energizing.

In the end, ensuring that I create time for activities I like keeps me going. It is true that those with successful careers will spend predominant parts of their life at work, so it is up to them to try to create a kind of equilibrium in their lives. **For women in particular, I would like to add that they should not attempt to be superwomen and have it all since that is not possible.** When you create a framework, but you are not mentally committed to it, it can result in unhappiness and failure. Do not get troubled by discussions about finding a perfect work-life balance. Instead, learn to live your life as you see fit and enjoy every moment. If something stresses you out too much, change it or opt out of it.

◆

- The qualities that make an excellent manager are effective communication and the ability to listen; the aptitude to recognize the 'weakest link' and the ability to work on it; the capacity to admit to mistakes, learn from them and remain open to making mid-course corrections; humility and passion.
- It is not how much you earn but what you do with it that creates wealth.
- Money must be allocated across debt, equity, real estate and other asset classes based on each one's appetite for risk.
- If something seems too good to be true, it probably *is* too good to be true.
- No risk, no return.
- The first five to ten years of your career must be spent in learning and strengthening your foundation. If this is not solid, it will be difficult to strategize effectively when you take on a higher role in the organization.
- Money will follow; do not chase money alone.
- Focus on excellence, no matter what you do.
- Learn how to handle both success and failure. Do not be afraid of failure and do not go overboard when you are successful.
- Value your team. It is all about people.
- Trends change faster than you think; you constantly need to think ahead of your times.
- Finally, your biggest competitor is yourself. Work every day to excel at your job and you will find success.

One of the best-known faces of Indian television, **SHEREEN BHAN** is a committed business journalist and news anchor. After completing her education at St Stephen's College, New Delhi, and the University of Pune, Shereen worked for the who's who in the media, from Siddhartha Basu to Karan Thapar. Finally, in the new millennium, she began her stint at CNBC-TV18, and since then there has been no looking back. Today, Shereen is the managing editor of the channel, and also the recipient of multiple awards including 'FICCI Woman of the Year' (2005) and 'Best Business News Anchor' (News Television Awards, 2013); she also regularly features on lists of the most beautiful women in India!

The daughter of an Indian air force pilot, who led a childhood of itinerancy, Shereen says she's still constantly on her toes! She writes, 'I can't really claim to have a work-*life* balance; my challenge is to balance all the work!'

◆

The Newsmaker
SHEREEN BHAN

Holding onto a metal handle for support, pulling myself up with every ounce of strength a seven-year-old could muster, I would clamber into a truck—a seven-tonne, as we would call it. Without a care for flying skirts or prying eyes, I would clutch the sides of that massive chunk of metal for dear life. Not once did I feel fear. This is how I'd go to school across different air force stations, from Halwara in Punjab to Jamnagar in Gujarat.

As the daughter of a fighter pilot in the Indian air force, change was the only constant. Every two years, we'd pack up our lives in steel trunks, say teary goodbyes to friends and make our way to our next stop to start afresh. I saw very early that adaptation is essential to survival. I learnt to cope with new teachers, new classrooms, new hierarchies of house captains, prefects and class monitors.

Through those years, I learnt another important lesson—the present is what matters, the past is history. So began the process of proving myself over and over. Each time I'd push myself, I'd confront fresh vulnerabilities that I would have to compensate for, and also new areas of strength. Consequently, my childhood was marked by a variety of pursuits—theatre, dance, writing and music; sports was a natural weakness. Unconsciously, I was making choices that would help me trace my future.

Never once, through those years of exploration, was I made to feel different because I was a girl. I skated on tar roads without worrying about bloodied knees, and scampered up trees to build makeshift dens where I would imagine new adventures every day. My mother was a homemaker and an entrepreneur—she very successfully started her own human resource (HR) consultancy once we moved to

Delhi—and, along with my father, taught us that marriage isn't the only goal in a woman's life, and being a girl is wonderful! Indeed, there are stories of how my sister—who, today, has her own dance academy in San Francisco—was handed most apologetically by the nurse to my parents when she was born; the nurse expected them to be upset at not having a boy but, much to the nurse's surprise, my parents beamed! Such acceptance cut across generations; my grandparents and the extended family treated women as equals—so much so, my father's mother drove around in an Ambassador without a care in the world!

The world I had inherited as a child was simple. We appreciated everything our parents could provide us and waited with stars in our eyes for our aunts and uncles from overseas to fly in with goodies. The excitement and envy a bag of sketch pens or a bar of Toblerone would produce may seem odd to today's children, but for us, such things were magical novelties. In hindsight, I realize that I grew up in a cocoon—a safe and relatively equal environment where one's gender, bank balance and zip code didn't matter. All that counted was ability and performance.

Then came New Delhi, and high school—a wholly different set of experiences that pushed me out of my comfortable bubble. Suddenly, where I went to school mattered, what I wore drew attention and who I hung out with established my standing in the social circuit. I navigated my way through my new surroundings and this entirely new set of tacit rules with a mixture of confidence, fear and trepidation. The cycle of learning and unlearning started again, but this time my choices were largely driven by the need to fit in and stand out, conform yet remain visible—not an easy balance to strike, least of all for a teenager! I tried to get noticed by showcasing my strengths. I attempted developing my leadership skills. The truth is, as I made my way through adolescence, the mechanics of the animal kingdom became only too obvious; I understood the import of Darwin's theory of survival of the fittest!

In hindsight, I wish I had let my hopes dictate my choices and not my fears. I decided to opt for science in classes eleven and twelve, not only because I thought I wanted to be a doctor but also because that is what all the really smart kids did. Fortunately for me, my aunt is one of Delhi's leading gynaecologists and I decided to spend time at her nursing home after my class ten Board exams. I soon realized that medicine was not for me; I didn't have the stomach for blood nor the strength to cope with loss. So I gave up my desire to be a doctor—but my fear of being judged by my peers stopped me from exploring the possibility of arts or commerce. I stuck it out with science, even though I had decided to abandon the only real reason I had for pursuing it.

Even as high school ended, the search for a college began. By now, I was sure that I wanted to do something creative, and so began the rounds of Delhi University and the impatient scanning of cut-off lists. I fell in love with the iconic St Stephen's College instantly, but it wasn't easy to enter its portals. Up against a couple of hundred people vying for just seven seats, I knew the odds were stacked against me. I desperately hoped I would make the cut. And as luck would have it—I was selected!

College exposed me to a different world altogether, a world driven by ambition and achievement—the college café burst at the seams with students talking about giving the Rhodes or Inlaks scholarship a shot, appearing for the common admission test (CAT) or studying for the civil services. With my nebulous dreams and uncertain ambitions, I must have felt inadequate, but the environment also compelled me to really find myself. I started to nurture the idea of getting into advertising or making documentary films; I joined the herd filling out applications for postgraduate courses outside India; I even signed up for campus placements. Caught in this mad frenzy of activity, college ended in the blink of an eye.

I waited for the results, still unsure about the exact path my future would take. Happily, the future opened itself out, almost serendipitously. My mother told me she had heard from a friend of hers about a communications course offered by the University of Pune. On a whim, I secured the forms. I liked what I saw and decided to apply. I got in.

Pune was my first real shot at being independent. I pushed myself to do things I would have earlier been too self-conscious to do. I sang in a band, acted in a film made by a graduate student of the FTII (the revered Film and Television Institute of India), taught an aerobics class and did voice-overs for C-DAC (the Centre for Development of Advanced Computing). I was on a mission to truly find myself.

It was in this phase of fresh confidence and self-discovery that I met Siddhartha Basu and Anita Kaul Basu, the founders of Synergy Communications and the brains behind several good-quality English shows. They took me under their wing, offered me real responsibilities and allowed me to explore the world of television—for this, I will be forever grateful. One of my tasks as an intern working on a current affairs programme, *A*

Question of Answers, was to prep the audience, get them into the groove and engage them in banter to calm their nerves. I pretended to run my own little chat show. I asked questions, provoked and prodded and made novices feel comfortable before the camera. Vir Sanghvi, who was the anchor of the show, saw my drill a few times and told me I was a natural for broadcast journalism. This was it—the turning point of my life. I realized I had a sense and smell for news.

In the months that followed, I graduated top of the university and walked right into a job with one of India's best-known television journalists, Karan Thapar. This was the story from the outset—I was spared the disappointments that newcomers are known to face, and was able to work with the best and brightest. Early in my career, I worked as a producer with noted journalist Tavleen Singh and actor-turned-activist Nafisa Ali. Then came TV18 and its founder Raghav Bahl. He was planning to launch a political channel. I don't know what Raghav saw in me, but a day after I met him, he called me back, put me into a studio with three in-house reporters and asked me to anchor a show discussing the Bhartiya Janata Party's (BJP) economic agenda. My heart was in my mouth, but I did it. The rest, as they say, is history. CNBC-TV18 has been my life for the last fifteen years.

◆

I love what I do, am passionate about what I create, am fiercely protective about my team and have a deep sense of ownership towards the brand that I work for. This makes even the hard days—and believe me, there are plenty of them—seem worthwhile.

I've also been blessed with some of the best mentors in the business—from Raghav Bahl, my former boss, who has always believed in me and offered constructive feedback, to Karan Thapar, who taught me to be absolutely thorough and check facts at least fifteen times! Karan would say, 'You are not here as an interviewer on a fishing expedition. Do your homework well and then ask pointed questions.' These are words that hold me in good stead even today. Outside the tiny world of the news media, I have found a mentor in the founder of Infosys, N.R. Narayana Murthy; I am lucky to know him personally, and have borne witness to his grace and humility.

Along with passion and firm mentorship, my professional life has been shaped by long hours of very hard work. I doubt I would

be where I am had I not pushed myself to do more, embraced new challenges and said yes to every assignment. The fact is that I work eighteen-hour days. When I began my career in the electronic media, I'd start at the crack of dawn and trudge on well past midnight. Nothing has changed since. To date, my day starts at 6.30 a.m. and I leave work only after anchoring my 10 o'clock show at night. There are no holidays—if I expect my team to work weekends, I have to be around as well. **I don't operate as a diva—walk in, get my make-up in place and anchor; I am with my co-workers in the trenches.** Some hours are spent with the reporters, some chairing interviews and events and some editing scripts and planning. I produce all my shows myself, do my own research and am there right from the stage of conceptualization to post-production—*Young Turks*, for instance, initially planned as a thirteen-episode programme and now in its fourteenth year, is a show I research, produce and anchor.

Given my schedule—mornings, afternoons and nights are spent fulfilling professional commitments, and I am always either going somewhere or returning—I can't really claim to have a work-*life* balance; my challenge is to balance all the work! In such circumstances, managing a home single-handedly is a huge challenge; there's little space for ancillary pursuits like music; movie nights or family get-togethers are rare; and one's social life is restricted to the workplace. Over time, friends and relatives have stopped inviting me to functions altogether, simply because they know I won't make it!

Having said that, I do make a very sincere effort to reach out to those who are close to me—a lazy Sunday brunch with family and friends is such joy!—but outings of this nature are by no means easy or spontaneous. I also try engaging with the little things I view as essential—reading Indian fiction, or just cleaning my home—on the rare weekend that is a holiday. But 'me-time' is an absolute luxury, not unlike the Toblerones I used to covet as a child. And as for extended vacations, I almost never get to take them!

At the end of the day, **if I manage to keep long hours at work, it is only possible because of a good support system of family and friends.** The last fifteen years would not have been possible without the unconditional support of my parents. My mother continues to be the chief supplier of good food and good sense in my life. She is also my chief fashion consultant!

◆

I have always been hard on myself. **I feel the need to prove myself every day. I wonder if this is a function of being a woman; if, at a subconscious level, I have a heightened sense of being judged and evaluated every minute; if, despite working in the electronic media, known for an open work culture, free of gender prejudices, as a woman I am programmed to self-scrutinize.** In my own career, people have, at times, focused on 'appearances' to the exclusion of all else—so I've had to work doubly hard to ensure that my craft speaks for itself. I don't enter a studio or leave for an interview without doing my homework thoroughly, and I do not give my guests the opportunity to question my credentials.

I do think women work differently—apart from overanalysing their career graphs and pushing themselves relentlessly, they look beyond strictly professional matters and tend to engage with their staff at a personal level. On my part, I am told I have a tendency to mother people! For instance, I worry about the safety of my young team members if they get home very late, and remain apprehensive about how they will report early the next day and meet deadlines! Male bosses, I suspect, may be quick to dismiss such concerns, but women bosses will reach out and sympathize.

As employees, women are unlike men in that they don't always assert themselves. In my own career, as I've worked my way up the organization, I have, at several points, been uncomfortable asking for what I rightfully deserve. I have not always stood up for myself, dreading confrontation and unnecessary attention. I have not bandied my achievements, for fear of being perceived as brash and pushy. **To date, I have not been able to have a real conversation about my compensation; I feel that talking money will make me seem aggressive or greedy. These are inhibitions that several women at the workplace have; it's wired into the collective unconscious.** But if there's one thing I've learnt, it's this—in every relationship, at home or at work, we need to be clear about what we want, draw boundaries and communicate candidly. I agree with Sheryl Sandberg's argument that women need to lean in a lot more. But equally, organizations need to empower women so they feel encouraged as decision makers.

◆

- Don't be a prisoner of your circumstances. Challenge yourself; you may be surprised.
- Hard work and patience are non-negotiable. As a young professional, you might get impatient to taste success. But success is known to arrive slowly, and only once you serve your time, get your hands dirty and multitask.
- Have a sense of purpose. As a professional, you can get caught up in the here and now, in the daily grind of earning money or seeking career advancements, and forget what inspired you to opt for an occupation in the first place. You need to keep your core values in the foreground, your priorities, what I refer to as 'business chakras'.
- Don't pigeonhole yourself and dabble in the same set of operations. Break the mould; be as versatile as possible.
- Most jobs are tough, and they only get tougher, both physically and mentally, as you climb the proverbial ladder. Learn to handle pressure.
- In all professions, being a team leader is vital. But so is establishing a rapport with people outside the immediate work environment, and maintaining relationships.
- There is nothing glamorous about television. A large part of a television journalist's job is back-breaking work—standing around for hours to get a twenty-second sound bite or waiting for interviews in the sweltering heat of Delhi, or staying up all night for just a potential conversation with a source. You need to swallow your pride every single day! The glamour begins and ends with short hair and make-up sessions before entering a studio; the rest of it is strenuous labour.

SHOBHANA BHARTIA wears many hats—chairperson and editorial director of the Hindustan Times Group; pro-chancellor of the Birla Institute of Technology and Science (BITS), Pilani; and an erstwhile member of the Rajya Sabha (2006–2012), during which time she introduced the Child Marriage (Abolition) and Miscellaneous Provisions Bill 2006. Besides, she is also a daughter-in-law, a mother to two children and a wife. If she manages to do it all, it is by being a stickler for punctuality.

In this, Shobhana is very much the daughter of her father, Krishna Kumar Birla. It was with his tacit encouragement that she started work at the media empire. With her nose for news, keen business sense and love for innovation, she made the newspaper professional, consumer-focused and profitable. Not surprisingly, this Padma Shri winner regularly features among the most powerful women in business (*Fortune*, 2011; 2012).

◆

The Paper Baroness
SHOBHANA BHARTIA

When visitors walk into my office, they inevitably notice a range of newspapers fanned out on a table. This is, perhaps, the most meaningful introduction to me. For **I am, first and above all else, a news enthusiast.** My morning begins with a perusal of the stories of the day—those that are breaking, and those that are tucked away in the inside pages—and a close reading of my own newspaper's front-page reports before they are sent to press. This quest for news is more than a habit, an obsession—it is the cord that connects me to my father.

Indeed, when I look back at my early years in Calcutta, I recall that despite coming from a family of entrepreneurs—my grandfather, Ghanshyam Das Birla, was an industrialist who invested in textiles, cement and chemicals, and my father, Krishna Kumar Birla, headed fertilizer combines, sugar factories and of course, Hindustan Times Media—dinner-table conversations were rarely about commerce and money. Rather, my father discussed current events, politics and the state of the world at large. During breakfast, no matter where my father was, in India or on a holiday abroad, he would have his office compile a news digest and read out the most interesting or pertinent nuggets to us. Conversations such as these widened my childhood universe. **I did not need to rely on imaginary friends or worry over petty triflings. Rather, I had more interesting diversions—my world was peopled with the newsmakers of the time, and I was concerned with the larger upheavals confronting the country.** Besides, I had the added advantage of being the primary object of my father's attention—despite having two sisters, I was, for all practical purposes, an 'only child' since my siblings, older than me, had married and moved away by the time I was twelve.

My father's retelling of the affairs of the country always struck a chord deep within me. **At the age of fifteen, I was so overwhelmed by my father's account of the floods in Orissa that I felt compelled to contribute to relief efforts in my own little way.** I spent long hours mulling over the quickest and most efficient means of making a difference. Finally, I gathered an enthusiastic band of friends, made tiny handicraft items, sundries and knick-knacks, and sold them to indulgent (and generous!) relatives and well-wishers. We raised much more than we had dared to hope for—one lakh rupees. My father was especially proud of our philanthropic zeal. When I asked him how I was to dispatch the contribution to the Prime Minister's Relief Fund, he took me directly to meet Indira Gandhi and hand over the cheque!

Given my interest in breaking stories and my deep involvement with current affairs, I suppose my destiny had been chalked out before I had had a chance to seriously consider the future. I may have dabbled in setting up a boutique with my sister, and may have sought temporary diversions to occupy my restless spirit, but my calling was one industry alone: the news media.

◆

In 1985, when my father announced that I, the youngest of his three daughters, would be joining his media empire, it surprised everyone in the family. However, I knew that my heart lay in journalism, and I was willing to weather questions and criticism. Besides, I had faith that my family's alarm would make way for encouragement once I proved myself.

What I was less prepared for was the response I received at the workplace. **I was viewed as a young, cossetted inheritor of a father's empire. Worse, the general belief was that I would be a passing sightseer—that I would dirty my hands a little, tire in a few days and leave. Most pervasive of all was the general air of condescension when I, a woman, assumed a position of authority.** And then there were those well-entrenched unions that opposed everything I believed in. There were so many prejudices and preconceptions to dismantle that I didn't know where to begin!

What saw me through was the fact that I have always avoided being complacent and riding on my father's hard-earned achievements. This must be a direct offshoot of my upbringing. When I was a child, instead of enrolling me in a local Birla-run school, my parents sent me to Loreto

House, a convent school where my surname was no advantage. I had to work as hard as any other student to build an identity for myself—and this held me in good stead in the future. Even today, I believe that **there is greater value in securing a professional break or advancement by working hard than in snagging a post by flaunting a name. Besides, while the former is permanent, the latter is as fickle as the times we live in.**

Therefore, I put my best foot forward—in hindsight, a wise move. While bigotries are deep-rooted, hesitant respect can only be earned by working hard and introducing innovation. I began by spending six months each in various departments—circulation, sales and editorial. Half a year may not be enough to become proficient in a sector, but it gives you a broad appreciation of the backroom toil and enterprise that build an organization.

I also sought an appointment with *The Washington Post*, went to the United States and met the publisher, Katharine Graham, to gain insights into the international market and how best to manage a brand. This foray was important since back then, the Indian media was incestuous; there was a common pool of editorial and managerial talent, and no fresh perspectives. I needed to hear a new point of view and interestingly, Katharine Graham offered exactly that; the meeting came with several moments of epiphany. **I learnt that while in the West it had been years since manual technology had been abandoned, in India we were still wrestling with column galleys that had to be physically pasted before being printed**; while global media organizations studied their readers and targeted them, in India there had been no such market analysis, and there was little synergy between the product and its consumers; while Katharine Graham was committed to producing a newspaper that was aesthetically sound, in India we were all too quick to make excuses for crooked columns and fading ink. There was much that needed to be changed.

In the months that followed, **I decided to reorient *Hindustan Times*, and make it profitable, professional and consumer-focused. This was easier said than done. For, *Hindustan Times* wasn't just an ordinary enterprise—it came with a formidable history.** It was at Mahatma Gandhi's behest that my grandfather got involved with the newspaper in 1924; Gandhiji's son, Devdas, had been the first editor; *Hindustan Times* had been the voice of the freedom struggle and a new independent India. How, then, could one approach it with a motive as base as profit; how could we presume to tinker with its design and content;

what need for a young, fresh, vibrant news digest, when there were grave issues to cover?

These would have been entirely valid questions had times been different, had liberalization not changed the demands of India's consumers. I remember spending hours with my father and senior employees and defending the need for change—be it through innovative advertising or colour pages or lifestyle supplements. In each instance, the first response would be of reluctance. I'd be told that innovative advertising would destroy the sanctity of page one; colour would vitiate the seriousness of the paper, make it a comic book; supplements on food and fashion could hurt the gravitas associated with the brand. While my father himself adopted the best practices in his fertilizer and sugar businesses, any alteration in the 'business' of newspapers worried him. However, **what option did we have but to pursue new revenue models? What could we do but keep pace with the times and reinvent ourselves? After all, the writing on the wall was obvious: survive or perish.**

So it was that, setting aside all opposition, *Hindustan Times* innovated. By early 2000, after we had spent more than a decade working together, my father asked me to run the newspaper empire. This was, by far, the best testimony I could have received.

◆

In a career this eventful, one is bound to learn from the glorious highs and from those unexpected failures. Some of the most significant insights I've gained concern the concept of leadership.

I believe **leaders display flexibility and the willingness to innovate and embrace transformation.** The inimitable Bernard Shaw said, 'Progress is impossible without change, and those who cannot change their minds cannot change anything.' When *Hindustan Times* was launched, as I've mentioned earlier, it was viewed as a symbol of anti-colonialism, rather than a news daily. However, time moved on, and we had to match steps with it. We had to redefine ourselves as a profit-oriented and profitable venture. And that's exactly what we did.

Equally, **leaders are responsible for identifying talent, then trusting their teams.** For me, personally, the model that holds the greatest appeal is a mix of traditional family-run mentoring and new-age professional practices. This is how *Hindustan Times* is managed, in any case. When I was asked to take over in 2000, I was clear that a professional (such as a chief executive officer [CEO]) would run all business operations; my job, as the promoter, would be to identify talent, create an environment to groom it and evaluate the performance of my team. As the promoter, it's important for me to step back and allow the CEO to take charge. Daily interference will only create friction and will upset any professional bond that could develop between us. Equally, it's imperative to create an atmosphere conducive to raising concerns and voicing dissent. Most of all, a promoter should never do anything that could undermine the position of the CEO. Anyone who tries to bypass the CEO, and reach the promoter directly, should be discouraged. It is for the promoter to ensure that the authority of the hired CEO is established. If a promoter cannot see herself doing that, she should run the business herself!

I believe that **leaders give some, take some, meet midway.** While introducing innovation, you must remember that change affects people, sometimes adversely. As a leader, you need to listen to the fears of your employees, empathize with their concerns and try safeguarding your vision, even while securing their interests. Often, this means meeting your colleagues halfway. I remember, at *Hindustan Times*, it took a while to introduce new printing technology; the fear was that such innovation would make people redundant. After considering all points of view, we made an open offer to our employees—we said that that we were willing to train them so they could operate the latest of machines. However, if they failed to transit successfully, or did not wish to involve themselves with industrial advances, they could retire under the voluntary retirement scheme. This eased some nervous tension.

A corollary is—**operate transparently and there will be little dissent.** If employees know you're concerned about their remuneration, work hours and job environment, and are working with them for their overall satisfaction, there's less likely to be an 'us versus them' situation.

Most importantly, **leaders know that mistakes are inevitable and that they must learn from past errors.** Any business owner who says she knew exactly how her organization worked on day one is lying. It is through trial and error that you really get to learn how a business functions. In my own instance, I recall our ambitious television venture not quite succeeding. We were to launch Home TV. We had the first-mover advantage; we had even managed to tie up with the best global partners. Despite everything aligning on paper, the endeavour fell through. In hindsight, I can spot all the errors—there were far too many partners in the venture; decision-making wasn't streamlined; and the channel had been positioned as a niche undertaking with highbrow entertainment, but little content for the masses. One must learn from such errors in judgement. Home TV may be an opportunity lost, but I've come out of it so much the wiser.

Ultimately, I think **this is the age of coopetition. We no longer live in an era where we can afford to isolate competition. We need to work with our 'rivals' to reach out to a larger range of people.** In my own way, I broke tradition by partnering with Bennett, Coleman and Company Limited to launch *Metro Now*, a morning tabloid in Delhi. Similarly, in 2002, when foreign investors were permitted to buy up to 26 per cent in local newspapers, we struck a deal, selling a 16 per cent stake in HT Media to the private equity firm, Henderson Global Investors. Further, we partnered with the *The Wall Street Journal*, and inked the *Mint* agreement in a record four months.

◆

At any given point, I've found myself with multiple commitments. There's *Hindustan Times*, of course; then there were duties to fulfil as a Rajya Sabha member; besides, I was also involved with the functioning of BITS, Pilani (founded by my grandfather). I also pursue fitness and believe in taking care of my health. I'm often asked how, under such circumstances, I make time for my family and play the roles of a daughter-in-law, mother and wife.

There is no easy answer to this question. To begin with, when my father expressed his inclination to have me at *Hindustan Times*, I had two very young boys. **My mother, a steadfast presence in our growing years, unwavering in her commitment to rearing us, reminded me, in her usual cut-and-dried, pragmatic style, of my responsibility towards my sons. Therefore, in deference to her wishes—and also sensitive to the validity of her stance—I worked on a half-day schedule for a few years, primarily with the *Hindustan Times Sunday Magazine*.** I remember, back then, even while at home and attending to my toddlers' demands, I'd scan all the newspapers, mark out those articles that may have been missed by my father and send him cuttings.

Once I was in the thick of my profession, I came to depend on the silent support of my husband. I also realized the need to imbibe one of my father's finest qualities—punctuality. When I was a child, my father was notorious for maintaining a daily plan for everything—so much so that even our time together would follow a definite schedule, and I was strictly told not to ramble. **I used to complain about my father's regimented calendar, but today, I realize that it's the only way to juggle multiple obligations. Like him, I, too, have become infamous as a stickler for punctuality. Like him, I don't keep people waiting and would not wait for people either.**

◆

As is evident, my father is my role model, not only because he instilled in me my love for current affairs, but also because he remained deeply spiritual, even while engaging with the world of business. When he'd write notes to the family, he'd always include a verse from the Bhagavad Gita, often to emphasize a point that may otherwise have been overlooked; when he'd interact with people, he'd follow the principles of the holy book. The Gita formed the bedrock of his morality and therefore, everything he did was transparent and sharply defined. However, what made him especially remarkable was his capacity to engage with all forms of wisdom, to distil the essence of each philosophical path without privileging one or the other. After his demise, when I went to his room, I found not only his beloved Bhagavad Gita by his bedside, but also the Bible and the Quran. When we speak of India's secular spirit, my father epitomized it.

All told, he made me the person I am.

◆

- Be passionate, even obsessed, with your area of work.
- Do not rely on a family's legacy or a surname; do not be content basking in the reflected glory of your parents' achievements. Carve an identity for yourself and chart your own professional path.
- Seek out mentors and consider their advice in all humility and seriousness.
- Do not be afraid to transform a brand, if the times demand such a move, or ask for innovation.
- You will make mistakes. This is fine, as long as you learn from them.
- Leaders display flexibility, operate transparently and trust their teams.
- Consider working with your rivals instead of isolating them.

One of the foremost women to serve in the Indian civil services, **SUDHA PILLAI** was appointed as member-secretary of the Planning Commission in 2010 in the rank of minister of state—the first woman to hold this office. In her four-decade-long career she has also served as union secretary of labour and employment and in the ministries of industry and corporate affairs. She was also the first woman to be appointed as principal secretary finance in the government of Kerala.

Born in Simla, Sudha was educated in Chandigarh and is a second-generation working woman. Having decided early on that she was meant to be an Indian Administrative Service (IAS) officer, she strove for excellence from the very beginning, securing a gold medal in her bachelor's and master's courses, getting an all-India second rank in the IAS examination, and pursuing a degree in public administration from Harvard. All though her career, Sudha focused on getting things done and made significant contribution to policymaking and implementation. Married to batchmate and former home secretary, G.K. Pillai, she is a mother of two and lives in Delhi.

◆

The Development Activist
SUDHA PILLAI

I am a second-generation working woman. My mother, who was born in Dera Ismail Khan (now in Pakistan), had begun her career as a schoolteacher at the age of twenty. She was a bright student and her father sent her to Lahore and Simla for her school and college education. **The fact that we had a working mother profoundly influenced my sister and me while growing up—we both expected to work when we finished our education.**

After the country was partitioned, Simla became the capital of Punjab. Both my parents worked for the state government, so they moved from Lahore to Simla. I was born in Simla on 1 May 1950. We shifted to Chandigarh in 1954, where I lived until I left for training in Mussoorie in 1972, after I got into the IAS.

When I was about seven years old, my mother told me a story about a time when I was a baby. One evening, according to her, as she sat with me on her lap in the garden of our home in Simla, a passerby, claiming to be an astrologer, told her that I would one day handle the affairs of three districts. This, translated into bureaucratic language, meant becoming a divisional commissioner. Astrology has not played a big part in my life, but this statement really affected me in some way. It boosted my self-confidence and made me more focused.

The atmosphere at home encouraged honesty, hard work and achievement. My father was a graduate of Forman Christian College, Lahore, and had master's degrees in English and public administration. He was, additionally, a scholar of Persian, knew thousands of Urdu ghazals and wrote books on public administration, some of which were cited by the likes of the Swedish Nobel laureate, Karl Gunnar Myrdal. In bureaucratic circles, he was acknowledged as an authority on local self-government matters and had a reputation for impeccable integrity. At home, my father was loving and engaged, earning our devotion and adoration. He was fond of telling stories at the dinner table, and taught us the importance of values through these tales. We always wanted to impress him and earn his praise; in our own way, we were aware of the fact that our parents were greatly respected. Apart from their wisdom and hard work, it was their courage and optimism that inspired me.

One very important factor that gave us a sense of well-being was my parents' faith in the future. They did not dwell endlessly on the trauma of Partition. The future beckoned us in the brand-new city of Chandigarh. I loved going to school. I still vividly remember my first day in nursery class. When I turned five, I was admitted to Senior Model School and was, along with two other children, promptly given a double promotion. This meant that I was almost always the youngest student in class through my schoolgoing years.

It was when I was nine or ten that I decided that I would try to join the IAS. I remember attending the school's annual day programme in the auditorium where, along with other students, I went up on stage to receive my prize from the director of public instruction, Serla Khanna (later Grewal). I even remember the name of the book I had won—*The Hungry Stones* by Rabindranath Tagore. The fact that my last name was also Khanna made me identify with her, albeit in my own childish way.

Childhood was not, however, only about studies and ambitious plans for the future. We used to play outdoors a great deal, read voraciously, eat both ripe and sour mangoes and mulberries in the summer, buy candy from J.B. Mangharam's and cakes from Bakewell, and hand-churn mango ice cream. Winters were gorgeous and Diwali meant several days of fun. I also enjoyed painting and, for my sister and me, buying a box of Reeves Tube Colours was enormously exciting.

The example set by my parents—the time and effort they invested in our education, their commitment to their professions and the stories at the oval oak dining table—moulded my values and taught me the meaning of sincerity and commitment, both in my personal and professional life. In very subtle ways, our parents taught us to focus on achieving excellence in our own work, to mind our own business, to be free of envy and greed, to respect others' views as well as others' belongings and, above all else, to say 'please', 'thank you' and 'sorry'. These internalized values were hugely liberating and helped a great deal while dealing with the far-from-ideal world that I got to inhabit for the next forty years. Of course, my teachers, both at school and college, left a deep imprint on me, but if I were to recall my happiest times, these would be going to the Central State Library in my teens with my father, and casually talking about Aldous Huxley and Bertrand Russell, Francis Bacon and Oliver Goldsmith, Henrik Ibsen and Jane Austen, Aleksandr Solzhenitsyn and Maxim Gorky.

◆

Both Punjab (to which I was originally allotted) and Kerala (where I shifted after marriage), moulded my work ethic early on. **When I began work as an assistant commissioner (under training) in Patiala, I was dismayed by the huge stacks of dusty, musty files I saw in cobwebby offices. However, village 'attachments' and close encounters with the problems villagers faced—and the simplicity, graciousness and robust common sense that helped them retain their dignity in the midst of deprivation and injustice—motivated me to push the system to solve their problems.** In Trivandrum (now Thiruvananthapuram), where I was posted as sub-collector, I felt emotionally integrated, despite (or perhaps due to) the fact that I was learning Malayalam at the rate of ten words per day from my office staff and petitioners. I have very vivid memories of all my postings which, though quite diverse, have had one thing in common—the need to keep up sustained, unremitting pressure to move things along. This has meant keeping an eye on the stacks of files and having zero tolerance for delays.

Teamwork and the fact some of the best ideas come from 'junior' staff help create bonds of affection and mutual respect in a vertical hierarchy. The fact is that there is no room for exaggerated ideas of one's own importance and one excellent value people can imbibe is taking their work seriously without taking themselves seriously. Another important element of my work ethic was creating conditions that would encourage integrity. This meant surprise inspections, a quick identification of those either slightly or fully compromised, a concerted attempt to proceed swiftly to pre-empt corrupt moves, along with an effort to pursue government court cases properly. By following these basic rules, serious procedural flaws could be avoided. Many years later, I was reading a book called *The Men Who Ruled India* by Philip Mason, which talked of the need for civil servants to ensure that they did nothing that would be contrary to 'public interest and private honour'. This concept really appealed to me.

The issue of integrity is really very simple. It is absolutely essential to—but not enough for—good governance. Taking integrity as the starting point, one should be working to achieve organizational goals. In other words, the need is to fully utilize support systems to produce the required results, to deliver the goods and, to use a cliché, be fair and just. All this may sound impossibly idealistic but it is not.

At Harvard—where I went at the ripe old age of thirty-five to do a second master's degree, this time in public administration—I took a course called 'equity in rural development policy'. **A statement that the professor made in class hit me with the force of a sledgehammer. According to him, the really needy have no access. They have to be sought out and are usually found in remote places. That very year, as district collector of Trivandrum, I learnt how true this statement really was.** The sixty-odd petitioners who came to my office every day had serious problems that needed urgent solutions. However, there were many more people who were invisible and who lived too far away and had no money to travel to the district headquarters. More importantly, they had no idea that they had any entitlements at all. Their poverty was stark and their lives a grim struggle for survival. The need for empowered village communities and accountable local governments could not be denied.

Apart from this realization, some other factors that began to define my work ethic were the urgent need to avoid a waste of time as well as public resources. **Delays caused cost overruns and distortions. Avoiding delays meant training oneself to be clear, concise and prompt; making clear recommendations; and taking decisions. This also meant discouraging adjournments, postponements and time-wasting tactics.** Fortunately, I had no problems with this approach over the years. My working style had two important personal and socio-psychological outcomes. Many of my junior colleagues told me that they enjoyed the experience of working with me and witnessing the fruition of their hard work. Secondly, it enabled me to go home happy every day, having had the satisfaction of getting pretty tangible outputs.

A result-oriented working style also enabled me to earn a reputation as a person who solved problems and helped people. It gave me the moral authority to say no to proposals which were undesirable, without being called names. I remember feeling that I was doing well, that I knew how to use the power attached to the position legitimately and that I had the aptitude for the kind of work I was required to do. In fact, I have had a great time in all my postings. So, in a way, my decision to join the IAS was a good decision after all, and I feel grateful for having been given the chance to learn so much and finding work that was so challenging.

◆

Leadership for me has meant the ability to forge a team and create a working environment where the desire for individual fulfilment works in tandem with the need to achieve common goals. A leader has to ensure that the goals to be achieved are socially desirable and that they truly represent the remit of the organization. In other words, **leaders have to ask their teams—what business are we in? It is the leader's job to ensure that her organization does not forget its own work and chase tempting distractions. As a matter of fact, a lot of our problems in governance arise from the usurpation of the roles of other, usually less powerful, entities.** Finally, the leader is, at heart, a kind and considerate human being who makes a team feel valued. I can look back and confidently say that I have seen several of my senior colleagues as well as ministers being great managers as well as inspiring leaders. I was lucky to have worked with such people.

The astounding fact is that when one is determined to put in that extra effort to get a desired outcome, life becomes very easy. Expectations at work begin to change—and in a very positive way, at that. Recently, I came across a very interesting formula in a presentation made by a young professional. According to her, **when implementing plans or schemes, it is important to look at the IOOI: that is, the input, output, outcome and impact. We sometimes feel very satisfied when inputs have been supplied and think that our job is done. It is for the leader to push the envelope and ensure that focus is maintained on the desired impact.**

◆

When I look back at my life so far, I realize that I was able to work and have a healthy family life because my husband helped at home. There were a couple of very hard years when we were in Delhi and had to rely on the childcare centre run by the Indian Council for Child Welfare at Deen

Dayal Upadhyay Marg. There were none of the sophisticated childcare provisions that we see in the government now, no crèches in any of the bhavans and no five-day week. We never had the courage to leave our children alone with domestic help. Our second-hand Ambassador car was a real gas guzzler, whose engine was forever being tuned. When we first set up house in the city, we had no gas connection. We had a Nutan stove that needed constant tweaking, but it didn't seem to matter. We managed to cook, even for friends and family members. Indeed, in spite of all these hardships that we laugh about now, our memories of those days are very happy because of our two adorable kids, our love for our jobs and a group of fantastic superiors. There were no files to be carried home. In fact, due to their sensitivity, this was strictly prohibited.

As sub-collector and district collector, you do get huge bundles of files tied in green cloth. I handled these when the children went to sleep. As a rule, I have never kept a file for more than twenty-four hours and have tried to clear them in the office itself. In fact, bulky bundles of dak and seventy to one hundred files a day was the norm in my last posting, but mostly these were dealt with during the working day. In general, I remember having a very lovely time with my children at different stages of their lives. They must have needed me more on certain days, of course, but they knew that they mattered the most and their parents could drop everything to rush to them. I don't know if I managed to strike a balance between my home and work life each day, but my most precious memories are of my two very young children helping me bake chocolate cakes and having to be bathed thereafter; of the frequent trips we took together to the local park as well as to Connaught Place; of picnics in Lodi Garden and, once, even a tonga ride in Chandni Chowk. I hope they, too, remember those days as much as they might remember having to study hard. The nice thing about being a parent is that you do not superannuate and can also hope to be around for your grandchildren.

Finally, I can say that my senior colleagues never expected me to do badly in my professional life. I relied upon good time management and hard work to justify their faith. I can also say that a helpful attitude at work, empathy and a sense of fair play are very important for success in one's career.

As far as your family is concerned, it is what makes your world go round. In the ultimate analysis, **children desire a feeling of security and need to feel loved, respected and cared for. They need good education and good food, and a sense that they are your number**

one priority. They also need discipline, which is why parenting is the most enduring, complex and meaningful profession in the world. The best contribution you can make to society is bringing up your children with love and complete dedication.

◆

- Be sincere and truly commit to all that you do, be it at home or at the office.
- To be a good leader, make an effort to really listen to your juniors.
- It is important to not take yourself too seriously.
- Integrity must be the starting point of your work; efficiency and performance orientation have to follow in quick succession.
- It is important for your team to know what the goal is and achieve it by working together. Train yourself and your team to keep a goal in mind and take quick decisions to minimize a wastage of time.
- Make space and time for your family; they are the most important people in your life.

SUNITA NARAIN is a writer and environmentalist and has been with the Centre for Science and Environment (CSE) since 1982. She is currently the director general of the centre; the director of the Society for Environmental Communications; and publisher of the fortnightly magazine, *Down To Earth*. In 2005, she was awarded the Padma Shri by the Indian government. She has also received the World Water Prize for her work in the space of rainwater harvesting. In 2005, she chaired the Tiger Task Force at the direction of the prime minister, to evolve an action plan for conservation in the country after the loss of tigers in Sariska. She was a member of the Prime Minister's Council on Climate Change as well as the National Ganga River Basin Authority, set up to implement strategies for cleaning the river.

Sunita Narain began her work in the early 1980s, as a co-researcher with Anil Agarwal, an eminent and committed environmentalist. In 1985, she co-edited the State of India's environment report, which highlighted why environmental issues in India are so important for the poor. Sunita has been committed to building the capacities of the CSE so that it can function as an independent and credible institution, influencing public opinion and advocating change.

◆

The Crusader
SUNITA NARAIN

To write about your own life is always a difficult task, but if you are a journalist and activist like me, then it is even more so. Over the years, I have trained myself to explore the outside world, to understand what is going wrong and what needs to be done to fix the problem. My task is then to identify the people working on seeking these solutions and taking their work to policy and practice. So, writing about my life and work is closely intertwined with writing of the problems that we, as environmentalists, confront and the answers we push for.

It is also a fact that bringing change is not easy. The problem is not that there are powerful interest groups that we are battling. The problem is that we are opposing conventional thinking and ideas of what is right and what is not. We can only succeed (and that, too, with great difficulty) if we maintain a single-minded focus on what needs to be done next. While doing so, once again, it becomes difficult to think of personal 'achievements' or milestones. It is a journey, nothing less. There are no pauses.

But let me try to think back on what has defined my own journey. How did I get to where I am today? Who gave me inspiration? What gave me the drive and passion to make a difference?

I grew up in a privileged world of knowledge. My grandfather, Sri Krishna, was an eminent journalist with a keen interest in gardening—an interest my mother, Usha Narain, shared. Hence, his house, located in New Delhi's busy Jantar Mantar area, was a maze of plants and books. When I look back upon my childhood, I realize that my own desire to protect the natural environment and to use knowledge as a tool for bringing change stems from these memories.

I was only eight years old when my father, Raj Narain, passed away while on a business trip to Europe. My mother was left with four daughters—of whom I am the eldest—to bring up. Against many odds, she took up my father's handicraft export business. Over the next decade, she provided all of us with the best education and fulfilled all our wants and needs. Today, when people ask me how I face difficult situations at work, I think only of the strength it took my mother to overcome the challenge of bringing up four daughters single-handedly. And it is important to remember that she did all this without the advantage of convention—it was against the norm for a widow to work at the time. She worked anyway, and without fear. It is for this reason that **I have always rejected the idea of gender disadvantage. My mother, and many other women of her generation, have shown us how much they were able to achieve despite the overwhelming odds stacked against them.** In fact, my mother gives me the inspiration to do much more with my own life—it would be a disservice to her life to do anything less.

◆

When I passed out of high school in the early 1980s, the environment was hardly an issue of public concern. It was certainly not a profession or space that my friends thought of joining. Yet, conversely, this was also the time when environmental issues had reached the global arena. In 1972, the world conference on environment had been held in Stockholm. India's then prime minister, Indira Gandhi, was one of the few leaders from the developing world who attended it. It was also in the 1970s that news had come of a movement in the remote Himalayas where women had hugged trees to protect them from woodcutters. The 'chipko' movement, as it became known, brought consciousness of how the environment was important for the very poor.

In fact, my involvement with the environment began with this movement. While in school, I happened to go to a conference being held at the Gandhi Peace Foundation in Delhi to discuss the 'chipko' drive. There, I met two other students from different Delhi schools who had similar interests. We joined hands to form a student organization in the field of the environment called Kalpvriksh—the tree of life. Our work together took us to the women of chipko. As we travelled through the Himalayas I began to see the connection between livelihoods and the environment. I still vividly remember asking why a particular patch of forest had been kept intact in the small district town of Chamoli and being told that women protected it because it was the only place that they could use for their early-morning ablutions. They needed privacy—something I took for granted—and trees were their curtain. The lessons I learnt during that trip have stayed with me all these years.

A year later, I met Anil Agarwal, who had just founded CSE and was beginning to attend to an ambitious project called the State of India's Environment (SOE). As I began working with him, I realized that the environment was about development. **For millions in India, the environment was not a luxury—something to worry about after becoming prosperous. The environment was about survival. People depended on it—on land, water and forests—and, without it, poverty would never be eradicated. I learnt that rejuvenating this natural asset was the way towards better economic growth.** This gave me the motivation I needed to pursue this work.

Those early years with Anil taught me a lot. When Rajiv Gandhi set up the wasteland development board to make planting trees a people's movement, Anil, who had pushed the idea, wanted to understand how this natural regeneration could take place. So we travelled to the villages where communities had come together to build a green future. There I saw the difference that the efficient management of natural resources could make to people's lives. (In India, forests are mostly owned by government agencies, but it is the poor who use them.) Anil and I quickly learnt to look beyond trees and at ways of deepening democracy, so these resources could be regenerated. **It became clear that without community participation, planting trees was not possible. For people to be involved, the rules for engagement had to be respected. To be respected, the rules had to be fair.**

This initiation helped me understand the challenges posed by climate change as well. Around the same time, data released by a prestigious research institution in the US completely convinced our then environment minister that it was the poor who contributed substantially to global warming by doing 'unsustainable' things like growing rice or keeping animals. Anil and I were pulled into this debate when a flummoxed chief minister of a hill state called us. He had received a government circular that asked him to prevent people from keeping animals. 'How do I do this?' he asked us. 'Do the animals of the poor really disrupt the world's climate system?'

We were equally foxed. It seemed absurd. Our work told us that the poor were victims of environmental degradation. Yet, here they were, painted as villains in the story. How?

With this question, we embarked upon our climate research journey. We began to grasp climate change issues, and quickly learnt that there wasn't much of a difference between managing a local forest and the global climate. Both were common property resources. What was needed, most of all, was a property rights framework which encouraged cooperation. One, **the world needed to differentiate between the emissions of the poor—from subsistence paddy or animals—and those of the rich—from, say, cars. Survival emissions weren't—couldn't—be equivalent to luxury emissions.**

Two, it was clear that managing a global common meant better cooperation between countries. As stray cattle or goats are likely to chew up saplings in the forest, any country could blow up the global climate agreement that was being negotiated if it emitted beyond what the atmosphere could absorb. Cooperation was only possible if benefits were distributed equally. This is where our grass-roots experience came in handy. We, at the CSE, developed the concept of per capita entitlements— each nation's share of the atmosphere—and used the property rights of entitlement to set up rules of engagement that were fair and equitable. But in all this, **we told climate negotiators to think of the local forest and learn that the issue of equity is not a luxury. It is a prerequisite. When I look back, this battle, based on moral principles but shaped by science and numbers, helped prepare me for future challenges.**

◆

In January 2001, Anil lost the long battle against cancer. I had already begun running the CSE a few years prior as his health had deteriorated, but the task ahead was formidable. How would I sustain the high quality of the organization's work without him? It seemed impossible.

Soon, I learnt to draw upon the ideas, perspectives and courage that he had instilled in me to perform my role. I will never forget how, in his last days—in fact, the day before he died—I was with him in Dehradun while trying to handle our campaign for clean air that was ruffling a lot of feathers in Delhi. The government had released the auto-fuel policy report, which debunked our advocacy of compressed natural gas (CNG) as the fuel that could clean up air. Despite his failing health, Anil gave me advice on how I should handle the issue; I cannot forget how, even in his last moments, he remained engaged with and committed to our cause. His passion keeps me fearless and motivated about my work even today.

My task was also made easier because colleagues who had worked with Anil and were steeped in his values stayed on at the organization.

But he was hard to replace. A formidable personality, he embodied the environmental consciousness of the country. How would the CSE continue to make a difference?

Then two things happened in quick succession in the early 2000s, and my ability to manage and lead was truly tested.

First, our work on cleaning Delhi's air was rapidly gathering momentum. In 2002, our campaign for the right to clean air reached its peak as the Supreme Court accepted our demand for a transition to CNG. But the transition happened with great difficulty. **Every time there was a court hearing, a CNG bus would mysteriously burn. It was part of the effort to prove that the solution we were suggesting was unviable. To argue our case effectively, we had to do in-depth research, seek technical responses from experts and build a public case for our issue.** It was difficult to explain why clean air was important for our health. It was even more difficult to convince everyone that the solution, untried across the world, would work in India.

But we did. The CNG transition happened. Delhi could see stars once again, as the air quality improved. It helped me understand that Anil had left behind a powerful institution, which had to keep making a difference.

The second campaign came to us by chance. We had just set up a laboratory to test toxins in water and food. One of our first efforts was to check for pesticides in drinking water. Samples were collected from different parts of the city and checked. But we found no common trend in them. So, when my colleagues showed me the results, I said, why don't we check bottled water? It seemed logical.

So, that's what we did. The results were shocking. **There was a cocktail of pesticides in each bottle of drinking water. But why, I asked? It was then that my training as a journalist came in handy. It was my job to question the results, find the answers.** My colleagues visited drinking water plants—posing as election agents for key politicians— to check if the water on route to the politicians' rallies was potable. They collected samples of the processed water and raw water, and we ran our tests again. Now the pieces fell together. The pesticides had come from the groundwater that had been bottled, and the companies had never tested or cleaned it. When we released the study, it led to a furore. Eventually, the Bureau of Indian Standards (BIS) agreed to change the quality standards for packaged drinking water and tighten the rules for pesticide residues.

But this was merely a trailer to what would happen when we'd test soft drinks and beverages for pesticides. My trial by fire happened when the government set up a joint parliamentary committee (JPC) to investigate our study. This was the fourth such joint parliamentary committee ever—after the Harshad Mehta, Ketan Parekh and the Bofors deal scandals. We had no idea how to respond to it.

It may be clichéd to say that such life experiences hone our skills. But these **adversities helped boost my courage to work and, because we could not afford to lose, build my desire for excellence. We had to ensure that we got it right the first time. There was no place for half measures or shortcuts.**

Hence, my colleagues and I prepared furiously for the JPC. We worked to convince the group of fifteen members of Parliament of our position, and we countered information that the other side presented. Finally, we got a report that not only vindicated our study but also gave recommended policy reforms in the area of pesticide management and food safety.

In retrospect, this challenging three-year period—between January 2001 (when Anil passed away) and January 2005 (when the JPC published its report on colas)—defined me and my role at the CSE. When I took over, I was hesitant, worried about how I would cope with the expectations of those I worked with and for. But **the two 'battles' not only forced me to think on my feet and work with my colleagues but also compelled me to lead from the front. They were not easy problems to tackle, but they helped me accept the strain of working in the public domain and for public interest.** I knew that if I went wrong—even if I erred in a single public response or fact—it would come at a heavy cost.

Another instructional moment came when I was first insulted during a tough no-holds-barred interview with a prominent TV editor of the time. The accusation was that I was not highly educated and so, had to be wrong when it came to the tough scientific issues concerning pesticide residue testing and analysis. This was followed by the allegation that I was doing this either for publicity or money. That was the day **I truly learnt that public scrutiny is tough and merciless, and I needed to be prepared for it. Ultimately, though, I understood that what really mattered was the message we were trying to spread—not just through the words we wrote but also based on how we wrote them and who we were.**

◆

I started work at the CSE when I was untrained and inexperienced—about twenty years old and just after I had completed my studies. I was new to the field of the environment, but I was hungry to learn. I also had the advantage of working in an organization that was young and small at the time (there were just four or five people employed full-time at the CSE then). So **I had no choice but to learn to do everything—from marketing to sales to even postage. I believe this was an invaluable experience. It made me much more than a writer, and prepared me for taking on the management of the institution. Learning from my mistakes is what has shaped my career.**

My first leadership challenge came when I was still a greenhorn. We had suddenly grown in size—new funding had led to new employees at the CSE, who brought with them different organizational cultures from the corporate world. We were still small, and mostly informal and unstructured. I realized, through many difficult interactions, that organizational cultures are very important. I remain concerned that, as it grows, the CSE will become 'institutionalized'—not a particularly good thing in our field. We need to remain committed to doing the work we do, but how do we do this and still build systems of management that ape corporate governance? How do we remain 'angry' but still worry about performance and schedules?

The most important thing, I believe, is to keep the institution's focus on its mission—why we are doing what we are doing. In this way, the organization becomes the means and not the end. So, yes, we need an efficient internal management system that is geared towards high performance and impact, but it not our only goal. I believe that it is important to build a sort of 'hybrid' culture, that is, a culture with the belief structure of a non-profit with the discipline of a corporate, so that we do not waste time with needless personnel problems. The organization also has to be outward-looking, even as it works efficiently and adheres to deadlines.

Hence, the CSE has built its existing systems of management keeping this in mind. We have tight internal systems for personnel and programme management but, at all times, the objective is to stay focused on the why. What we do is designed to achieve the outcomes that we have jointly discussed and decided upon.

This is not easy. We work on the interface between action and policy. Our work is to drive that ever-ephemeral thing called change, which is not easy to measure or verify. It is also clear that while we need highly skilled people to work with us, they need to be equally passionate—mad, in fact. But our academic training does not combine these two traits. So our effort is to ensure that qualified staff knows the 'why' and understands that our objective is to make a difference in the policy and practice of the environment. The CSE has over 150 people working for it now, but we want to remain a high-impact institution, hopefully for a long time.

I strongly believe that the only way we can succeed is if we remain an 'outlier' institution. We cannot conform to the common idea of what a research or advocacy institution should do. Instead, the CSE should be nimble in ideas and action—not unlike guerrilla movements—and yet be structured in thought and output.

My own contribution to the evolution of the organization is to ensure that I remain a thought leader who drives the culture of impact and influence. I am very fortunate as my senior colleagues have stayed and grown with me and we can run the CSE as a collegiate. This is obviously not easy, but **I believe that leadership is never asserted but accepted without fight or fuss.**

The future, I think, will be much more of the same for me. I believe that India faces a huge challenge in trying to reinvent the way it manages growth so that it is both inclusive and sustainable. We cannot afford the high-cost ways of the already developed world to clean up our environment. These countries had the money to invest in cleaning and they did. But because they never looked for big solutions, they always stayed behind the problem—local air pollution is still an issue in most Western cities, even if the air is not as black as ours.

In India, we want to emulate the already rich countries and their disastrous ways, with much fewer resources and much more inequity and poverty. The fact is, we cannot find answers in the same half-solutions they invested in. This is our challenge. We can do things differently to redefine growth without pollution, but only if we have the courage to think differently. This is what the real fight is about: changing the idea about the idea itself.

◆

I am often asked if I get scared while taking on big interests working against the environment. It is true that our work requires us to raise tough questions, but it does not mean that we are

adversarial or at war with the other side. I strongly believe—and explain precisely this to my colleagues—that we have to remain committed to our convictions, but we must equally stay open to the ideas and positions of others. We cannot, and should not, personalize our issues, but instead look to the processes and institutions that need to be reformed. This helps us maintain our perspective, but it also allows us to stay an honest institution. So, the courage it takes to fight against polluters—however powerful—comes from the conviction that we are not doing anything wrong.

Does being a woman make this fight even harder for me? The fact remains that I work in an extremely male-dominated industry, particularly since I am required to leave the softer world of activism and, armed with scientific knowledge, enter the hard world of business and government. However, the honest answer is no. There is no doubt that I have to work harder to explain myself, to constantly prove my credentials and worth. But it is also clear that this has worked to my advantage—when I know that a task will not be easy, I cannot take it for granted.

This is not to undermine the fact that most women find it really tough to break the glass ceiling. But it is also a fact that **many of us have the privilege of working in creative and open environments where we are accepted as equals and allowed to achieve our dreams. This is not a small luxury. We need to celebrate it and find ways of expanding the space for others to be able to do the same.**

Where finding a work-life balance is concerned, my work usually takes up my life. But this does not mean that I do not enjoy life. I do. I run, I swim, I read and I (hope to) travel. But I have to confess that what drives me primarily is the passion for my work and my belief that I can do something that will make a difference. As I get older, though, **I often think of the way my mother lived her life to the fullest and it makes me want to do more to get the balance right between work, family, and friends.** I cannot say that I have got it right yet, but there is still time.

◆

- Believe strongly in what you do. This will give you the motivation you need to pursue your ideas and make them a reality.
- Learn from your mistakes.

- As a leader, it is important for you to convey to your staff the reasons guiding a certain task. This improves output and efficiency in an organization.
- Have the courage to think differently and challenge the norm.

VIJAYALAKSHMI IYER took over as chairman and managing director of the Bank of India (BoI) in November 2012 after an illustrious career in banking. Her portfolio includes several years spent working for the Union Bank of India and a couple of years as the executive director of the Central Bank of India. She has won several awards for her exemplary leadership and initiatives, including the Skoch Group Financial Inclusion Award and the Golden Peacock Award for women achievers.

As one of seven children in a middle-income family, Vijayalakshmi had to study commerce out of necessity rather than interest, since her father could not afford to send her to a medical college. Soon after graduation, she joined an electric company for a measly sum of money to support her family and continued to pursue her postgraduate course in the evenings. She got a job at the Union Bank of India soon afterwards, and while she continued to rise at work, she suffered a severe blow in her personal life when she lost her husband to cancer in 1997. With the help of her two daughters and mother-in-law, however, she picked herself up once more and reached new heights in her career.

◆

The Inclusive Banker
VIJAYALAKSHMI IYER

You don't choose your family. They are god's gift to you,
as you are to them.—Desmond Tutu

I was born into a family of four brothers and two sisters living with all the travails typical of a Mumbai household—nine members occupying a (barely) 500-square-foot apartment, where making ends meet every month was no mean feat.

Despite this practically Dickensian situation, my parents ensured our childhoods remained optimistic and peaceful. For my father, a great stickler for values who treated his sons and daughters on a par, the priorities were straightforward: to give the best possible education to his kids and instill indispensable lessons in honesty and hard work. He strove every day to fulfil that goal. Playing a perfect second fiddle, my mother kept the family intact and in great shape. My mother and father worked in absolute harmony with each other in every sense.

My parents took special care to engage us so that we never felt the need for excess. Perhaps they could afford none. I fondly recall playing cards or carom at night with them; moments of togetherness during those evening hours that each of us relished. My early schooling, meanwhile, was normal, if not extraordinary. We looked up to our eldest sister who, besides being beautiful, was an outstanding student all through her school and college life. An MBBS (medicinae baccalaureus and bachelor of surgery) gold medallist from the University of Mumbai, she set the bar high for the rest of us, creating a competitive spirit among us during our formative years. Where I was concerned, my triumph lay in topping my school in the Secondary School Certificate

(SSC) exams, despite never having secured the first position until class nine.

As a leading light of the South Indian community, my father was philosophical and spiritual but never orthodox in his views. He started meditation centres, dance and music classes, and even invited other scholars to enlighten us. His social work extended to founding schools and developing housing societies for our community. For me, my father was my role model in everything I did. Thus, his passing away in October 1985 at the age of sixty-seven was a tremendous personal jolt to me; it took me a year to reconcile to this loss.

Family compulsions, rather than acute personal interest, dictated my choice of commerce as a curriculum major. I had modelled myself on my elder sister who chose medical science, but my father was helpless and didn't have sufficient funds. He, however, did the next best thing—he inspired me to take up commerce which, he believed, had greater employment prospects. I readily conceded, and have had no regrets.

Without concrete career plans, I completed my graduation from ML Dahanukar College of Commerce, Mumbai. All I wanted was employment immediately after my graduation. By then, my father's basic responsibility of running a large family had become onerous. Hence, I joined a private sector electric company for a measly monthly salary of ₹250 and pursued a postgraduate course in the evening.

One day, when on a routine stroll with my parents, I walked into the college premises, only to notice that the Union Bank of India had invited applications for the posts of clerk and officer. However, the last day of application was the very next day. I realized that I met all the eligibility criteria and, moreover, getting a bank job was considered a status symbol in those days. I applied, confident about my ability to get the job. However, on the day of the written test, things went terribly wrong: my mother was hospitalized due to a severe migraine attack and I lost my way en route to the examination centre, only to reach the venue an hour late. I was in tears.

However, destiny stood by me; the exam began behind schedule due to the late arrival of question papers. There, I virtually took my first step towards a long and distinguished banking career. I strove for perfection in everything, leading to greater responsibilities. In fact, I scaled many defined points in the bank's hierarchy in just a few years, a rarity in a public sector bank (PSB).

◆

While opportunities came frequently at work, my personal life began unravelling—my husband was diagnosed with carcinoma in the lungs. His doctor's diagnosis shrank not only his lifespan (to three months), but also my world of happiness; I confronted total emptiness. He was just forty, a father to two lovely daughters, aged twelve and nine. As he was undergoing a very painful cancer treatment, my family stood by me to lessen my trauma. He survived another twenty-two months, only to succumb to the inevitable on 22 January 1997.

I was devastated and felt completely at a loss about my future. Sensing my extreme misery, my mother-in-law stepped in and bravely guided me through my duties in life, especially towards my children. I am proud to acknowledge her immense contribution to my life; I owe every bit of my success to her. I also acknowledge my daughters, who handled the vicissitudes of life well and ably supported me through my life's critical decisions. **The lessons I learnt from my loss were plenty; as they say, when life knocks you down, let your reason get you back up. We need to become wiser and emerge stronger from every experience in life.**

It was Hippocrates who said, 'Healing is a matter of time, but it is sometimes also a matter of opportunity.' While on a recovery path at work and in my personal life, the Reserve Bank of India's (RBI) initial circular on risk management in 1997–98 came as a key break in my career. Given the heightened focus on risk in the banking system, the RBI insisted that risk management functions be overseen by a competent person who would not be subject to normal transfer policies for a period of at least seven years. The mantle fell upon me to set up an integrated risk management department at the Union Bank—an opportunity that ensured not only a prolonged stay in Mumbai but also a greater balance in my career and family life.

In banking, setting up a division has its own challenges—more so while starting a risk management department. However, I had a chance to frame various risk policies, processes and systems to identify, measure, monitor and manage risk in all aspects of banking. The sheer magnitude of the task called for close liaising among various functional heads, field functionaries, and regulators. Aligning the business's interests with practical planning was highly critical.

I had a free hand in designing and developing the blueprints for training programmes in risk management. With utmost care and concern, I ensured that these programmes were designed in line with the needs and expectations of the bank as well as the regulators. **The most gratifying moment came when the RBI judged the Union Bank's Internal Capital Adequacy Assessment Process (ICAAP) documents as the best among all PSBs. For me, it was well-earned success; the risk management department was usually at the receiving end of criticism, and I felt singularly happy to have won recognition both from within the organization and outside for the department I had set up.**

My stint in the department was eventful, productive and rewarding. I waded through uncharted terrain, gauging the true spirit of a new technical subject that was gaining currency worldwide. I learnt that taking ownership of a situation helps shape our behaviour and priorities.

Recognizing my contribution to risk functions, I was elevated to the position of deputy general manager of information technology functions, and later made the general manager for both the risk and information technology departments. I had the mandate of automating operations of the bank in all its 4,000 branches. Parallely, we brought in alternate channels of banking such as automated teller machines (ATMs), point of sale (POS), Internet banking, etc. We relentlessly endeavoured to set up training programmes for improving the business potential of these new channels and teaching people how to leverage new technology. **I realized that a well-defined strategy, coupled with a supportive team, could institute even mega projects within defined timelines.** These challenging and stimulating roles, spanning six years, significantly added to my career's all-round growth. Looking back, I consider these assignments the milestones that put me in the limelight, as very few individuals in the banking sector had such diverse expertise at the time.

◆

In September 2010, I was made executive director of the Central Bank of India. Headquartered in Mumbai, the bank was known as a 'tough bank' to work in and my assignment was considered 'difficult' in industry circles. Theoretically, an executive director's post is second in a bank's hierarchy, but in practice, the role is not well defined. In the initial few months, as a member of the board and various committees, I got a sense of operational issues, developmental problems, systemic flaws and a lack of team spirit in the organization's working culture. I comprehended why industry circles called the bank 'tough'.

In the Central Bank, there was large-scale disagreement within the management and office politics was rampant; back then, the bank was struggling with performance issues. Customer confidence in the bank was on a serious decline. **The need of the hour was building a cohesive senior management team and reinstating the bigger objectives of the organization. Often, I had to stand up for these objectives. Being a woman with an adjusting nature helped me bring together the various factions within the senior management.** This in turn enabled me to bring about the desired change in the work culture across the credit, risk, treasury, human resource and information technology departments. One of the most satisfying outcomes of this overhaul was achieving the desired connect between the headquarters and field offices. Employees at all levels began to feel more comfortable discharging their functions effectively. Even though it was difficult to lead from a secondary position, I was able to kindle passion and drive among our employees, so together we could work towards the organization's goals.

To stop and reverse the decline in customer service, I sought a technology-centric solution that also improved the bank's retail orientation. I became instrumental in rolling out core banking solutions across all branches on a fast track. In less than two years, the bank was invigorated and displayed technical prowess. The initiation of various structural, operational and motivational strategies steered the overall re-engineering of the bank's operations, besides enhancing its ability to face the challenges of the future.

My greatest discovery at the Central Bank was that building human capital and realigning it, so each entity would communicate in the same language, was not just imperative but also highly critical for business survival. There has to be a great deal of complementariness across various levels of management if an organization is to be successful, besides a degree of accountability for performances. My term as executive director made me work holistically.

◆

In November 2012, I was a strong contender for the post of chairman and managing director of the BoI. Reportedly, many industry colleagues and a few co-workers tried to thwart my elevation to the post of BoI chief, their lone contention being that I was not experienced enough to handle a bank that large (given my exposure to the much smaller Union Bank). Moreover, many of my seniors were occupying top positions in smaller banks. However, the fact was that, by late 2012, as I (along with many industry colleagues) was being elevated, several key vacancies came up simultaneously in large banks. Normally, these would have gone to senior bankers, but now we all had an equal chance. **On 5 November 2012 at around 8 p.m., a notification came that I would be elevated to the post of chairman and managing director of the BoI. It was one of the most important days of my life.**

A warm welcome awaited me, even though I felt that many were apprehensive about the bank's future direction as I was the first lady chairperson of the organization. Personally, I was thrilled at the opportunity of heading a much bigger bank; being chosen for the post was gratifying and I had come a long way since December 1975 when I had joined the Union Bank. **In a male-dominated industry, it is tough for a woman to break the glass ceiling. The only way to the top is to go that extra mile.**

Before taking charge, I had analysed the balance sheet of the bank for the preceding ten years; my observations were worrisome. The BoI, a contender for the top slot until 2009, was now in third position among nationalized banks, having lost its market share in deposits and advances, even as peers surged ahead at an 18-20 per cent annual growth rate. The BoI's credit growth on the domestic side was in single digits. Analysts who were tracking the bank had recommended a 'sell', consistently citing it as an underperformer. Productivity and profitability had hit a nadir. I knew I had a tough task at hand.

Here was a 106-year-old bank—with a consistent profit record and several product innovations—that had apparently failed to grasp the changing market dynamics. I gauged that the primary reason for its decline was the failure to understand and absorb the true spirit of the large transformational exercise undertaken across the organization in the preceding two years. The BoI had taken a step in the right direction by enlisting a consultant's support for reorganizing itself vertically into departments such as large corporate, mid-corporate, retail, and small and medium-sized enterprises (SME) to meet competitive pressures and skill shortages due to mass retirement. However, it could not ensure that these changes were well implemented. Field staff hardly appreciated the need for change. Coordination was clearly missing, while the overconfidence of the senior management was aggravating the problem. Worse, the top echelons of the bank refused to even discuss the crisis.

It was clear to me that **this was a classic case of the message getting**

lost in translation; the senior management never lent a patient ear to the field staff, refusing to acknowledge bare facts and failing to carry out mid-course corrections. No one listened to either the customer or the employee. All one could hear was that the corporate office had issued all the necessary instructions but the field offices had refused to respond to them. A fierce blame game was raging between the head office and field officers, much to the chagrin of customers, several of whom left the bank. A pall of gloom had descended on the BoI.

Nothing was lost yet, I reassured myself. The bank had attained great heights; it was just passing through its share of trials and tribulations. I took comfort in many of the known strengths of the bank—a rich legacy, transparent practices and a strong foundation. Operationally, it had tremendous strength and the quality of the staff, by and large, was very good. But there was no time to admire the monolith as I had to pull the trigger on several fronts.

My immediate priorities were re-engineering and energizing human resources and improving the bank's brand equity. Customers often spoke of the bank's inadequate customer-centricity. Banks always have to be imaginative while providing services, however mundane, or while taking a new idea to clients. Further, when a bank attains a certain size and looks at gaining market share, it must strategize innovatively. Clearly, the BoI had to work harder to broaden its customer base and grab big businesses with its original pitch.

My experience with change initiatives in my previous roles had given me great insight into the critical nature of the execution process. **By nature, humans resist change, and to bring about any kind of innovation determined efforts are required. I coined the term 'Perform to Potential' for the first year to uncover our inherent abilities, while in the subsequent year, I offered the tag line, 'Poised to Grow—Work More, Work Better.'**

To identify an issue early and then effectively tackle it, I established two hotline portals directly to my office—one for employees and the other for customers. Different stakeholders could directly send me their views about service issues or suggestions regarding the desired products. These two hotlines had a huge psychological as well as directional impact, as both our employees and our customers knew I was just a call away.

◆

A strategy that I endorse for all leaders is communicating tough decisions directly. I believe that having a face-to-face dialogue in the midst of a crisis is effective and crucial. Thus, I broke tradition and travelled across India to meet the nearly 44,000-strong staff to talk about the change in management, our state of affairs, the concerns of customers and those of the community of analysts and, of course, the remedial actions to be taken. The agenda for bringing about effective change was communicated honestly and with conviction. Fortunately, everyone gave me a patient hearing and nodded approvingly at my explanations; I would never have depended on a chief executive officer (CEO) circular to do this job.

It was time to walk the talk. **I have always felt that people expect much more from women who hold high offices than from men in similar positions. Hence, I laid down a clear action plan for reducing the turnaround time of proposals and improving the quality of service.** I empowered lower-rank officers by delegating more decision-making powers to them, effectively bringing in more hands to direct the bank's strategy. The internal machinery was rejigged through bi-weekly meetings that discussed pertinent issues of the bank. I pushed the senior management to assume the role of problem solvers. They responded willingly and we cut the turnaround time of proposals from ninety to twenty-one days.

To strengthen our employees' skills further, we initiated vocational training and e-modules where retired personnel also pitched in with guidance. Several long-term, structural corrections followed, leading to a decisive and fundamental change in attitude across the board. It is critical to build a sense of individual growth among employees and pride for the organization they work for.

My skills of responding to rapidly changing market conditions were put to the test, almost on a regular basis. **For a leader, and especially for someone surrounded by sceptics, I would recommend sticking to the basics. I focused on riskless business areas, such as public sector undertakings and retail, to provide steady growth before going in for the big opportunities.** Riding on our initial successes and with the support of a motivated team, I decided to take private banks head-on and also convert the BoI from merely a lending institution to a financial conglomerate. We launched several innovative products and specialized services, while on the service front I pursued a merchant banking licence, Aadhar-based biometric authentication and transaction banking. To expand our niche capabilities, I reinvigorated subsidiaries and joint ventures such as STCI Finance, BoI Axa Investment Managers and Star Union Dai-ichi Life Insurance. Customer call centres were introduced for recovery mechanisms. I also constituted a senior management team to monitor asset quality and our top hundred clients. Both employees and customers saw the changing dynamics and gladly accepted them.

Finally, I needed to ensure that our success stories reached those who mattered; hence, I revamped the communication mechanisms at the bank. I introduced effective ways of improving its visibility through press, media and investor meetings. The results were striking; the bank received far more coverage and greater, but considerate, scrutiny. This affirmed my belief that communication is crucial for success.

◆

When I began my career in banking with the Union Bank, it felt like an exciting adventure. I put in a lot of hard work and my dedication eventually paid rich dividends. However, **the personal setback I suffered had a debilitating effect on me. Eventually, though, it showed me the fragility of life, and how little control we have over it. Perhaps that sense of uncertainty made me focus on my job and aim for and achieve higher standards.** It also brought me closer to my daughters.

A thirty-nine-year-old career cannot be without its share of ups and downs. I am lucky to have found the opportunities that have helped me rise to the top from fairly humble beginnings. As a leader, my determination and courage have helped me engage with my employees and persuade them to work together and take the organization in a decisive direction.

It was George Bernard Shaw who said, 'Life isn't about finding yourself. Life is about creating yourself.' I may have succeeded in finding myself to an extent, but I definitely need more time to create myself.

◆

- I am often amazed at one of greatest virtues of our brain—its malleability. It can be trained and conditioned so that we can extricate ourselves from the ordeals of the past. Believe in the power of your mind, where the whole world resides. What holds us back, whether in our careers or our personal lives, is not some external reality but our own thought processes.

- Leadership is all about change and transformation. Continuously challenging the status quo, setting a direction, staying grounded and driving an empowered team to deliver with precision and ownership are some key lessons for a successful leader. At the same time, a leader's life and position are not always cosy. Since she challenges the status quo, she is often faced with adversities and failure, which may be overwhelming and humiliating.
- Our life is the most precious gift, so spend at least ten minutes on yourself. It helps you discover your blind spots and deal with different situations. Time spent reflecting should help you improve.
- Take care of yourself. The stress you face today is enormous, and to deal with it you must develop your own coping mechanisms. You will need lots of energy to face the challenges of life.
- All of us have the potential to be leaders—stay focused and you could emerge a winner!

A 1968-batch Indian Administrative Service (IAS) officer of the union territories (now AGMUT) cadre, **VINEETA RAI** is the first woman to have held the post of revenue secretary in the ministry of finance. Besides, in a career spanning thirty-six years, she has held various key positions in the government, from posts in the department of banking and insurance and the ministry of urban development to those in the ministry of health and family welfare, and home affairs. Additionally, she has been a government-nominated director to several public sector corporations.

With degrees in history from Miranda House (Delhi) and Brandeis University (USA), Vineeta is a voracious reader. A mother to two children, she says that negotiating a work-life equilibrium is challenging, and professional ascents are particularly difficult since institutional sexism is a real threat. According to Vineeta, 'Neither our laws and policies, nor our institutional mechanisms have been able to overcome the entrenched biases of those in charge.'

◆

The Admirable Administrator
VINEETA RAI

Whether we choose our own path or it is chosen for us by circumstance, it is what we bring to it that shapes our journey. The playing field is never a level one. Besides, what we call fate or luck is only a combination of our values, principles, aspirations and will.

In my case, my choices were determined by a range of early influences, including my parents, the environment I grew up in and the education I received—all of which promoted equality. I was the eldest in a family of three girls and a boy. From the very outset, **all four of us were encouraged by our parents to pursue our own interests and inclinations. There was no question of gender conditioning, never a suggestion that 'girls don't do this'.** Perhaps this approach stemmed from my parents' varied professional interests and their personal convictions. My mother, a product of a liberal education and one of the few Indian women to travel to England for higher studies (in the mid-1930s), was a trailblazer. And my father, a civil servant, was free of gender biases and, in fact, eschewed them. My parents taught us early in life and by example, 'Whatever you do, do it with passion and commitment.'

They also encouraged us to involve ourselves with extracurricular pursuits. I recall a childhood surrounded by books; there were shelves of them in almost all the rooms in our house. From fairy tales sourced from different countries (Baba Yaga, the witch from Russian folklore, was a favourite) and Arthur Mee's children's encyclopaedia, to Enid Blyton's delightful stories and Louisa May Alcott's *Little Women*, I read everything I could lay my hands on. Stories of these worldly characters and other-worldly figures spurred my imagination, aroused my sympathy and made me aware of a world beyond my immediate environment. Later, the reading list widened to include Dickens, Chekhov, Tolstoy and Tagore. And then there were the inspirational biographies of remarkable women and men—of Toru Dutt, for instance, who, in her short life of twenty-one years, wrote and translated prolifically in English, French, Bengali and Sanskrit, or Pandita Ramabai, the social reformer, who strove for women's emancipation. **Reading nurtured a quality I value greatly—empathy. To be able to understand human beings, see the world as the Great Masters saw it and visualize situations and circumstances from another's point of view is vital for any kind of growth.** Later, this quality came to hold special relevance in my profession, which is essentially about dealing with and understanding human beings and having a genuine interest in their well-being.

Along with reading, music dominated our early lives and we absorbed it almost without conscious effort. My mother was an accomplished singer of Hindustani classical styles and my father's eclectic taste exposed us to Western classical music. My own attempts at learning Indian classical singing came to naught (despite a wonderful guru of the Gwalior gharana) because my musical sense (or rather, the lack of it) did not match my ardent interest in the art form. Nonetheless, **music, much like reading, has remained a buffer during times of professional and personal tensions; it has brought me immense joy and has kept me from boredom.**

◆

I spent my early years in Patna. In the 1950s, Patna was a beautiful city along the banks of a placid and pristine River Ganga. It came with a glorious historical past and was the nucleus of the great empires of the Mauryas and Guptas. It was the centre of learning and wisdom. Scholars like Aryabhata and Chanakya had received patronage from the Mauryas and Guptas; Nalanda, that great seat of learning, was in the vicinity; and Lord Buddha, Mahavira and Guru Gobind Singh had stories linked to spaces in and around Patna. As a child, I used to visit the city's magnificent ruins. Therefore, history for me became more than a textbook narration of facts. Indeed, I owe my sense of historical perspective and my keen interest in the past to Patna.

In those days, much more than now, touring was an integral and important part of the life of a civil servant, be it as a district magistrate or a chief secretary. **My father, as chief secretary, toured extensively;**

this involved visits to villages and district headquarters, as also industrial hubs like the steel township in Jamshedpur, the coal mines in Dhanbad and the fertilizer factory in Sindri, the largest in Asia. I often went with him on these tours and saw first-hand what the work of a civil servant entailed. My father's passion for and commitment to dealing with issues and people during these visits made a lasting impression on me. Although at that time I was too young to make a decisive career choice, the experiences and the exposure I received during this impressionable period undoubtedly influenced my later career decision to join the civil services.

When I was twelve years old, we moved to Delhi. While the capital was not as fast-paced as it is today, moving from a sheltered small town to a big city and a new school made me grow up in a hurry, in a bid to cope with a new life; this was further hastened by my parents' departure to the US for a year. By the time I finished school in 1961, I was quite sure that after my graduation as a history honours student, I would appear for the civil services exam, with the IAS being my first choice.

My father neither encouraged nor discouraged me. But as a civil servant and a human being, he was my greatest inspiration. He was remarkable and knew how to use his power and authority for public good. He was a visionary and was associated with the setting up of many national institutions, like the Border Security Force. Dr Verghese Kurien, who was the father of the milk cooperative movement, acknowledged my father's contribution to his efforts in his autobiography. My father was a conciliator, never an appeaser; he was a principled realist, but never cynical. He respected his political superiors, but also challenged them. He saw possibilities where others saw failure. Even when he became disillusioned with the falling standards in public life, he never lost faith in the future of the country. When I joined the civil services, he told me to 'do unto others as you would have them do unto you', and that 'the means are as important as the end'.

There were a number of other factors that influenced my decision to join the civil services. These included my meetings with young IAS officers in Delhi, who believed that the services would provide a unique opportunity for active participation in the growth of the nation; as also my interaction with the times I lived in, the 1960s, an era of high idealism. **In the 1960s, the leaders who had fought for our independence— including Pandit Nehru, Govind Ballabh Pant and Lal Bahadur Shastri—were still at the helm of affairs; political parties were still**

principled and disciplined; members of Parliament such as Nath Pai from the Praja Socialist Party, with firebrand speeches, were there to inspire each of us. It was but natural that we would wish to be a part of the change. And the public services seemed to offer an immediate avenue for participation.

◆

When I began work in the IAS, I was allotted the union territories cadre. In a career spanning thirty-six years, I worked in the (then) union territories of Delhi, Arunachal Pradesh, Goa and Chandigarh. Each posting was unique and each an enriching experience, affording me the opportunity of understanding people and public administration, and the rich diversity of India. In the government of India, I worked in the ministries of home affairs, health and family welfare, urban development, and finance (where, prior to retiring, I was secretary for insurance and banking, and then, revenue secretary). This was a period when public sector banks—many of which had high non-performing or stressed assets—were revived, enabling them to become active partners in the country's economic growth. The steps taken to ensure this, in my time, included the empowerment of the debt recovery tribunals, the passing of the Securitization and Reconstruction of Financial Assets Act 2002, and the consequent setting up of asset reconstruction companies. My tenure also saw the revitalization of the Infrastructure Development Finance Company (IDFC) which had not grown despite substantial government equities. Schemes for the turnaround of the Industrial Finance Corporation of India (IFCI) and the restructuring of the Industrial Development Bank of India (IDBI) from a term lending institution to a universal bank, were also completed during this period. In the department of revenue, tax reforms for both direct and indirect taxes were initiated based on the recommendations of a committee headed by eminent economist Dr Vijay Kelkar; as revenue secretary, I was closely associated with these reforms. The simplification and rationalization of procedures and computerization were other major initiatives undertaken around the same time to promote transparency and voluntary compliance by taxpayers. The modalities of implementing the value-added tax (VAT) regime throughout the country were also finalized. As a result of all these initiatives, we not only saw revenue collections—both direct and indirect—exceeding budget estimates, but also saw upwardly increased 'revised estimates'. A decade has passed since then, but I do not recall this happening again.

I am writing somewhat at length about my tenure here because my postings got me a great deal of media coverage and publicity. **As the first woman officer to head the departments of banking, insurance and revenue, I was acknowledged for having broken the glass ceiling. I do hope, however, that I will also be remembered for the role I played in spearheading various initiatives and reforms.**

Of course, professional achievements are not without setbacks. There are bound to be ups and downs in a long career. I have had my share of disappointments, amongst them being a premature transfer—a tool used by politicians to get rid of 'inconvenient' officers when they cannot be upbraided with penal or punitive action. During those days, I took comfort in the fact that I was true to my work ethics. I also held on to a guiding principle—nishkam karma. Roughly translated, this means that we should do our work with conviction, without concerning ourselves with rewards and acclaim. We ought to pay heed to our moral compass and stand up for the principles we cherish. We may make mistakes, but we have the solace and satisfaction of knowing that our intentions and actions were honest. This principle has held me in good stead to this date.

◆

Although an IAS officer is put in a position of authority very early in her career (as a sub-divisional officer), what constitutes administrative leadership is rarely articulated or given importance. Political leadership alone is foregrounded. **In my view, administrative leadership is perhaps as important as political leadership because an administrator is the instrument through which the government's political aims and objectives are translated into programmes and policies.**

Some leadership qualities, especially relevant to the services, are:

i.   faith in the basic tenets of the Constitution—including fundamental rights, the directive principles of state policy, democracy, secularism and the rule of law—to which civil servants swear their allegiance before beginning their service;

ii. full knowledge about the organization and the officers who staff it, their strengths and weaknesses—essential for suitable mentoring;

iii. personal dignity and discipline, since the services enjoy statutory protection;

iv. the capacity to nurture juniors, so they reach their full potential—give them credit where credit is due, condone minor faults with grace and stand by subordinates and accept responsibility when they commit an error of judgement in good faith;

v. a desire to earn the respect of juniors and of the public at large, not by throwing one's weight around, but by working with dedication;

vi. striving to be fair, and when the occasion demands, compassionate and understanding;

vii. learning to listen to others' points of view, without presuming to know it all.

My father summed up all of this in a few words—a leader is 'sparing in censure, generous in praise, and [exercises] self-denial in the matter of credit'.

I was once asked whether these are inherent qualities or if the attributes can be developed during the course of one's career. In my view, these qualities can be acquired through proper training and orientation. In the Second Administrative Reforms Commission, of which I was member-secretary, we devoted a great deal of time and thought to developing leadership potential, and made a number of recommendations regarding changes in the civil services exams and in-service training programmes.

◆

The value of professionalism has also not been given adequate importance. Individuals who enter the civil services are products of their social and economic milieu, just as those who enter other professions and occupations. They are, therefore, as influenced by class or region, and are as likely to have beliefs and biases, as the rest of society. An assortment of approaches is indicative of the diversity of our society and the multiplicity of our social and political beliefs. But **if the objectives of the Constitution are to be achieved, if equality, secularism and a harmonious social order are to be established, the members of the civil services need to be moulded through training and orientation so as to be professionally competent.**

I remember discussing the importance of professionalism in the civil services with my father who aptly said that professionalism can act as an effective moderator of, or a strong curb on, personal feelings and predilections. He gave the example of a good doctor who will not let his personal likes and dislikes influence his treatment of a patient; the doctor may be intensely religious, but he will treat an atheist with all the skill and care he is capable of. Similarly, a lawyer dedicated to his profession may abhor murder but, if required, he will defend a murderer in court. Similarly, civil servants may continue to have their personal views on social and economic issues, but while at work, a strong sense of professional obligation will make them conform to the social and economic platform of the government of the day.

◆

Within the first ten years of service, I got married and had two children. Fortunately, I had (and have) a supportive spouse, my mother lived in the same city and Sarojini—who came to my family when I was just two months old and helped my mother raise all four of us—lent a hand, so I could raise my children effectively. I was lucky to have had an excellent support system.

Even with this, **all of us who work need to, in varying degrees, find a work-life balance; we need to make adjustments to ensure that we can spend adequate quality time, if not 'quantity time', (alas!) with our children while doing justice to our professional commitments.** Negotiating an equilibrium is difficult, and there are no hard and fast rules regarding how best to achieve this.

Speaking from my own experiences, when my children were much younger, I cut back on social outings so I could spend time with them. But no amount of time is enough! When children are that young, there are everyday hassles—minor ailments, incomplete homework, early-morning tantrums, exams, report cards full of 'Cs' and 'Ds'! Yet, my advice would be: **leave your domestic worries at home. Do not whine about them at office—it is unprofessional. But if your child really needs you, put your child first.**

Let me give two instances from my own life. In 1988, I was offered a posting as a joint secretary in the prime minister's office (PMO). It was an honour to be considered for such a coveted posting. But my children were very young and needed my time and attention; besides, I was aware of the long hours of work expected by the PMO (including weekend work commitments). Therefore, I chose to decline the offer and conveyed this to the principal secretary who recorded my views. However, several colleagues and friends kept asking me 'what the real reason was'! Perhaps, the truth was too simple to believe—my children needed me.

Earlier, in 1985, I had an opportunity to be a visiting fellow at Oxford University for one academic year. Against the advice of my parents, my spouse and well-wishers, I decided to take my children with me because I thought the exposure would be good for them; I would also worry less and concentrate more on my studies if they were with me. The decision meant that I had to closely regulate my work schedule, seek the support of my tutor and forgo trips to Scotland and other places. But it was all worth it when years later, my daughter wrote in an essay:

> In 1993, at the age of eighteen, I moved halfway across the world from New Delhi to California to study molecular biology at the California Institute of Technology. That move decided the trajectory of my life and I would not have had the confidence to make that life-changing journey had my mother not taken my brother and me with her to Oxford.

She also attributed her interest in art and music to her visits to concerts, art galleries and museums in London and Paris.

◆

There's no denying the fact that women have to work much harder (than men) to make it in a man's world—in part because they juggle multiple commitments. I recall, during a workshop I had organized, men and women had been divided into two gender-specific groups; both had to list what they did at home and at work, and what they thought they could do. Many men, at the end of the effort, were left a tad discomfited—they had very little to show for what they did at home ('wake up, shower, drive to work, return, eat dinner'), and there was much they could do (but didn't). Women, on the other hand, seemed to be running home, dealing with the children, getting food organized, managing house help, going to work and planning the next day's schedule! Until we reach a place of absolute gender equity, the truth is—women end up doing the work of two people.

Moreover, **gender discrimination is pervasive—even today, men often take decisions for women.** I recall an instance when a concerned officer decided to exempt women officials from election duty since he felt it would be inconvenient for them to be away from their familial duties for long hours. A delegation of these women met me, regretting the officer's decision—'manning' booths gave them a sense of achievement and power. If only they had been asked...

While my home environment was one of absolute equality and I did not personally encounter any gender discrimination at work, I got a sense of its pervasiveness after joining the civil services. In this, the civil services is like every other profession; here, and elsewhere, sexism is covert. I personally know of incidents narrated to me by women colleagues and officials—incidents involving snide comments or sexually offensive remarks. But for various reasons, the injured parties would choose not to complain.

Statistics capture this scenario, and when these statistics are translated into real-life situations what we see is horrific, uncivilized and unacceptable. As a magistrate, I have witnessed incidents of violence against women and gender discrimination. Prejudices are expressed before women are even born in the form of female foeticide, and continue through their life cycle. Worse, women themselves perpetuate the discrimination and indignity they have suffered by abusing other women.

Unfortunately, **neither our laws and policies, nor our institutional mechanisms have been able to overcome the entrenched biases of those in charge. Institutional discrimination is very real.** A case in point is when I worked as a regional advisor on gender population and development for a United Nations organization across South and Central Asia. As in India, in the rest of Asia, too, gender discrimination is rampant; though individual women may reach top posts, as in our country, the norm is to prevent them from occupying strategic positions of authority. The government of one Central Asian republic found an ingenuous way of perpetuating such inequity; the retirement age for women working in the government was to be four years earlier than that of their male colleagues. The government proudly informed us that women would still get their full pension. I complimented them on their 'welfare measure', but couldn't help observing that the decision ensured that women were virtually debarred from occupying the topmost positions in their government—after all, most key posts are within reach during the last two-three years in office. My comment was an eye-opener for the women officers, who had not realized the implications of this new scheme. Consequently, they petitioned for a change in this policy.

This is the story everywhere. **Policies and programmes, including those impacting women, are often made without consulting them. Equally, institutions and institutional mechanisms set up at**

workplaces to combat sexual harassment inspire little confidence. Indeed, many women prefer not to approach them and suffer terrible indignities in silence. The sad truth is that a lot of the mechanisms just do not work. I recall a case when a younger woman colleague in my department was courageous enough to lodge a written complaint against a senior officer for sexual harassment. An enquiry committee, constituted as per the Vishaka guidelines, gave a wishy-washy report despite credible evidence confirming harassment. I recommended action against the delinquent officer to my minister. However, even he gave the offending officer the benefit of the doubt; the officer, therefore, got away scot-free. On another occasion, when I was home secretary in the Delhi administration, I learnt that a woman had complained of marital violence to the Crime Against Women cell; she accused her husband, who was a senior police officer. No action was taken and the officer was let off with a warning by his superiors. It is on being confronted with such examples that women hesitate to even complain.

While governments and organizations are quite willing to acknowledge women's practical gender needs (health, education, etc.), they resist confronting strategic issues involving the sharing of power. It is, therefore, not surprising that even after the passage of so many years, our Parliament has not been able to pass the Women's Reservation Bill. It is also not surprising, if we study placements for top posts in our government, that no woman officer has yet been appointed as cabinet secretary, despite two senior women officers having been eligible for the post. The posts of home and defence secretary, too, continue to be male bastions.

In my career, I have worked with women officers who have been outstanding in every respect; they are intelligent, diligent and committed to their professions. And their numbers are only growing. Their presence and involvement will undoubtedly benefit organizations and the people of this country at large. It is, therefore, imperative for workspaces to create an environment that allows women employees to work with dignity, security and confidence. **Such gender equity, however, cannot be promoted in a vacuum. Both men and women need to push for it. We need to remember that women's rights are human rights, and that sustainable development is not possible if half the population is denied its right to be an equal partner.**

◆

- Let your mind run free. If you're a parent, let your child's spirit run unhindered; let her read books, soak in music, dance, sing out of tune if she must and chase butterflies. If you're an adult, invest time in cultivated hobbies; some of the finest minds have had their moments of epiphany while pursuing 'pastimes'.
- Do not limit yourself. Equally, do not enter a vicious circle—where you question your immense capabilities, close the doors on opportunities, feel disillusioned and incapable and, therefore, once again start questioning your abilities. You need to break out of this cycle and remind yourself each day that you have the calibre to transform your dreams into reality.
- As a woman, remember that you have to work harder than a man.
- Integrity is paramount and encompasses within it truth, morality and justice. The American motivational writer, Zig Ziglar, summed it up aptly: 'With integrity you have nothing to fear, since you have nothing to hide. With integrity you do the right thing, so you will have no guilt.'
- Do not clock in and clock out; your work contract may specify timings, but there's much that can be gained during the 'off hours'.
- There's value in housekeeping, too. While the responsibilities of a homemaker are as demanding and exacting as those of professionals, the homemaker is not paid for her time and effort and thus, her value gets overlooked, goes unrecognized. We must begin by acknowledging the huge role she plays in keeping society functional.

ZIA MODY is a legal consultant, the founding partner of AZB & Partners, one of India's largest law firms, and an authority on corporate mergers and acquisitions law. She has been regularly listed by *Business Today* as one of the twenty-five most powerful businesswomen in India.

Born in 1956, the daughter of Zena and Soli Sorabjee spent her early years in Bombay, moved to Cambridge (UK), then Harvard Law School (USA), worked with Baker & McKenzie in New York City, before returning to her city of birth, Bombay. Married to business tycoon Jaydev Mody, and mother to Anjali, Aarti and Aditi, Zia says that while she worked overtime at her firm, her husband and mother-in-law helped her keep hearth and home together.

◆

Big Mamma
ZIA MODY

If there is one enduring image from my childhood, it is of my father at the dining table lost behind piles of briefs. More often than not, these wouldn't be the collected works of Shakespeare and Keats—writers and poets my father loves deeply—but reams of legal text. Suddenly, he'd get up, attend to a phone call, discuss the next day's matter and let slip a startlingly perceptive comment regarding a case. As an awestruck ten-year-old, I'd observe my father examining files, eavesdrop on his conversations and try following his arguments. How exciting his work life seemed, how deliciously challenging! I became a lawyer by osmosis.

I also imagine, from the very outset, my personality fit the requirements of the trade. My mother likes pointing out that I was very argumentative. And as a five-year-old, enrolled in JB Petit High School, I was notorious for negotiating my way through all situations. Back then, reluctant as most kids are to wake up and leave for school, I'd tell my paternal grandmother, my bapaiji, that I'd get ready only after she completed a game of mahjong with me. My poor dutiful grandmother was compelled to arrange the set at 5.30 a.m. and hurry through a game, in order to get me dressed for school!

Years later, **when I told my father of my career ambitions and my desire to study law abroad, he expressed some surprise. For he, more than anyone else, knows that law is a jealous mistress**—after funding an expensive course, would I abandon the profession midway? I assured him of my commitment to the field. And I had my mother backing me to the hilt—my father couldn't oppose her!

I come from a family of highly empowered women—my great-grandmother was the daughter of a Zoroastrian priest; my grandmother, my nanima, Shirin Fozdar, was one of the rare women

to graduate from Elphinstone College in the 1920s; and my mother, Zena, was on the board of counsellors for Baha'is in Asia and is vice chancellor of the National Spiritual Assembly of Baha'is in India. At home, my mother's word tends to be law; it's why we think of her as an 'alpha mom'.

My mother made it clear—she wanted me to study abroad, chase every dream. In some ways, she wished to fulfil her own ambitions through each of her children—my three brothers and me. My mother had met my father while performing in a college play—she was on stage and he was backstage. They fell in love and got married when she was only eighteen. While pursuing immense personal fulfilment, she feared she had lost out on a higher education; she often jokes that she would have ended up far better than my father, had she had a few more degrees!

So it was that with her vocal support I first went to Cambridge, then Harvard.

However, I must point out that while law has always been a presence, my childhood was marked by the pursuit of many pastimes. My mother insisted on enrolling me in every conceivable class—piano, Indian dancing, pottery, sewing, horse riding. I was even a part of one of the first batches of Tarla Dalal's cooking class! I occasionally resented the constant scramble from school to workshop, the daily hodgepodge of activities, but in hindsight I realize that each hobby, no matter how fleeting, has shaped me.

Of all my childhood pastimes, horse riding stands out, not least because I'd find myself at the Mahalaxmi Race Course six days a week—for the horses and, if truth be told, to be courted on the racecourse by my future husband! Horse riding is in my blood—my grandfather had been a steward at the racecourse and my father remembers all the horses and their handicaps. How much I loved those majestic beasts, especially the creatures that would not be tamed! One in particular, known for his rebelliousness and for challenging all his riders—Scarius was his name—won me several prizes at the Amateur Riders' Club.

Once I went abroad to study, I lost touch with my most beloved of pursuits. There was too much schoolwork to complete; besides, I couldn't evoke the same enthusiasm for horse riding. In Mumbai, I knew the horses, their temperaments, their very specific idiosyncrasies; in New York, there was distance. However, **what remains is an abstract love for horse riding. To date, if there is a race I watch, I sit at the edge of the seat. What also remains is an early lesson—in strategy—a skill I use extensively today.** As an adolescent, while racing, I'd always calculate my points; if I saw that I wasn't going to win, I would be okay losing so that I could help one of my friends place better!

◆

Post-Harvard, I secured a job as a corporate associate in New York with Baker & McKenzie. For four years, I learnt the ropes in Manhattan, getting into complex transactions and being a part of negotiations. Then I returned to India.

In 1984, bright-eyed and fresh out of New York City, when I first entered my chambers in the male-dominated Bombay High Court, I was dressed as was customary in America—in a short formal skirt. My senior, the wonderful Obed Chinoy, looked at me through big owl-like glasses and said nothing. On the second day, he told me, almost apologetically, '*Kal se jara salwar-kameez pehan lo.*' (Please wear a salwar-kameez from tomorrow.) Overnight, I had to change my wardrobe.

That's when it hit me—I had moved from free-thinking Manhattan to an India that was still grappling with the presence of women at work. **While in New York my challenge was to be better than I had been the previous day, in India I had to be better than *all* men—or I risked being overlooked.**

Yet, no matter how hard I tried, in a country where few women lawyers were arguing counsel, and many hung around the courts waiting to get married, no one was willing to take me seriously. Worse, just when my presence started becoming acceptable, I went the family way! **If a woman in court was an oddity in the 1980s, a pregnant one was unheard of. There are stories still doing the rounds of me, heavily pregnant, rushing down the corridors of Bombay High Court.** I was the subject of every joke. In the last month of my pregnancy, the judge said he'd hear me out on the condition that it would be my last appearance in a while! On another occasion, a senior counsel, while introducing me, told the court, 'I appear with my learned friend, and *her* little friend.'

These were moments of levity on days that were otherwise littered with obstacles. **Clients weren't convinced that I could deliver results; solicitors were wary of 'pushy' women juniors; most avoided what they called my 'monkey mail' of daily questions.** Confronted by constant scrutiny and judgement, I found it hard to secure clients. With some difficulty, I bagged my first brief, a small matter, a writ petition of Zenith Industries vs. the Union of India. This first brief came from an old family friend, Aziz Parpia. When I was about to mark my second brief and quote my fee—a princely sum of 4GMs (gold mohurs) or ₹60—the inimitable Obed Chinoy peered through his glasses and advised me to work pro bono. After all, if I charged no fee—never mind if I happened to be a woman—clients would flock to my doorstep.

This is exactly what happened. And, hungry for work, I took everything that came my way—whether it was a testamentary matter, a customs matter or a property dispute—even if it meant relearning the laws surrounding a subject. The schedule I set for myself back then was harsh, but also, in a strange way, valuable—today, when I'm in meetings, much to my partners' astonishment, I can cite obscure excise case laws when they least expect it!

The trouble with being a female counsel is this—the only way of making a mark is by arguing in court, but few clients want a young woman junior lawyer to argue cases! It's a chicken-and-egg puzzle. I had to wait patiently for my breakthrough case—and finally, it came in the form of a non-governmental organization (NGO), the Bombay Environmental Action Group, filing cases against some builders for floor space index violations; prominent South Mumbai high-rises such as Pratibha and Om Chambers were implicated. While the NGO had a case, it had no money, and Shyam Chainani, who was leading the effort, decided to work with junior lawyers like me. We worked for free, worked overtime, argued on behalf of the NGO and against very senior lawyers on the other side. Most importantly, we won every single case! Eight floors of Pratibha were ordered to be demolished. I felt a rush of early confidence. My comrade-in-arms was Navroz Seervai—we were young and delightfully naive.

I also saw that in a space which clearly privileged men, I could overcome all gender biases and win, as long as I had facts on my side. Over-preparation became a shield and a habit. I'd surround myself with piles of books—much like my father—to investigate just one proposition. And since I could not rote learn as much as I would have liked to, I'd meticulously jot down everything on tiny slips of paper—so much so that my opponents would say, 'Take away Zia's parchis to win!'

I suppose I soon got quite a reputation as an information gatherer, a scrupulous fact checker and a truth hound. Once, while arguing a very important case, the opposing side kept interrupting me to say that I was incorrect. Time and again, I had to break the flow of my speech and cite sources as evidence to show that I was in fact being wholly accurate. After this cycle had repeated itself a few times, the judge told the opposing team's lawyer, 'Please sit down. When Mrs Mody makes a statement, we take it as correct.' The pat on the back took a while to come—but when it did, I couldn't have asked for more.

I like believing that my experiences in the 1980s and my constant presence in court made it easier for future generations of women lawyers to come to the fore. **Women, especially in the legal sector, bring enormous value to work—they're natural debaters, phenomenal multitaskers and, unlike men, who engage in some posturing, have a well-rounded approach to negotiations and settlement discussions.**

Of course, as a lawyer, I'm often asked if the judiciary has done enough to foster gender equality. Well, I do think the Supreme Court has tried its best—the Vishaka judgment stands testimony to this. But the issue of gender equity is complex, and asks, not just for legal intervention, but for a change in the nation's DNA. In my view, this change can only be expedited if the socio-economic status of women improves, if they become financially independent and self-sufficient. Women's empowerment and microfinance are interlinked.

◆

After about a decade of counsel practice, international clients, who wanted to invest in India, were being referred to me. This was a direct function of India opening up to foreign investment and new business laws being developed. Much to my father's dismay, I switched to table practice; I became a corporate lawyer. While the rollercoaster of emotional highs and lows in court can be exhausting, I admit I sometimes miss litigation. My band and gown still hang behind the door in my room. I always threateningly joke—if some seniors don't show up and things get difficult, I will simply wear my gown and begin, 'Your lordship!'

Around 1995, I started a small proprietorship called the Chambers of Zia Mody with a small band of fabulous lawyers, backed by a loan of ₹30 lakh from HDFC. I remember, when I requested Deepak Parekh not to charge me prepayment interest penalty, he joked, 'But good Parsis don't take loans!' Today, life has come a full circle—Parekh brought HDFC to our firm and is one of our most valued clients and a dear friend.

Life has come a full circle in others ways, too. In 2004, the Chambers of Zia Mody had a change in name—it morphed into AZB & Partners—'A' signifying Ajay Bahl; 'Z' to convey my own name; 'B' for Bahram, the son of Naval Vakil, who had offered my father his first brief. Together, we started offering advice for overseas deals, and honed our skills as mergers and acquisitions experts. As young lawyers, we'd debate relentlessly, agitate and argue, sometimes through the night—no office in the building was noisier! All that sound and fury paid—we grew from a motley band of twelve to about 300 lawyers, with a strong presence across the country.

However, **I refuse to get complacent. I still oversee significant matters and like to be involved when critical views are taken; I am always available to my clients on my BlackBerry; and I do not schedule a time for going back home—4 a.m. departures from the workplace are not unheard of, if the day (and night) demands it.**

The fact is, I'm notorious for being a workaholic. I thrive on sixteen-hour days and carry work with me seven days a week—and when I feel indulgent, six-and-a-half days. I always tell my team, 'No sacrifice of time, no good lawyer.' Especially in the early years of your career, for the first decade or two, the axioms to follow are constant perseverance, constant hard work; only then can you constantly prove yourself.

If you're hungry for achievement, your profession should travel with you, whether you are in the office or outside. A while ago, when I had been waiting for a flight, I ran into Anil Agarwal, the chairman of Vedanta Resources. During a quick chat, I learnt that he knew one of my brothers; a couple of days later, at Anil's behest, the three of us met for a joint meal. I ambled in with my tiffin box, and the conversation that followed was stimulating, even revelatory, offering glimpses into each of our personalities. The next day, I got a call from Anil, who asked me, 'Zia, can you help us with a Cairn India deal? We intend to take it over.' During our dinner interaction, Anil had never once mentioned a takeover; I imagine he first wanted to size me up. It made me realize all over again—you never know when you're talking to a potential client, or who is sizing you up when!

I also think **if you are a deep, thoughtful, intense professional, you need what I call 'digestion time'. After playing with a thought at work, you should mull over it at home, understand its intricacies, its hidden potential, its veiled drawbacks.** To date, if a client calls at work and says, 'I need an answer today,' I listen, perhaps offer an initial response, but often say, 'Look, I need to think about it more.' Thinking takes time, and often extends well beyond designated office hours.

◆

Today, I still use the skills I picked up as a litigator—which card to put down first on the table or how to sniff out the weaknesses of the other side. Besides, I enjoy negotiating a good settlement, resolving deal breakers and presenting the most up-to-date facts on the topics being discussed. A huge payback is the trust and confidence not only of our clients, but also of the opposing party. And of course, the best payback is when the opposing party becomes our client the next time around!

The value guiding everything we do, though, is absolute honesty. **All my partners at AZB know and believe that what matters most is the reputation of the letterhead. And if a matter doesn't smell right because the client is not transparent with you, do not touch it.**

When I was young, my father, during those endless phone calls, would say the same thing every time, 'No, we must not do anything wrong; no, the affidavit has to be correct; no, the judge will expect this.' Those early impressions drive my professional conduct today.

In my chambers, when I was a young junior counsel of the Bombay High Court, the message used to be, 'You are an officer of the court; the client comes later.' Clients may not always be right, but *you* should always be seen doing the right thing. Your integrity is paramount. Once, while attending to a case, the other side's counsel suggested we settle—a perfectly reasonable solution. Then he added, 'I have told my client that whatever Zia decides is fine.' Shocked, I went to my own client, explained what had transpired and told him, 'You will not be happy with what I am about to tell you. Get another lawyer.' It was my client's turn to be shocked—after all, wasn't the deal in the bag? Despite multiple warnings, he refused to let me go. So, I decided the case against him. It was the last time he came to me for a settlement, but I know I did what was right.

In the next decade, I want AZB to be an 'institutionalized' law firm—people-oriented as well as process-oriented. Eventually, we want to scale up, and this can only be done by us partners by empowering the young lawyers in our team. **Given the hours I spent mentoring my juniors in the early days, I'm not surprised that my moniker is 'Big Mamma'!**

◆

There's no doubt that law consumes me completely. It forecloses every other possibility, including an idyllic work-life balance. I very often did not give enough priority to my husband and our three daughters, especially in the early days. I remember abandoning my chickenpox-stricken daughter's bedside for courtroom obligations; not being attentive enough to my children and poring over briefs after a quick dinner; missing the birthday parties of some of their friends. Once, as my girls were to leave for school at 7.30 a.m., I entered home, dog-tired after another all-nighter at my office. My eldest, Anjali, saw the state I was in and said, 'I'm never going to be a lawyer!' True to her word, she's now a furniture designer, except, oddly enough, she is as obsessed with her job as I am! Perhaps the only personal commitment I have tenaciously observed is attending (almost) every parent-teacher meeting; otherwise, I fear, I've had to compromise on 'we time' to build our firm.

Given my work hours, I have learnt to let go of domestic responsibilities and lent others the space to bring up my girls. One mainstay was my mother-in-law. As a child, my mother could travel, secure in the knowledge that my bapaiji (her mother-in-law) was looking after my siblings and me; likewise, later, I could commit to work, aware that my empathetic mother-in-law was rearing my three daughters so well and happily.

And of course, there's my husband. I met Jaydev when I was ten; he was the boy who had moved next door. As a young girl, I'd be glued to the window watching him walk down our compound road—he was (and is) incredibly handsome! As an adolescent, I'd meet him while riding horses at the Race Course. At twenty-eight, I returned to India to marry him. He remains not only my best friend, but an anchor and the force behind my career. **When my girls were much younger, Jaydev would tweak his busy schedule and juggle his own professional commitments to fit them in—take them to countless classes or ferry them to eat chaat at Babulnath!** While I was eternally away at work, he was the parent my girls could approach to gratify their childhood whims and impulses. They are terribly spoilt by him.

◆

In my journey as a lawyer, some names stand out for the mentoring they offered and the encouragement they unstintingly provided. First on the list, rather predictably, would be my father, Soli Sorabjee, whose humour and fierce intelligence remain my safety net even today. When I struggled as a young junior at the Bombay High Court, he told me to wish that my seniors would fall sick every day—that, if nothing else, would grant me a breakthrough case to argue myself! While he's always around to advise me,

I haven't worked extensively with my father; we inhabit different cities. There are even fewer cases we've fought on opposing sides—but, of these, one stands out. I recall, I walked into court and found my father already seated; he hadn't even told me he would be appearing against me! Once I calmed my rattled nerves, I decided to put my best foot forward—except, this was of little use. My father spoke for precisely five minutes and won the case. We went into appeal and I had to open the case before the judges in the division bench. I simply said, 'I was at a clear disadvantage, My Lord, if you see the appearances against me.' The judges had a hearty laugh; they knew exactly what I meant. Nobody stood a chance against Soli Sorabjee's courtsmanship—not even his daughter!

Then, there's Obed Chinoy, my senior, who instilled in me the need for precision and thoroughness. If ever there was a lacuna in a legal proposition, if a date happened to be missing, he would assert, 'Stop! Fill the gap! Why is this detail not here?' One missing fact, he taught me, amounted to a wrong result. Fali Nariman, ever a lover of knowledge, on his part would tell me, 'Read, read and read. And not just the law, my dear! First the facts. Then the law!'

In the US, Ruth Ginsberg, a Supreme Court judge, again with a frightening but quiet intelligence, was my icon; but mentorship I found in Norman Miller, a senior partner at Baker & McKenzie. He taught me corporate law. As a young overexcited corporate associate, I believed the other side was always wrong, and by winning every point I had to prove it! Miller taught me calibration and objectivity. He said, 'Look at the other side's point of view first. If you want a deal, there is no win-lose. There has to be win and a little win at least, if not win-win. Everybody should be happy.' Today, when we negotiate, my attempt is to make the other team accept a particular point. When I speak, my aim is not to demolish the adversary, but take the whole room with me.

Beyond the world of work, if there's one person I hold in high esteem, it's my maternal grandmother—Shirin Fozdar—feisty, tough, a woman of infinite energy and enthusiasm! She travelled the world, had five kids and was convinced that her faith (the Baha'i faith) would see her and her family through life. She was, and remains, my hero.

◆

- Love what you do; if you work because you love to, not because you have to, you are almost always guaranteed a success story. And success is synonymous with satisfaction.

- Work double time if you have to. And there's no such thing as 'off hours'.
- You only get one or two chances because of your lineage; the rest depends on your hard work and intelligence.
- Ambition is necessary. Women are quick to get overwhelmed by insecurities—a function of social conditioning—and let opportunities slip them by. A hunger for success alone will help them overcome self-doubt.
- Make honesty your first name.
- Do not forget the basics; as a corollary, do not forget why you have entered your profession. Money and power should not make you forget your early ideals.
- Ignorance is death.
- Complacency, too, is death. You are only as good as your last email. Work as though it is your first day on the job!
- Innovate and learn to accept technology.
- After those endless hours of work, make time to give back to a world that has been kind to you. Who says you have to be very rich to give? You just need enough for yourself, and then you're free to offer the plenty that's left. The best legacy you can leave your children is a willingness to open hearts and palms.

Acknowledgements

I was keen to have a diverse group of contributors in this volume to ensure that a variety of voices were heard. I thank the eminent contributors who readily acceded to my request in spite of their busy schedules, all because they believed in the need for a book such as this. For those of you penning down your thoughts and experiences for the first time, I am sure this was often frustrating, made worse by the persistence of the publishing team to adhere to deadlines. But the outcome is here for you to see, and I hope it encourages you to share your thoughts and write more often. You are role models who inspire others and many will follow in your footsteps.

This book would not have happened without the commitment and support of Ritu Vajpeyi-Mohan, Dharini Bhaskar and Prerna Vohra at Rupa. The endless follow-ups and stringing together very different writing styles could not have been easy. I would like to thank the entire team at Rupa for making this book a possibility.

To Neera Bali, for assisting me through the process in her ever efficient and calm manner. To my mother and Noni, for the strong women you are and for representing how women can influence their children and those around them. And, of course, Rashid, Rumaan and Kemaya, who are my most objective critics—you remain my strength and my inspiration.

The royalties from the sale of this book will go to Grassroots Trading Network for Women—a not-for-profit organization working to strengthen, support and expand market opportunities for poor producers, with a particular focus on women.

Index

Banking and Capital Markets
Arundhati Bhattacharya, 19
Chanda Kochhar, 42
Kaku Nakhate, 74
Naina Lal Kidwai, 147
Shanti Ekambaram, 216
Vijayalakshmi Iyer, 258

Consulting
Anjali Bansal, 2
Bharti Gupta Ramola, 32

Fast-Moving Consumer Goods (FMCG)
Avani Davda, 25
Sangeeta Pendurkar, 193

Government
Nirupama Rao, 159
Sudha Pillai, 239
Vineeta Rai, 269

Information Technology/Information Technology Enabled Service
Aruna Jayanthi, 11
Debjani Ghosh, 61

Law
Pallavi Shroff, 168
Zia Mody, 281

Manufacturing
Kiran Mazumdar-Shaw, 85
Mallika Srinivasan, 118
Meher Pudumjee, 129

Media/Digital Media
Kirthiga Reddy, 96
Lynn de Souza, 109
Shereen Bhan, 223
Shobhana Bhartia, 231

Stock Exchange and Credit Rating
Chitra Ramkrishna, 53
Roopa Kudva, 185

Hospitality and Healthcare
Jyotsna Suri, 69
Preetha Reddy, 179

Not-for-profit
Mirai Chatterjee, 138
Shaheen Mistri, 203
Sunita Narain, 247